AF837396

Essays on Non-Classical Logic

Advances in Logic – Vol. 1

Essays on Non-Classical Logic

Editor

Heinrich Wansing

Dresden University of Technology, Germany

World Scientific

New Jersey • London • Singapore • Hong Kong

Published by

World Scientific Publishing Co. Pte. Ltd.

P O Box 128, Farrer Road, Singapore 912805

USA office: Suite 1B, 1060 Main Street, River Edge, NJ 07661

UK office: 57 Shelton Street, Covent Garden, London WC2H 9HE

British Library Cataloguing-in-Publication Data
A catalogue record for this book is available from the British Library.

ESSAYS ON NON-CLASSICAL LOGIC
Advances in Logic — Volume 1

Copyright © 2001 by World Scientific Publishing Co. Pte. Ltd.

All rights reserved. This book, or parts thereof, may not be reproduced in any form or by any means, electronic or mechanical, including photocopying, recording or any information storage and retrieval system now known or to be invented, without written permission from the Publisher.

For photocopying of material in this volume, please pay a copying fee through the Copyright Clearance Center, Inc., 222 Rosewood Drive, Danvers, MA 01923, USA. In this case permission to photocopy is not required from the publisher.

ISBN 981-02-4735-4

Printed in Singapore by Mainland Press

Contents

Preface

This volume contains the invited and various contributed refereed papers of a workshop on non-classical logic, held October 5–6, 1999 at the University of Konstanz (Germany) as part of the 18th Congress of the *Allgemeine Gesellschaft für Philosophie in Deutschland*. In addition to these papers, two further papers have been invited. As a result, the present collection of essays covers quite a broad range of up-to-date topics in non-classical logic. The problems addressed range from methodological issues in paraconsistent logic (Urchs) and deontic logic (Wansing) to relations between the revision theory of truth and infinite Turing machines (Löwe). The papers give a lively picture of what is going on in contemporary non-classical logic. Recently, for instance, the new interest in game logics has led to a re-activation of the almost forgotten framework of dialogical logic. In the present volume, the versatitlity of this approach is carefully discussed (Rückert) and put to work in interesting applications (Rahman). Moreover, there are contributions to the very active fields of substructural logic (Robering) and classification of concepts of negation (Shramko). Mathematical and foundational aspects of modal and temporal logic, i.e., two core areas of non-classical logic, are dealt with in the papers by de Rijke/Sturm and Blackburn. Moreover, there is a contribution to an important issue in philosophical logic, namely truthmaker theory (Read).

I would like to thank Jürgen Mittelstraß for inviting me to organize the workshop in Konstanz, Dov Gabbay for supporting the publication of the present book, and Sebastian Bauer for LaTeX-nical assistance.

Heinrich Wansing

Dresden

May, 2001

Preface

Chapter 1

Fine Grained Theories of Time

Patrick Blackburn

In recent years there has been a fruitful exchange of ideas between philosophical logic and Artificial Intelligence (AI), most notably in the study of logics of belief. In the case of temporal logic, however, interaction has been minimal. This is surprising. Central areas of AI (for example, planning) raise interesting issues about temporal representation and reasoning, and the philosophical tradition (most notably the modal approach to temporal logic pioneered by Arthur Prior [41]) has provided detailed maps of temporal logic. But, by and large, philosophical logic and AI have gone separate ways.

Why is this? An examination of some well-known AI temporal representation formalisms, such as those of Allen [1] and McDermott [34], suggests some answers. For a start, both Allen and McDermott take as fundamental the ability to *refer* to times: one names a time and asserts that something holds, or does not hold, *at that particular time* — but temporal reference isn't possible in Prior's original tense logic, nor in the richer interval-based tense logics subsequently developed. Furthermore, the AI tradition takes the *sorted* nature of temporal information seriously. For example, a central motivation for Allen's approach is to capture the distinction between properties, events, and processes. But, while sortal distinctions play an important role in natural language semantics (see, for example, Vendler [54] and Dowty [22]), in the logical tradition they have been rather marginal. Sorting a first-order language does not lead to new expressivity,[1] so most logicians have paid little attention to sortal diversity.

The main claim of the present paper is that the divergence of interests between philosophical logic and AI is only apparent. By sorting the atomic symbols of various modal logics of time we will obtain systems in which reference to times is possible, and in which the ontological variety important in both AI and natural language semantics can be mirrored. In an extended case study we'll examine Allen's temporal logic, first through the eyes of sorted Priorean tense logic, and then via a sorted version of Halpern and Shoham's [33] interval-based logic. We'll succeed in capturing all the main ideas of Allen's system, and will do so in a way that avoids the problematic aspects of his account of properties. Moreover, as we shall see, sorting *modal* languages does not yield syntactic sugar: it brings about genuine expressive gains, and these gains are relevant to temporal reasoning.

But the paper has a secondary aim: to explore the idea that natural languages can guide the design of knowledge representation formalisms. The fundamental difficulty of applying logic to AI is not so much finding *some* logical representation, but finding a *good* one. The logical landscape is vast: how do we locate the places of interest? The idea that natural languages might be a useful guide is appealing (see, for example, the remarks in Chapter 6 of Turner [52]) and this paper tries to takes it seriously. The sorted systems considered here were not developed for use in AI; they are parts of richer languages designed with the needs of natural language semantics in mind (see Blackburn [6, 9]). Only subsequently was it observed that these systems offered an interesting perspective on temporal knowledge representation.

We proceed as follows. We first review Priorean tense logic, emphasizing its natural language origins, and noting the (surprising) blend of expressive strength and weakness it offers. In the second section we address its principal weaknesses (the lack of temporal reference), and show how to overcome it via sorting; the upshot is a simple extension of Priorean tense logic in which reference to both points and intervals is possible. In the third section we make our first attempt to model Allen's framework. The attempt is partially successful: we are able to model Allen's account of properties. However, although our sorted tense logic can refer to intervals, its semantics remains point-based, and this blocks a sortal account of Allen's treatment of events. So, in the fourth section we take the obvious step: we apply the sorting strategy to a richer interval-based tense logic, the logic of Halpern and Shoham [33].

[1] Any formula of a sorted first-order language can be regarded as an abbreviation of an ordinary first-order formula over a richer signature; see Enderton [23].

The sorted modal languages used in this paper are a special case of what are now known as ***hybrid languages***. Like tense logic itself, hybrid languages, and the idea of sorting on which they build, trace back to the work of Arthur Prior. Work on hybrid languages has blossomed in recent years (a historical sketch is given at the end of Section 2), and the paper concludes with some general remarks on hybridization and temporal knowledge representation.

1.1 Priorean Tense Logic

What is the logic of time that underlies everyday discourse? Philosophers have given a variety of answers. According to Quine [43], natural languages contain no special logic of time of any great interest: tenses are simply idiosyncrasies, and should be paraphrased away. Arthur Prior's vision was very different. According to Prior, there are interesting logics of time, and the mechanisms natural languages use to encode temporal information deserve serious study. His views led him to develop *tense logic*, a simple bi-modal language for representing and reasoning about temporal information.

Two main ideas fire Priorean tense logic, and both are abstractions from natural language. The first is syntactic. Prior observed that natural language tenses work rather like modal operators. Tenses 'operate' on sentences, enabling us to situate the state of affairs described in the underlying sentence in various temporal locations (for example, the past, the present, or the future). The second (and deeper) idea is semantic. Prior observed that everyday discourse presupposes an internal, or observer centered, view of events. Past, present and future are not absolute notions: they make sense only relative to a context. Tenses, and temporal indexicals such as today and yesterday, exploit the fact that everyday discourse is temporally situated: by uttering a sentence we implicitly fix a time (the *utterance time*) and natural languages typically specify temporal information relative to this important *deictic centre*.[2] This semantic intuition is neatly mirrored in the Kripke semantics for Priorean tense logic.[3]

[2]For a linguistic analysis of tense based on the notion of deictic centre, see Comrie [19].

[3]This brief sketch does little justice to Prior's conception. For a detailed (and elegant) exposition, Prior's book *Past, Present and Future* [41] is particularly good. Incidentally, it's not historically anachronistic to treat Kripke semantics as if it was part and parcel of Prior's conception. Not only were the intuitions underlying Kripke semantics shared by Prior (as a reading of *Past, Present and Future* will make abundantly clear), Prior was actually one of the pioneers in its development: as early as 1955 Prior had used what we would now call Kripke models over the frame $\langle N, < \rangle$ (the natural numbers in their usual order); see pages 22–23 of *Past, Present and Future* for further details.

One word of warning. Prior writes elegantly and clearly, but if you are unused to philo-

Let's make our discussion precise. A language of (propositional) Priorean tense logic is an ordinary language of propositional calculus augmented by two unary modalities F (the *future* tense operator) and P (the *past* tense) operator. That is, Priorean languages contain a denumerably infinite set VAR of distinct propositional variables (typically written p, q, r, and so on), the two punctuation symbols) and (, some truth functionally adequate collection of Boolean connectives (for example $\wedge$ and $\neg$), and F and P.

We make formulas (or sentences) from these symbols as follows. Firstly we stipulate that the set of atomic symbols of the language (hereafter called ATOM) is to be precisely VAR, the set of propositional variables. We then define WFF, the set of well formed formulas of the language to be the smallest set such that: ATOM $\subseteq$ WFF; for all $\phi, \psi \in$ WFF, $(\phi B \psi)$ and $\neg\phi \in$ WFF, where B is any binary Boolean operator; and for all $\phi \in$ WFF, $F\phi$ and $P\phi \in$ WFF. A wff of the form $F\phi$ is read as 'it will be the case that ϕ' (that is, ϕ will hold in the future) and a wff of the form $P\phi$ as 'it was the case that ϕ' (that is, ϕ did hold in the past). We introduce two defined operators G and H, the duals of F and P respectively. $G\phi$ is defined to be $\neg F \neg \phi$ and $H\phi$ is defined to be $\neg P \neg \phi$. $G\phi$ reads 'it is always *going* to be the case that ϕ', and $H\phi$ reads 'it always *has* been the case that ϕ'. The *length* of a formula ϕ (written $|\phi|$) is the number of primitive symbols it contains.

The semantics of Priorean tense logic is defined in terms of *frames* and *Kripke models*. A frame $\mathbf{T}$ is an ordered pair $\langle T, < \rangle$ where T is a non-empty set, and $<$ is a binary relation on T. The elements of T are thought of as instants (or points) of time and $<$ is thought of as the relation of temporal precedence: if $t < t'$ we say that t' is later that t, or t is earlier than t'. In short, frames are a simple set theoretic rendition of a pervasive view of time: that time is rather like a river, a flow of temporal elements from earlier to later. Actually, because we have placed no constraints on the temporal ordering $<$, we're admitting 'flows' that look more like swamps than rivers. No matter. We'll define our semantics in terms of arbitrary frames, but when it comes to applications we shall restrict ourselves to working with a *linear* conception of time. To be more precise, we shall then assume that we are dealing only with frames $\langle T, < \rangle$ that are *strict total orders* (STOs).[4]

---

sophical argumentation, you may him find him tough going. But Prior can't be understood by relying purely on secondary sources: relatively few commentators on his work in temporal logic seem to have read him in detail, and sometimes (particularly in discussions of natural language semantics) notions are ascribed to Prior which bear little or no resemblance to his views. One secondary source worth noting is Ohrstrom and Hasle [36]; indeed this would be an excellent adjunct to the present paper. Nonetheless, Prior was a highly original thinker, arguably one of the key philosophical logicians of the 20th century, and there is no substitute for tackling his (often demanding) writings in the original.

[4]That is, $<$ must be *transitive* (that is, $\forall t \forall t' \forall t'' (t < t' \wedge t' < t'' \rightarrow t < t''))$, *irreflexive*

Given a frame $\mathbf{T}$ $(= \langle T, < \rangle)$, a *valuation* V on $\mathbf{T}$ is a function $V : ATOM \longrightarrow Pow(T)$. That is, a valuation assigns to each atom a set of times, the times where that particular piece of atomic information is true. In short, *valuations specify information distributions.* The composite semantic entities known as *models* (or *Kripke models*) are ordered pairs $\langle \mathbf{T}, V \rangle$ where $\mathbf{T}$ is a frame, and V is a valuation on $\mathbf{T}$. If $\mathbf{M} = \langle \mathbf{T}, V \rangle$ is a model, then $\mathbf{T}$ is called the frame *underlying* the model, and we say $\mathbf{M}$ is *based on* $\mathbf{T}$. And now for the satisfaction definition:

$$
\begin{array}{lll}
\mathbf{M}, t \models a & \text{iff} & t \in V(a), \text{ for all } a \in \text{ATOM} \\
\mathbf{M}, t \models \neg\phi & \text{iff} & \mathbf{M}, t \not\models \phi \\
\mathbf{M}, t \models \phi \wedge \psi & \text{iff} & \mathbf{M}, t \models \phi \text{ and } \mathbf{M}, t \models \psi \\
\mathbf{M}, t \models F\phi & \text{iff} & \text{there is a } t' \text{ such that } t < t' \;\&\; M, t' \models \phi \\
\mathbf{M}, t \models P\phi & \text{iff} & \text{there is a } t' \text{ such that } t' < t \;\&\; M, t' \models \phi
\end{array}
$$

If $\mathbf{M}, t \models \phi$ then we say that $\mathbf{M}$ *satisfies* ϕ at t, or that ϕ is *true* in the model $\mathbf{M}$ at t. We say that ϕ is *globally true in a model* $\mathbf{M}$ iff for all $t \in T$, $\mathbf{M}, t \models \phi$. We say that ϕ is *valid on a frame* $\mathbf{T}$ iff for all valuations V on $\mathbf{T}$, $\langle \mathbf{T}, V \rangle \models \phi$. That is, a wff ϕ is valid on a frame $\mathbf{T}$ iff it is globally true no matter what the information distribution is, and in such a case we write $\mathbf{T} \models \phi$. A wff is *valid* iff it is valid on all frames $\mathbf{T}$, and in such a case we write $\models \phi$. Finally, a wff ϕ is *satisfiable* iff there is some model $\mathbf{M}$ and a point t of the frame underlying $\mathbf{M}$ such that $\mathbf{M}, t \models \phi$.

Summing up, Priorean tense logic is a simple language, whose syntax to some extent mimics the tenses of natural language. More importantly, its semantics is built on internal, observer centered, ideas: the fundamental semantic notion, $\mathbf{M}, t \models \phi$, relativizes truth to a time t, the *point of evaluation*, and we can think of this relativization as a first attempt to capture the notions of utterance time and deictic center. Furthermore, the satisfaction definition treats the tense operators as devices which scan the states $<$-accessible from the point of evaluation for information. This models one of the most important facts about tensed sentences, their context dependence.

Now that we know what Priorean tense logic is, and something of the intuitions that guided its design, a different type of question beckons: what exactly is Prior's formalism when viewed from a *logical* perspective? The answer, a rather surprising one, emerged in the 1970s: Priorean tense logic is essentially a fragment of second-order logic.[5]

(that is, $\forall t(t \not< t)$), and *trichotomous* (that is, $\forall t \forall t'(t < t' \vee t = t' \vee t' < t)$. Actually, various non-linear conceptions of time are both interesting and useful; one such conception underlies McDermott's [34] system of temporal knowledge representation. But we're going to discuss Allen's [1] system, and we only need linear frames for that.

[5]The detailed development of this answer is due to several logicians, including Thoma-

The second-order nature of Priorean tense logic reveals itself when the following question is raised: what general constraints on the flow of time can be imposed using Priorean wffs? Put more simply, what can the Priorean language say about *frames*? Now, it's straightforward to see that certain first-order constraints are expressible. For example, its easy to see that $FFp \to Fp$ is valid on precisely the frames that are transitive. That is, for any frame $\mathbf{T}$ $(= \langle T, < \rangle)$, we have that $\mathbf{T} \models FFp \to Fp$ iff $<$ is transitive, and thus we say that $FFp \to Fp$ *defines* transitivity. As a second example, consider *density*.[6] This is a natural constraint to impose for many applications, and it is definable by means of a Priorean wff: $\mathbf{T} \models Fp \to FFp$ iff $<$ is dense.

On the other hand some very simple first-order constraints on the flow of time are *not* definable using Priorean wffs: in fact neither *irreflexivity*, *antisymmetry*, *asymmetry*, *right directedness*, *trichotomy*, nor *right discreteness* are definable.[7] These constraints are relevant to temporal reasoning: irreflexivity, antisymmetry and asymmetry forbid various kinds of temporal whirlpools, right directedness points time's river towards the future, trichotomy underlies the linear conception of time, and discrete time models may be the models that best reflect physical reality. Thus, regarded as a medium for talking about frames, the Priorean language has some striking weaknesses.

Now for the surprise. Although Priorean languages have these first-order limitations, they nonetheless succeed in stepping across the boundary into second-order logic: they can express constraints that no first-order language can. Van Benthem [5] gives a number of nice examples. One of them is ϕ^Z, a conjunction of five Priorean formulas, one of which is the following rather mysterious looking wff (actually a bidirectional variant of the Löb formula used in modal

---

son [49, 50, 51], Fine [24], Goldblatt [31] and van Benthem [4]; this work is still some of the most interesting in modal logic. The first frame incompleteness result (which signaled the presence of second-order phenomena) was proved (by Thomason [49]) in the setting of Priorean tense logic, but a second-order perspective is needed for most modal languages. For further discussion and history, see Blackburn, de Rijke and Venema [11].

[6]That is, $\forall t \forall t' (t < t' \to \exists s (t < s \land s < t'))$.

[7]Irreflexivity and trichotomy were defined in Footnote 3. Antisymmetry means $\forall t \forall t' (t < t' \land t' < t \to t = t')$, asymmetry means $\forall t \forall t' (t < t' \to t' \not< t)$, right directedness means $\forall t \forall t' \exists s (t < s \land t' < s)$, and right discreteness means $\forall t \forall t' (t < t' \to \exists s (t < s \land \neg \exists s' (t < s' < s)))$. I won't prove that these properties are not definable (this would take up too much space) but the examples are all standard, and for further discussion and proofs the reader is advised to consult van Benthem [5], or Blackburn, de Rijke and Venema [11].

provability logic):[8]

$$(H(Hp \to p) \to (PHp \to Hp)) \wedge (G(Gp \to p) \to (FGp \to Hp)).$$

As van Benthem shows, ϕ^Z comes close to defining $\mathbf{Z}$ $(= \langle Z, < \rangle)$, the set of integers in their usual order, up to isomorphism. To be more precise, he shows that ϕ^Z defines $\mathbf{Z}$ up to isomorphism on the class of strict total orders: that is, ϕ^Z is valid on a frame $\mathbf{T}$ that is a STO iff $\mathbf{T}$ is isomorphic to $\mathbf{Z}$. This is something that cannot be done in first-order logic.[9] The magic lies in the variant of Löb's formula. On transitive frames this guarantees that only a *finite* number of points lie between any pair of points t and t' of the frame. This is a second-order constraint, and it is its ability to enforce this property that enables Priorean tense logic to come so close to defining $\mathbf{Z}$.

For further discussion of tense logic as second-order logic (and in particular, for an account of *why* this perspective exists at all) the reader should consult van Benthem [5]. Here I merely wish to draw a methodological moral. Prior was lead to tense logic for philosophical reasons: he believed that only a logic based on internal, observer centered, ideas could do justice to our conception of time and the language we use to talk about it. This lead him to reject classical analyses and explore the use of modal languages. But the consequences of this (seemingly modest) decision are dramatic: we wind up with a temporal language that cuts the cake of expressivity on strikingly new lines. Evidently natural language can lead us in unexpected directions, so the question to pose next is: what else does it have to teach us?

1.2 Referential Tense Logic

We don't have to look far for further lessons. Although Priorean tense logic neatly captures the deictically centered nature of natural language tenses, it fails to get to grip with a linguistic fact of equal importance: tenses are typically *referential*. For example, an utterance of Vincent accidentally squeezed the trigger doesn't mean that at some completely unspecified past time Vincent

[8]The other conjuncts of ϕ^Z are $FFp \to Fp$ (which, as has already been mentioned, defines transitivity), $P\top \wedge F\top$ (which defines those frames in which there is no first point of time and no last point of time; $\top$ here is shorthand for $p \vee \neg p$), $F(p \wedge q) \to F(p \wedge Fq) \vee F(p \wedge q) \vee F(q \wedge Fp)$ (this defines the class of frames in which time doesn't branch to the future), and $P(p \wedge q) \to P(p \wedge Pq) \vee P(p \wedge q) \vee P(q \wedge Pp)$ (this defines the class of frames in which time does not branch towards the past).

[9]Any first-order formula φ (or indeed, any set Σ of first-order formulas) which putatively has the same effect as ϕ^Z has at least one infinite model, namely $\mathbf{Z}$ itself. Thus by the upward Löwenheim Skolem theorem, φ (or Σ) must have models of every infinite cardinality. The uncountable models cannot be isomorphic to $\mathbf{Z}$.

did in fact accidentally squeeze the trigger, it means that at some *particular*, contextually determined, past time he did so.[10] But the referential aspect of the English simple past tense cannot be straightforwardly mirrored in Priorean languages. The natural representation we have for the trigger-squeezing sentence is P(Vincent accidentally squeeze the trigger), but while this correctly places the accidental squeezing in the past, the referential force of the English original eludes it. Although Prior abstracted tense logic from natural language, nowadays formal semanticists regard his abstraction as rather crude, and prefer to work with systems such as Kamp's DRT in which temporal reference is possible.

So let's extend Priorean tense logic to make temporal reference possible. Now, in extending tense logic we have to be careful not to destroy those features that made it interesting in the first place. Priorean tense logic is a *simple* system motivated by general features of natural language. We should look for extensions that involve minimal tampering with the syntax and semantics of the Priorean original, and be guided by natural language in our search. An idea that emerges naturally from these desiderata is to *sort* Priorean tense logic.

Here's an important intuition about natural language: different sorts of information comes in different sorts of packets, and knowing what kinds of packets there are, and what types of information they contain, is an important part of knowing a language. To give a simple example, suppose that while shopping in a crowded department store you overhear a snippet of conversation: '...runs on Sunday...'. Now, you wouldn't be able to tell anybody *what* was running: you didn't hear that part of the conversation, and the topic might have been a person, a train, a course, or an egg. Nor could you say *when* the running took place or will take place: certainly on a Sunday, but which one? Indeed no particular Sunday may have been referred to: if the habitual reading of the present tense was intended, the intent may have been to quantify across several Sundays. Nonetheless, as even this discussion of what we don't know shows, we certainly can glean *something* from the overheard words: minimally that some process (a running) is supposed to take place (either regularly or once) on the day of the week that is neither Monday, Tuesday, ..., nor Saturday. Languages are highly structured, and even on the basis of rather minimal input, our knowledge of this structure may enable us to deduce part of what was (or was not) intended. Part of this structure involves semantic *classifica-*

[10]For example, if the previous sentence had been The car jolted unexpectedly, we would normally interpret Vincent accidentally squeezed the trigger to mean that Vincent accidentally squeezed the trigger at, or just after, the time of the unexpected jolt. For a good introduction to tense, temporal reference, and their interaction, couched in terms of Kamp's Discourse Representation Theory (DRT), see Kamp and Reyle [37].

tions and *contrasts*. For example we know that 'Sunday' can be classified as a day-naming-word, and that its denotation contrasts with the denotation of other day-naming-words such as 'Tuesday'. Knowing the various classifications and contrasts and how they are encoded is an important part of knowledge of language, and it is this (rather Saussurean) intuition that I'm going to cartoon in tense logic.

Sorted first-order languages are well understood, but what on earth is a sorted *modal* language? Let's consider the matter. Like most modal languages, Priorean tense logic lets us build information representations using Boolean operators and modalities. Ultimately, complex representations are built up out of the atomic symbols. However in Priorean languages, as in other modal languages, there is only one kind of atomic symbol: propositional variables. Why not introduce a second sort of atomic sentence, syntactically distinct from the first? Indeed, why not introduce a third, a fourth or a fifth new sort of atomic sentence, each distinct from the propositional variables and each other? Syntactically these items would be on a par with the familiar propositional variables: we'd build up sentences using these new symbols, or some mixture of these new symbols and propositional variables, exactly as before. Semantically, however, each sort would be distinct: each sort would encode a different type of information, or to put it another way, each sort would have a different characteristic intended meaning. These characteristic meanings would be captured by placing constraints on the functions that were permitted to interpret the items in each sort: only those functions which respected the intended meaning would qualify as valuations.

Let's apply this idea to the problem at hand. We'll first add a new sort to Priorean tense logic to make it 'point referential'. So, let NOM, the set of *nominals*, be a set of symbols such that VAR$\cap$NOM$= \emptyset$. We typically represent nominals by the letters i, j, k and so on. Define the set of atoms of our language, ATOM, to be VAR$\cup$NOM. This single atomic level change is the *only* syntactic change we make: the wffs are made up out of the elements of ATOM exactly as for Priorean languages. That is, all atoms are wffs, and we can freely form new wffs from other wffs using the Boolean connectives and tense operators. The only difference is that now the atomic symbols are subdivided into two categories, nominals and propositional variables. Note that the wffs fall naturally into three classes. First there are wffs like $FFp \to Fp$, which contain only propositional variables. We'll call these *purely Priorean* wffs. Second there are wffs like $i \to \neg Fi$ which contain only nominals. We'll call these *purely nominal* wffs. Finally there are wffs such as $F(i \wedge p)$ which contain both sorts of atom, and we'll call these *mixed* wffs.

We want nominals to enable us to refer to points of time. To achieve this we're going to insist that in any model, *nominals are to be true at one and only one time.* Nominals will 'name' the unique time they are true at. So, let **T** be any frame. By a valuation for our language is meant a function $V : ATOM \longrightarrow Pow(\mathbf{T})$ such that for all $i \in$ NOM, $V(i)$ is a singleton. This atomic level change is the *only* semantic change we make. As with Priorean tense logic we define models **M** to be pairs $\langle \mathbf{T}, V \rangle$ where **T** is a frame and V a valuation, and we define the concept of a wff ϕ being satisfied in a model **M** at a point t (that is, $\mathbf{M}, t \models \phi$), and the various other semantic notions, *exactly* as we did for Priorean languages.

Thus we have our first sorted modal language (or *hybrid language*, as they are usually called). The language has two sorts, nominals and variables, and is called *nominal tense logic.* Nominals encode information about the identity of times: on encountering a nominal we may not know which time it names, but we *do* know that it names some (unique) time. We inherited propositional variables from tense logic. They encode arbitrary information, and on encountering one we are none the wiser.

What has sorting achieved? In a nutshell: expressivity. For a start, we have complete freedom to use the standard logical to combine referential and other information as we see fit. For example, using the wff

$$P(i \wedge \textsf{Vincent accidentally squeeze the trigger})$$

we can insist not only that Vincent did accidentally squeeze the trigger, but that he did so at a particular time, the time named by i. That is, the *syntactic* encoding of information is completely uniform: everything is a formula. The symmetry is broken only where it really counts: at the *semantic* level.

The expressive increase is reflected in a crop of new validities. For example, consider the purely Priorean wff:

$$F(p \wedge q) \wedge F(p \wedge r) \rightarrow F(q \wedge r).$$

This is *not* valid. From the information that there is a future time where p and q are true, and also a future time where p and r are true, we cannot conclude that there is a future point where q and r are true together. However the following mixed analog *is* valid:

$$F(i \wedge q) \wedge F(i \wedge r) \rightarrow F(q \wedge r).$$

There is only one point at which i is true, so given the truth of the antecedent, the truth of the consequent follows.

But the expressive gains run deeper: with the aid of nominals we can enforce many new constraints on frames. Recall the six examples given earlier of frame properties not definable in Priorean languages. All six conditions are definable in our enriched language (indeed, definable using only purely nominal formulas) as the following result shows:

Theorem 1.2.1 *Let* $\mathbf{T} = \langle T, < \rangle$ *be a frame. Then:*

$\mathbf{T} \models i \to \neg Fi$	*iff*	$<$ *is irreflexive;*
$\mathbf{T} \models i \to \neg FFi$	*iff*	$<$ *is asymmetric;*
$\mathbf{T} \models i \to G(Fi \to i)$	*iff*	$<$ *is antisymmetric;*
$\mathbf{T} \models Pi \vee i \vee Fi$	*iff*	$<$ *is trichotomous;*
$\mathbf{T} \models FPi$	*iff*	$<$ *is right directed;*
$\mathbf{T} \models i \to (F\top \to FHH\neg i)$	*iff*	$<$ *is right discrete.*

Proof: Straightforward, and left to the reader. □

Indeed, with the aid of nominals we can define $\mathbf{Z}$, the integers in their usual order, up to isomorphism. We see this as follows. Let ϕ^{STO} be

$$(i \to \neg Fi) \wedge (Pi \vee i \vee Fi) \wedge (FFi \to Fi).$$

The first conjunct defines irreflexivity, the second trichotomy, and the third transitivity, thus ϕ^{STO} is valid on precisely the STOs. Now, as we have discussed, van Benthem has shown that the purely Priorean wff ϕ^{Z} defines $\mathbf{Z}$ on the class of STOs — hence $\phi^{STO} \wedge \phi^{Z}$ is valid on precisely those frames isomorphic to $\mathbf{Z}$. Summing up: nominals can see temporal structure that propositional variables are blind to. Sorting has *not* lead to syntactic sugar: nominal tense logic is a genuinely richer than Priorean tense logic.

Our first referential sort looks promising, so let's introduce another. Much work in both temporal knowledge representation (e.g. Allen [1]) and natural language semantics (e.g. Dowty [22]) insists on the importance of extended *periods of time*, or *intervals*. We will now introduce a third sort, the sort of *interval nominals*, and constrain their interpretation so that the set of points at which any interval nominal is true is an interval. Thus, even though we will continue to work with a point-based semantics, we will gain a partial handle on interval structure. For certain purposes, admittedly, this handle will turn out to be inadequate, and we'll eventually be forced to sort in the richer setting of interval-based semantics. Nonetheless, it's interesting to see how far we can go with simpler equipment.

So choose a third denumerably infinite set INOM, mutually disjoint from both NOM and VAR. We call the elements of INOM interval nominals, and typically represent them using e, d, c, and so on. Next we define ATOM to be VAR $\cup$

NOM ∪ INOM. Once again, this is the only syntactic change we make: wffs are made from this expanded set of atoms in the usual way.

What about the semantics? The following seems a plausible characterization of what we mean by an interval: *an interval is an unbroken stretch of time.* Let's make this precise. Let $\mathbf{T}$ $(= \langle T, < \rangle)$ be a frame. A *convex* subset of T is a subset S of T such that $(\forall s, s' \in S)(\forall t \in T)(s < t < s' \Rightarrow t \in S)$. That is, convex subsets are unbroken stretches of time. We shall insist that when interpreting our language on a frame $\mathbf{T} = \langle T, < \rangle$, for all interval nominals e, $V(e)$ must be a non-empty convex subset of T. As before, no constraints will be placed on the denotations of variables, and nominals must denote points. A function $V : \mathrm{ATOM} \longrightarrow Pow(T)$ that respects these constraints is called a valuation, and a model is a pair $\langle \mathbf{T}, V \rangle$ where $\mathbf{T}$ is a frame and V a valuation on $\mathbf{T}$. Semantic concepts such as satisfaction and validity are defined as before. We call this three-sorted modal language *referential tense logic.*[11]

Now, in the following section we will use referential tense logic to model (parts of) Allen's system, and Allen views temporal precedence as linear. So what can we do with referential tense logic when working with STOs? The key observation is that over STOs the *universal modality* $\Box$ and its dual $\Diamond$ are definable, and both modalities interact elegantly with nominals and interval nominals. Now, $\Box\phi$ is true at a time t iff ϕ is true at *all* times. Over STOs this means we need can define $\Box\phi$ to be $H\phi \wedge \phi \wedge G\phi$. The dual operator $\Diamond$ is thus $\neg\Box\neg\phi$ (that is, $P\phi \vee \phi \vee F\phi$) and clearly $\Diamond\phi$ means that ϕ is true at *some* time. Now for the crucial point: these operators interact beautifully with our two referential sorts. For example $\Box(i \rightarrow \phi)$ (and indeed, $\Diamond(i \wedge \phi)$) can be regarded as a 'jump' instruction. Because nominals are true at exactly one point, these wffs are true iff the information ϕ holds at the point named by i. In effect, these wffs shift the point of evaluation to the point named by i and test for the truth of ϕ there. Matters are similar with interval nominals: $\Box(e \rightarrow \phi)$ is true iff the information ϕ holds at *all* points in the interval named by e. Such combinations are precisely what we shall use to model Allen's HOLDS predicate. Indeed if we wanted to work with nominals or interval nominals over *non*-linear time flows — on such flows $\Box$ cannot be defined in terms of the tense operators — it would be an excellent idea to introduce the universal modality as an additional primitive.[12]

---

[11] Referential tense logic is a subsystem of the richer many-sorted languages defined in Blackburn [6, 9] that deal with clock-expressions, days, months, years, and temporal indexicals such as yesterday, today, tomorrow and now.

[12] In fact, virtually everyone who has worked with nominals has examined the effects of introducing the universal modality as a primitive, precisely because its combination with referential sorts is so effective. Indeed in Goranko and Passy [32], the standard reference on the universal modality, one of the main motivations given for being interested in the universal modality in the first place is because of its smooth interaction with nominals. A number of

So: we now have a simple looking bi-modal language in which reference to both points and intervals is possible. But has this increased expressivity come at a computational cost? Pleasantly enough, at least when working with linear time, the answer is *no.* I'm now going to show that the satisfiability problem for the referential tense logic of any class of STOed frames is no worse than the satisfiability problem for the Priorean tense logic of the same frame class. I'll do this by (polynomial time) reducing the former problem to the latter. At the heart of the following argument is the following observation: although the language of Priorean tense logic is not referential, it *is* possible (at least when working with linear time), to simulate temporal reference by making use of certain defined operators.

We've already met two of the defined operators we'll need, namely the universal modality $\Box$ and its dual $\Diamond$. In addition we'll use the *difference* operator D. The difference operator is a modality that explores the inequality relation on frames. That is, $D\phi$ is true at a point t in a model iff ϕ is true at a point t' such that $t' \neq t$. Because we are working with STOed frames, $D\phi$ is definable: $P\phi \vee F\phi$ suffices.[13] With the help of these operators we can define operators U and I that will enable us to simulate referential sorts. Define $U\phi$ to be $\Diamond(\phi \wedge \neg D\phi)$. That is, $U\phi$ is true if ϕ is true at a *unique* point. The U operator gives us a way of simulating nominals. Define $I\phi$, to be $\Diamond\phi \wedge \Box(P\phi \wedge F\phi \rightarrow \phi)$. That is, $I\phi$ is true in a model iff ϕ is true somewhere, and, in addition, the set of points at which ϕ is true is convex. Thus I gives us a way of simulating interval nominals.

We now define, for any wff ϕ of referential tense logic, a corresponding purely Priorean wff ϕ^b with two pleasant properties. First, the length of ϕ^b is linear in the length of ϕ. Second, ϕ is satisfiable iff ϕ^b is. As a first step, let β be any bijection from VAR $\cup$ NOM $\cup$ INOM to VAR. We use β as the base clause for a simple substitution translation σ: $\sigma(a) = \beta(a)$, for all atoms a; $\sigma(\neg\phi) = \neg\sigma(\phi)$; $\sigma(\phi B \psi) = \sigma(\phi) B \sigma(\psi)$ for all binary Boolean connectives B; $\sigma(F\phi) = F\sigma(\phi)$; and $\sigma(P\phi) = P\sigma(\phi)$. Thus, given a wff of referential tense

recent papers on hybrid languages (notably Areces, Blackburn and Marx [2], Blackburn [10], and Blackburn and Tzakova [17]) have examined the consequences of introducing only the 'jump' operators noted above as primitive. That is, instead of adding a primitive universal modality, these papers add a primitive operator $@_i$ for each nominal i, where $@_i\phi$ means "jump to the point named by the nominal i and test for the truth of ϕ there". For some hybrid languages the use of primitive $@_i$ can be preferable to introducing a primitive universal modality (for example, on complexity theoretic grounds; see Areces, Blackburn and Marx [2]). Moreover, the $@_i$ operators support elegant proof theories (see Seligman [47], Blackburn [10]).

[13]Like the universal modality, the difference operator is now a standard tool in modal logic; de Rijke [45] is the best source for further information. The difference operator also plays an important role in the proof-theoretic analyses of nominal tense logic in Demri [20] and Demri and Goré [21].

logic ϕ, $\sigma(\phi)$ is a purely Priorean wff that has exactly the same form as ϕ: all we have done is substitute propositional variables for the atoms in ϕ.

We are now ready to define $\phi^\flat$. Let $i_1, \ldots, i_n$ and $e_1, \ldots, e_m$ be the nominals and interval nominals that occur in ϕ. Then we define $\phi^\flat$ to be:

$$U(\sigma(i_1)) \wedge \cdots \wedge U(\sigma(i_n)) \wedge I(\sigma(e_1)) \wedge \cdots \wedge I(\sigma(e_m)) \wedge \sigma(\phi).$$

If ϕ contains no nominals or interval nominals we simply omit the relevant conjuncts from $\phi^\flat$. Thus when ϕ is purely Priorean, $\phi^\flat$ is just $\sigma(\phi)$.

Lemma 1.2.2 *For any wff ϕ of referential tense logic, $|\phi^\flat|$ is linear in $|\phi|$.*

Proof: Left to the reader. □

Lemma 1.2.3 *Let ϕ be any wff of referential tense logic, and* **T** *be any* STO. *Then ϕ is satisfiable in a* **T**-*based model iff $\phi^\flat$ is satisfiable in a* **T**-*based model.*

Proof: Let ϕ be a wff of referential tense logic, let $\mathbf{T}$ be a STO, let $\mathbf{M} = \langle \mathbf{T}, V \rangle$, and suppose that $\mathbf{M}, t \models \phi$. Let $V^\flat$ be any valuation such that $V^\flat(p) = V(\beta^{-1}(p))$ for all propositional variables p, and let $\mathbf{M}^\flat$ be the model $\langle \mathbf{T}, V^\flat \rangle$. $V^\flat$ assigns singletons and convex subsets to all propositional variables which are β images of nominals and interval nominals respectively. Thus for all nominals i, $U(\sigma(i))$ is globally true in $\mathbf{M}^\flat$, and for all interval nominals e, $I(\sigma(e))$ is globally true in $\mathbf{M}^\flat$. Clearly $\mathbf{M}^\flat, t \models \sigma(\phi)$. Thus $\mathbf{M}^\flat, t \models \phi^\flat$.

Conversely, suppose there is a model $\mathbf{M}^\flat = \langle \mathbf{T}, V^\flat \rangle$ and a point t in $\mathbf{T}$ such that $\mathbf{M}^\flat, t \models \phi^\flat$. Let V be any function from ATOM to $Pow(\mathbf{T})$ such that (a) $V(\beta^{-1}(p)) = V^\flat(p)$ for all propositional symbols occurring in $\phi^\flat$, (b) $V(i)$ is a ngleton, for all nominals i such that $\sigma(i)$ does not occur in $\phi^\flat$, and (c) $V(e)$ is a convex subset for all interval nominals e such that $\sigma(e)$ does not occur in $\phi^\flat$. V is a valuation: in particular, the relevant constraints hold for all nominals and interval nominals whose σ images *do* occur in $\phi^\flat$ because all conjuncts of the form $U(\sigma(i))$ and $I(\sigma(e))$ are true in $\mathbf{M}^\flat$. Thus $\mathbf{M} = \langle \mathbf{T}, V \rangle$ is a model, and clearly $\mathbf{M}, t \models \phi$. □

Theorem 1.2.4 *Let $\mathcal{S}$ be a class of* STO*s. Determining whether an arbitrary wff of referential tense logic is satisfiable in a model based on a frame in $\mathcal{S}$, is linear time reducible to the satisfiability problem for Priorean tense logic on $\mathcal{S}$.*

Proof: To test whether a wff ϕ of referential tense logic is satisfiable in a model based on a STO in $\mathcal{S}$, we need merely form $\phi^\flat$ (which by Lemma 1.2.2

we can do in linear time) and attempt to satisfy ϕ^b on some such model (which by Lemma 1.2.3 is a necessary and sufficient condition for the satisfiability of ϕ in such a model). But ϕ^b is purely Priorean. □

As a simple application of this result, we have that the satisfiability problem for the referential tense logic of $\mathbf{Q}$ $(= \langle Q, < \rangle)$, the rational numbers in their usual order, is NP-complete. We argue as follows. Clearly this problem is NP hard, as it contains the satisfiability problem for propositional calculus as a special case. On the other hand, the previous theorem tells us that the problem of satisfying Priorean wffs in $\mathbf{Q}$-based models gives us an upper bound for the problem, and from the work of Ono and Nakamura [39] we know that the satisfiability problem for Priorean wffs on $\mathbf{Q}$-based models is solvable in NP-time. Thus the NP-completeness result for referential tense logic follows.[14]

To close this section, some historical remarks and pointers to the literature on hybrid languages. Arthur Prior [41] introduced nominals into tense logic (he called them *world propositions*). Arthur Prior wasn't primary interested in making temporal *reference* possible, rather he was interested in *quantifying* over times in a modal framework.[15] Thus in Prior's hybrid languages it was possible to bind nominals using $\exists$ and $\forall$. Robert Bull was the first to investigate sorting technically; his paper on the subject (Bull [18]) is an overlooked classic of temporal logic. Among other things, Bull introduced a three-sorted language: propositional variables, nominals, and a *course-of-history* sort (that is, atomic formulas constrained to be true at the points on some *path* through the frames; Bull's pioneering work predates by more than a decade the use of path-based temporal logics in computer science).[16] Bull allowed both nominals and course-of-history symbols to be bound using $\exists$ and $\forall$, and contained a primitive universal modality, thus his system had massive expressive power.

[14]Note that the proof of Theorem 1.2.4 hinges on the definability of U and I, which in turn hinges on the fact that $\Box$ and D are definable when working with STOs. If we were working on a class of frames in which these operators were not definable, then adding them as primitives *can* have consequences for computational complexity. For example, in Blackburn and Spaan [14] it is shown that the satisfiability problem for multimodal languages with nominals over deterministic frames is NP-complete. The universal modality is not definable over this class of frames, and if it as added as a primitive, the satisfiability problem becomes EXPTIME-complete. Furthermore, recent work has shown that over some classes of frames, the satisfiability problem for nominal tense logic can be more complex than the satisfiability problem for Priorean tense logic. For example, the satisfiability problem for Priorean tense logic over the class of all frames is PSPACE-complete, but the satisfiability problem for nominal tense logic is EXPTIME-complete; see Areces, Blackburn and Marx [2].

[15]Prior does not seem to have fully appreciated the importance of temporal reference, though he did write a paper which uses sorting to handle the temporal indexical now (see Prior [42]), and he sometimes used sorting to handle clock-expressions.

[16]Goranko [30] investigates standard path-based temporal logics using hybrid languages.

Following Prior's death in 1969, work on hybrid languages seems to have lain dormant till sorting was reinvented by the Sofia school in the 1980s. Their work concentrated on the use of nominals in propositional dynamic logic (PDL); Passy and Tinchev [40] is an encyclopedic discussion of the subject, and Gargov and Passy [26] show that nominals permit an elegant treatment of looping and determinism in PDL.

Although the Sofia School did interesting work on systems in which nominals could be bound by $\forall$ and $\exists$, one of their most important legacies was the attention they devoted to *weaker* systems, a topic which has dominated work on hybrid languages in the 1990s.[17] A key paper on nominals in the setting of uni-modal logic (sometimes with the addition of a primitive universal modality) is Gargov and Goranko [27].[18] Blackburn [6] considers the effects of enriching Priorean tense logic with nominals, interval nominals and various other sorts.[19] Shortly thereafter, papers began to appear which considered hybrid languages based on novel primitives, notably the jump operators $@_i$ mentioned in Footnote 12, and a binder $\downarrow$ which binds nominals to the point of evaluation; see Goranko [29, 28] and Blackburn and Seligman [12, 13]. The recent Areces, Blackburn and Marx [2] isolates the crucial systems and proves a number of fundamental expressivity, interpolation and complexity result. Over the same period there was intensive work on both Hilbert-style (Blackburn and Tzakova [15, 17]) and a wide range of non-Hilbert style proof systems (Seligman [47], Konikowska [38], Blackburn [10], Demri [20], Demri and Gore [21], and Tzakova [53]). Hybrid languages — especially the weaker systems — are now far better understood than they were in 1990. For further information on hybrid logic, see Carlos Areces's hybrid logic homepage at `http://www.hylo.net`.

One of the strengths of work on hybrid languages is that it has usually been guided by questions arising in concrete applications: Bull's work on paths was motivated by the need to define a strong future tense operator for branching time, the work of the Sofia school was influenced by issues by theoretical computer science, and my own early work on the subject was influenced by natural language semantics. This interplay between theory and practice continues to

[17] Many tasks, such as proving general completeness results, are relatively easy for hybrid language containing $\forall$ and $\exists$; isolating well-behaved weaker systems is more demanding.

[18] This paper contains a beautiful expressivity result: as far as frame definability is concerned, it is irrelevant whether we enrich a modal language with the difference operator D, or with both nominals and the universal modality. One direction of this equivalence is obvious: as we saw above, the D operator is strong enough to simulate nominals, and clearly $\phi \wedge \neg D \neg \phi$ defines the universal modality. But the reverse direction is neither obvious nor easy to establish.

[19] The key results for nominals can be found in Blackburn [7], while interval nominals and other natural language inspired sorts sorts are discussed in Blackburn [9].

the present day. For example, the AVM notation used in computational linguistics turns out to be syntactic sugar for multi-modal logic enriched with nominals; see Blackburn [8] and Blackburn and Spaan [14] and Reape [44]. More recently it has become clear that hybrid languages offer a natural framework for discussing description (or terminological) logics; a preliminary overview can be found in Blackburn and Tzakova [16], and for a comprehensive examination, see Areces [3]. Finally, modal logics of relative similarity and rough sets have recently been enriched with nominals (see Konikowska [38]). Thus the discussion of temporal knowledge representation which follows is very much in the spirit of a longstanding tradition.

1.3 A First Look at Allen's System

Let's make our first attempt to bring together ideas from philosophical logic and AI: we'll attempt to capture the leading ideas of Allen's [1] theory of time in referential tense logic.

Allen's system

Allen's system is a quasi first-order language in which various relationships between intervals can be expressed, properties can be asserted to hold over intervals, and events and processes (for which Allen's blanket term is occurrences) can be said to occur at intervals.

Allen adopts a linear view of time, and he makes use of all thirteen possible relations that can hold between two intervals in an STO. These thirteen mutually exclusive binary relations are the equality relation $=$, and in addition B(efore), M(eets), O(verlaps), S(tarts), D(uring), and F(inishes) and their inverses, $\overline{B}$, $\overline{M}$, $\overline{O}$, $\overline{S}$, $\overline{D}$ and $\overline{F}$. The relations are best introduced by example. Consider the frame $\mathbf{Q}$, the rational numbers in their usual ordering. Then:

$$\begin{array}{ll}
B([0,1],[2,3]) & \overline{B}([2,3],[0,1]) \\
M([0,1],(1,2]) & \overline{M}([1,2],[0,1)) \\
O([0,2],[1,3]) & \overline{O}([1,3],[0,2]) \\
S([0,1],[0,2]) & \overline{S}([0,2],[0,1]) \\
D([1,2],[0,3]) & \overline{D}([0,3],[1,2]) \\
F([1,2],[0,2]) & \overline{F}([0,2],[1,2])
\end{array}$$

Allen has a two place relation symbol for talking about each of these relations, thus his language contains such items as BEFORE, MEETS, FINISHES and so on. Axiomatic constraints on the thirteen relations and their interrelationships are stated using this vocabulary. Two typical axioms are:

$$\text{MEETS}(t_1, t_2) \wedge \text{MEETS}(t_2, t_3) \rightarrow \text{BEFORE}(t_1, t_3),$$

and

$$\text{MEETS}(t_1, t_2) \wedge \text{DURING}(t_2, t_3) \rightarrow \\ \text{OVERLAPS}(t_1, t_3) \vee \text{DURING}(t_1, t_3) \vee \text{STARTS}(t_1, t_3)$$

This should give the flavor of Allen's notation for talking about intervals. As is clear from these examples, Allen makes use of the standard Boolean connectives and variables over intervals. Moreover, he uses the quantifiers $\forall$ and $\exists$. In short, this part of his system is an orthodox first-order theory of interval structure.

Allen's then introduces *properties* and *occurrences*. Intuitively, properties P are those states of affairs expressed by such English predicates as is tattooed, is a killer and is covered in blood. When we combine a property with a noun phrase we form a property sentence. These sentences have the following characteristic: they can be true at an interval iff they are true over all its subintervals. For example, Mia is a married is true over the interval 1993 A.D. iff Mia is a married is true over all subparts of that year.

Occurrence sentences have quite different temporal characteristics. Allen subclassifies occurrence sentences into event sentences and process sentences, but I'm only going to discuss event sentences here. A typical event predicate is jumped onto the table. Intuitively such a predicate denotes an activity that involves some idea of product, outcome, or culmination. Now consider the event sentence Honey Bunny jumped onto the table, and suppose that T is an interval of time over which Honey Bunny successfully jumped onto the table. Then if T' is a proper subinterval of T it is *not* true of T' that Honey Bunny jumped onto the table. There may be other intervals T'' over which Honey Bunny jumped onto the table — perhaps Honey Bunny jumped onto several tables in turn — but T cannot contain such T'' and vice versa.[20]

To deal with properties and events Allen introduces two further binary predicates, HOLDS and OCCUR. HOLDS takes a property symbol P and an interval term T, and the resulting expression HOLDS(P, T) asserts that the property P holds over the interval denoted by T. Similarly, OCCUR takes an event symbol E and an interval T, and the resulting expression OCCUR(E, T) asserts that the event E happened over the interval T. These two predicates

[20]In passing, I don't think this style of analysis is a good way of capturing the notion of outcome; more promising, in my view, are the ideas of Moens and Steedman [35]. But I'll stick to Allen's approach in this paper.

are governed by axioms which reflect the intuitions about properties and events just discussed. First, Allen demands that:

$$\text{OCCUR}(E,T) \ \& \ \text{IN}(t,T) \Rightarrow \neg\text{OCCUR}(E,t).$$

An event cannot occur at two intervals, one of which is a subinterval of the other. Second, he demands that:

$$\text{HOLDS}(P,T) \Leftrightarrow (\forall t)[\text{IN}(t,T) \Rightarrow \text{HOLDS}(P,t)]$$

where $\text{IN}(t,T)$ is defined as $\text{DURING}(t,T) \vee \text{STARTS(t, T)} \vee \text{FINISHES}(t,T)$. The truth of a property sentence at an interval trickles down to all proper subintervals.[21]

So far so good. However Allen then goes on to elaborate his account of properties, and here matters become rather murky. The elaboration concerns the property terms: Allen allows property symbols to be combined using certain functions named *and*, *or* and *not*, and from some of the axioms Allen introduces to govern these functions, for example

$$\text{HOLDS}(and(P,Q),T) \Leftrightarrow \text{HOLDS}(P,T) \ \& \ \text{HOLDS}(P,Q),$$

it's clear that he wants an 'internal logic' of property terms that mirrors the 'external logic' of formulas. Indeed, Allen also introduces functions *exists* and *all* which can bind variables in property terms. The intention is clear: Allen wants to treat properties as term-like entities that behave in a formula-like manner (and in fact, Allen explicitly says he wants properties to name complex logical expressions). But some of his axioms seem rather unmotivated. Moreover, the structure of property terms is never fully specified, and it remains unclear exactly what can and cannot be done in this part of his system.[22]

Nonetheless, Allen's theory has been one of the most influential accounts in AI of temporal representation and reasoning, and certainly its leading intuitions are natural. Can they be captured in referential tense logic? As we shall see, we can successfully capture the ideas that underly Allen's treatment of properties. We'll do so by treating referential tense logic as akin to a low level programming language and define a set of high level macros over it. First we'll define analogs of Allen's interval-relating predicates such as MEETS and STARTS. This is easy to do using the referential sorts, and the macros we define automatically inherit the correct logical behavior from the semantics

[21] This is a simplification. Allen also introduces an stronger axiom, $\text{HOLDS}(P,T) \Leftrightarrow (\forall t)[\text{IN}(t,T) \Rightarrow (\exists s)[\text{IN}(s,t) \ \& \ \text{HOLDS}(P,s)]]$. His reasons for doing so aren't relevant to our discussion, and, as Galton [25] shows, this stronger axiom leads to difficulties.

[22] Similar criticisms of this aspect of Allen's work have been made by Turner [52] and Shoham [48].

of referential tense logic. We then define an analog of the HOLDS predicate. This is where our sorting strategy *really* pays off. After all, in referential tense logic all types of information are treated in syntactically uniform fashion. In particular, referential information is represented using nominals and interval nominals, and these are *formulas*. Thus all types of information can be freely combined using the logical symbols. We simply don't need to add a separate 'internal logic' — a genuine logic is already hard-wired into the semantics of referential tense logic.

Simulating Allen's system

Our first task is to show that we can simulate Allen's interval relation symbols. As referential tense logic uses interval nominals to pick out intervals, this means we must show that given two interval nominals, say e and d, we can assert that any of the thirteen relations discussed above holds between their denotations. This is easily done. For any interval nominals e and d we define:

$$
\begin{array}{lll}
\textbf{Equals}(e,d) & =_{def} & \Box(e \leftrightarrow d) \\
\textbf{Before}(e,d) & =_{def} & \Box(e \rightarrow \neg d \wedge Fd) \wedge \Diamond(\neg e \wedge \neg d \wedge Pe \wedge Fd) \\
\textbf{After}(e,d) & =_{def} & \Box(e \rightarrow \neg d \wedge Pd) \wedge \Diamond(\neg e \wedge \neg d \wedge Fe \wedge Pd) \\
\textbf{Meets}(e,d) & =_{def} & \Box(e \rightarrow \neg d \wedge Fd) \wedge \neg\Diamond(\neg e \wedge \neg d \wedge Pe \wedge Fd) \\
\overline{\textbf{Meets}}(e,d) & =_{def} & \Box(e \rightarrow \neg d \wedge Pd) \wedge \neg\Diamond(\neg e \wedge \neg d \wedge Fe \wedge Pd) \\
\textbf{Overlaps}(e,d) & =_{def} & \Diamond(e \wedge d) \wedge \Diamond(e \wedge \neg d \wedge Fd) \wedge \Diamond(d \wedge \neg e \wedge Pe) \\
\overline{\textbf{Overlaps}}(e,d) & =_{def} & \Diamond(e \wedge d) \wedge \Diamond(e \wedge \neg d \wedge Pd) \wedge \Diamond(d \wedge \neg e \wedge Fe) \\
\textbf{Starts}(e,d) & =_{def} & \Box(e \rightarrow d) \wedge \Diamond(d \wedge \neg e) \wedge \Box(e \wedge d \rightarrow H(d \rightarrow e)) \\
\textbf{Co-starts}(e,d) & =_{def} & \Box(d \rightarrow e) \wedge \Diamond(e \wedge \neg d) \wedge \Box(d \wedge e \rightarrow H(e \rightarrow d)) \\
\textbf{During}(e,d) & =_{def} & \Box(e \rightarrow d) \wedge \Diamond(d \wedge \neg e \wedge Pe) \wedge \Diamond(d \wedge \neg e \wedge Fe) \\
\textbf{Contains}(d,e) & =_{def} & \Box(d \rightarrow e) \wedge \Diamond(e \wedge \neg d \wedge Pd) \wedge \Diamond(d \wedge \neg e \wedge Fd) \\
\textbf{Finishes}(e,d) & =_{def} & \Box(e \rightarrow d) \wedge \Diamond(d \wedge \neg e) \wedge \Box(e \wedge d \rightarrow G(d \rightarrow e)) \\
\textbf{Co-finishes}(e,d) & =_{def} & \Box(d \rightarrow e) \wedge \Diamond(e \wedge \neg d) \wedge \Box(d \wedge e \rightarrow G(e \rightarrow d))
\end{array}
$$

Though somewhat ungainly, these definitions have the required effect. For example, consider the definition of **Starts**(e,d). The first conjunct asserts that the interval named by e is a subinterval of the interval named by d. The second conjunct guarantees the existence of a time where d is true and e is not, thus the force of the first two conjuncts is that the interval named by e is a proper subinterval of that named by d. Now consider the third conjunct. This says that at any time where both e and d are true, then at all previous times, if d is true, e is true also. To put it another way, we can't find any time t where both e and d are true and such that at some earlier time t' we have that d holds and e doesn't. That is, both intervals must start at the same time, and thus the net affect of the three conjuncts captures what is required.

So we can define expressions that correspond to Allen's predicates. Moreover, the logic of these expressions is the logic desired by Allen. For example, consider Allen's axiom

$$\text{MEETS}(t_1, t_2) \wedge \text{MEETS}(t_2, t_3) \rightarrow \text{BEFORE}(t_1, t_3).$$

The macro

$$\mathbf{Meets}(e, d) \wedge \mathbf{Meets}(d, c) \rightarrow \mathbf{Before}(e, c),$$

is a formal analog of this. And this macro is valid: expanding it into referential tense logic yields:

$$\begin{aligned}&\Box(e \rightarrow \neg d \wedge Fd) \wedge \neg\Diamond(\neg e \wedge \neg d \wedge Pe \wedge Fd)\wedge \\ &\Box(d \rightarrow \neg c \wedge Fc) \wedge \neg\Diamond(\neg d \wedge \neg c \wedge Pd \wedge Fc) \\ &\qquad \rightarrow \Box(e \rightarrow \neg c \wedge Fc) \wedge \Diamond(\neg e \wedge \neg c \wedge Pe \wedge Fc),\end{aligned}$$

which cannot be falsified.

If we want, we can extend these macros to take nominals as well as interval nominals. That is, we could allow ourselves to write down such expressions such as $\mathbf{Before}(i, j)$, and $\mathbf{Starts}(i, e)$, where i and j are nominals. $\mathbf{Before}(i, j)$, which is just

$$\Box(i \rightarrow \neg j \wedge Fj) \wedge \Diamond(\neg j \wedge \neg i \wedge Pi \wedge Fj)$$

says that that point named by i is properly before that named by j; while $\mathbf{Starts}(i, e)$, which expands into

$$\Box(i \rightarrow e) \wedge \Diamond(e \wedge \neg i) \wedge \Box(i \wedge e \rightarrow H(e \rightarrow i)),$$

says that that point named by i is the earliest point in the interval named by j.

With the first task accomplished, let's turn to the second: mimicking the way Allen's system deals with properties. Can we define a macro **Holds** that has the properties Allen desires of HOLDS? Such a macro must mirror the downwards persistence property:

$$\text{HOLDS}(P, T) \Leftrightarrow (\forall t)[IN(t, T) \Rightarrow \text{HOLDS}(P, t)],$$

and furthermore must possess a suitable 'internal logic'.

The required macro could hardly be simpler. For any wff ϕ and any interval nominal e we define:

$$\mathbf{Holds}(\phi, e) \;=_{def}\; \Box(e \rightarrow \phi).$$

In short, **Holds** is just the canonical combination of universal modality and referential sort noted in the previous section. It's clear that it behaves appropriately. First, it satisfies downwards persistence. To see this, let $\mathbf{In}(e, d)$ be defined to hold iff $\mathbf{During}(e, d) \vee \mathbf{Starts}(e, d) \vee \mathbf{Finishes}(e, d)$. A little thought reveals that $\mathbf{In}(e, d)$ holds iff $\Box(e \rightarrow d) \wedge \neg\mathbf{Equals}(d, e)$, and thus (as we would hope) the **In** macro expresses that the interval named by e is a proper subinterval of that named by d. Then for any any interval nominals e and d and any wff ϕ we have that the following expression is valid:

$$\mathbf{Holds}(\phi, e) \wedge \mathbf{In}(d, e) \rightarrow \mathbf{Holds}(\phi, d).$$

We also inherit from the semantics of referential tense languages an internal logic of **Holds** analogous to the internal logic of HOLDS that Allen seems to want. For example we have that all instances of

$$\mathbf{Holds}(\neg\phi, e) \rightarrow \neg\mathbf{Holds}(\phi, e)$$

and

$$\mathbf{Holds}(\phi \wedge \psi, e) \leftrightarrow \mathbf{Holds}(\phi, e) \wedge \mathbf{Holds}(\psi, e)$$

are valid. In passing, note that we can extend the use of **Holds** to nominals: $\mathbf{Holds}(\phi, i)$, which is just $\Box(i \rightarrow \phi)$ states that the the property ϕ holds at the point picked out by i. But the main point is this: we *don't* need to try to "construct" a logic of property terms by introducing new logical functions and trying to constrain them with suitable axioms. Everything we need is already in place.

To sum up, referential tense logic captures Allen's calculus of properties, and does so fairly cleanly. Firstly there's the (fairly obvious) point that because we can refer to intervals in this language, we can simulate Allen's predicates. Secondly there's the rather more subtle (and far more important) point concerning syntactical uniformity: because *all* types of information, including referential information, is handled using formulas, we didn't have to introduce 'logical functions'; the ordinary connectives sufficed.

But now that we've seen what can be simulated, let's turn to what *can't*, namely Allen's treatment of events. At first sight there seems to be an appealing way to to model events in referential tense logic. Until now we've used sorting as a tool for achieving temporal reference, but surely there are more obvious ways of using it? In particular, up till now we've treated ordinary propositional variables as placeholders for arbitrary information: properties and events are implicitly lumped together as things to be represented using propositional variables. But why not enforce sortal constraints here as well?

For example, we could subdivide the variables VAR into two syntactically distinct sorts PVAR and EVAR. The elements of the former sort would be taken as ranging over primitive property sentences, and the latter over primitive event sentences. By imposing appropriate constraints on valuations we could try to capture the distinction and thus model the full scope of Allen's work in a four-sorted version of Priorean tense logic.

Nice idea, but it won't work. It's impossible to state constraints on tense logical valuations that capture Allen's notion of event: valuations in a point-based setting automatically enforce property-like behavior. Suppose q is an element of EVAR, that is to say, a variable earmarked to represent events. We want to say that q can never be true at two intervals t and t' such that one is a proper subinterval of the other. However in Priorean tense logic, saying that q is true over an interval t amounts to saying that q is true over all points in that interval. This means that if t is not a singleton interval, then q is true over *all* proper subintervals t' of t. Unless we restrict ourselves to the special case of point-events, no constraint on valuations is going to give us what we want: q cannot help but be some sort of property. The point-based semantics underlying referential tense logic tense logic is perfect for properties, and this very perfection renders it disastrous for events.

But the statement of the problem makes the remedy clear. The difficulty has nothing to do with modal languages, nor with the idea of sorting: it's simply that a point-based temporal semantics is too impoverished to support distinctions we wish to draw. So let's use a more appropriate semantic setting. In the following section we'll take as our base a certain interval-based language. Sorting this will give us what we want.

1.4 A Sorted Interval-Based Language

Interval-based languages, like languages of Priorean tense logic, are modal languages: they contain sentence operators reminiscent of those in Priorean logic, and adopt the internal view of time inherent in Kripke semantics. The crucial difference is that *wffs are evaluated at intervals.* This enables more sophisticated temporal distinctions to be drawn, and in particular, it's going to allow us to model occurrences. Actually, it will improve matters in other ways as well. The language we'll sort is that of Halpern and Shoham[48]. This is the interval-based language that naturally arises by abstracting from Allen's formalism, so our sortal analysis of Allen's work will be far neater than in referential tense logic.

The language of Halpern and Shoham contains: a denumerably infinite collection of propositional variables VAR, whose elements we write as p, q, r and so on, Boolean connectives, the punctuation symbols, and the one place sentence operators $\langle A\rangle$, $\langle\overline{A}\rangle$, $\langle B\rangle$, $\langle\overline{B}\rangle$, $\langle E\rangle$ and $\langle\overline{E}\rangle$. These deal with six of the fundamental relations between intervals in linear time. $\langle A\rangle$ picks out an interval that begins immediately after the current one, while $\langle\overline{A}\rangle$ picks out an interval that finishes immediately beforehand. $\langle B\rangle$ picks out an interval contained in the current one that begins when the current interval begins, while $\langle\overline{B}\rangle$ picks out at interval of which the current one is a beginning. $\langle E\rangle$ and $\langle\overline{E}\rangle$ are analogous to $\langle B\rangle$ and $\langle\overline{B}\rangle$ respectively, but pick out endings instead of beginnings. As we shall see, operators dealing with Allen's other relations are definable using these primitives.

Let's sort this language to make it referential. We'll add two referential sorts: SNOM, the *stretched interval nominals*, and PNOM, the *point-interval nominals.* (To simplify the terminology a bit, we'll usually refer to stretched interval nominals simply as *interval nominals*, and call point-interval nominals *point nominals.*) Stretched interval nominals will be used to name genuinely extended time periods — 'stretched out' periods of time — while point interval nominals will denote certain special point-like intervals. We assume that SNOM and PNOM are denumerably infinite sets, that VAR, SNOM and PNOM are mutually disjoint, represent the elements of SNOM as e, d, c, and those of PNOM by i, j, k. We'll call this language *referential interval logic.*[23]

The ingredients are in the bowl: now to mix them. Define ATOM to be VAR $\cup$ SNOM $\cup$ PNOM, and let WFF, the set of well formed formulas (or sentences) of our language be the smallest set containing ATOM that is closed under the application of the Boolean and interval operators. We introduce the following defined operators: $\langle D\rangle\phi =_{def} \langle B\rangle\langle E\rangle\phi$, $\langle L\rangle\phi =_{def} \langle A\rangle\langle A\rangle\phi$, $\langle O\rangle\phi =_{def} \langle E\rangle\langle\overline{B}\rangle\phi$, $\langle\overline{D}\rangle\phi =_{def} \langle\overline{B}\rangle\langle\overline{E}\rangle\phi$, $\langle\overline{L}\rangle\phi =_{def} \langle\overline{A}\rangle\langle\overline{A}\rangle\phi$ and $\langle\overline{O}\rangle\phi =_{def} \langle B\rangle\langle\overline{E}\rangle\phi$. As should be clear from the informal readings of the primitive operators, these defined operators deal with Allen's other relations. For example, $\langle D\rangle$ picks out an interval during the current one, while $\langle O\rangle$ picks out a 'future overlapping' interval. We define the duals $[A]$, $[\overline{A}]$, $[B]$, $[\overline{B}]$, $[E]$, $[\overline{E}]$, $[D]$, $[\overline{D}]$, $[L]$, $[\overline{L}]$, $[O]$ and $[\overline{O}]$, in the usual way. For example, $[\overline{E}]\phi =_{def} \neg\langle\overline{E}\rangle\neg\phi$.

Now for the semantics. Let $\mathbf{T}$ $(= \langle T, <\rangle)$ be an STOed frame (in the usual sense of tense logic) and let $I(\mathbf{T})$ be the set of all closed intervals $[t, t']$ $(= \{s \in T : t \leq s \leq t'\})$ on $\mathbf{T}$. The intervals in $I(\mathbf{T})$ fall naturally into two disjoint

[23] An aside. Referential interval logic is technically well behaved. In particular, the referential sorts we have introduced blend naturally with the analysis of Halpern and Shoham's system given in Venema [55], for nominals provide a natural tool for exploiting "rules for the undefinable" similar to those used by Venema.

subclasses: $S(\mathbf{T})$ and $P(\mathbf{T})$. $S(\mathbf{T})$ is the set of all those intervals $[t, t']$ such that $t \neq t'$. We call $S(\mathbf{T})$ the *stretched intervals* on $\mathbf{T}$; they model extended and connected stretches of time, or proper intervals. $P(\mathbf{T})$ is the set of intervals $[t, t']$ such that $t = t'$; we call $P(\mathbf{T})$ the point-intervals on $\mathbf{T}$. Clearly such intervals are point-like.[24]

Given an STO $\mathbf{T}$, a valuation on $\mathbf{T}$ is a function V with domain ATOM and range $Pow(I(\mathbf{T}))$ that satisfies two constraints. First, for all stretched interval nominals e we insist that $V(e)$ is a singleton, and that if $[t, t']$ is the unique element in $V(e)$, then $[t, t'] \in S(\mathbf{T})$. That is, each interval nominal must denote a unique stretched interval. Second, for all point nominals i we insist that $V(i)$ is a singleton, and that if $[t, t']$ is the unique element in $V(i)$, then $[t, t'] \in P(\mathbf{T})$. That is, each point nominal must denote a unique point interval.[25]

A model $\mathbf{M}$ is a pair $\langle \mathbf{T}, V\rangle$ where $\mathbf{T}$ is an STOed frame and V a valuation on $\mathbf{T}$ of the kind just described. We now define what it is for a model $\mathbf{M}$ $(= \langle T, <, V\rangle)$ to satisfy a wff ϕ at an interval $[t_1, t_2] \in I(\mathbf{T})$:

$$
\begin{array}{lll}
\mathbf{M}, [t_1, t_2] \models a & \text{iff} & [t_1, t_2] \in V(a), \text{ for all atoms } a \\
\mathbf{M}, [t_1, t_2] \models \neg\phi & \text{iff} & \mathbf{M}, [t_1, t_2] \not\models \phi \\
\mathbf{M}, [t_1, t_2] \models \phi \wedge \psi & \text{iff} & \mathbf{M}, [t_1, t_2] \models \phi \text{ and } \mathbf{M}, [t_1, t_2] \models \psi \\
\mathbf{M}, [t_1, t_2] \models \langle A\rangle\phi & \text{iff} & \exists t_3 : t_2 < t_3 \text{ and } \mathbf{M}, [t_2, t_3] \models \phi \\
\mathbf{M}, [t_1, t_2] \models \langle \overline{A}\rangle\phi & \text{iff} & \exists t_3 : t_3 < t_1 \text{ and } \mathbf{M}, [t_3, t_1] \models \phi \\
\mathbf{M}, [t_1, t_2] \models \langle B\rangle\phi & \text{iff} & \exists t_3 : t_3 < t_2 \text{ and } t_1 \leq t_3 \text{ and } \mathbf{M}, [t_1, t_3] \models \phi \\
\mathbf{M}, [t_1, t_2] \models \langle \overline{B}\rangle\phi & \text{iff} & \exists t_3 : t_2 < t_3 \text{ and } \mathbf{M}, [t_1, t_3] \models \phi \\
\mathbf{M}, [t_1, t_2] \models \langle E\rangle\phi & \text{iff} & \exists t_3 : t_1 < t_3 \text{ and } t_3 \leq t_2 \text{ and } \mathbf{M}, [t_3, t_2] \models \phi \\
\mathbf{M}, [t_1, t_2] \models \langle \overline{E}\rangle\phi & \text{iff} & \exists t_3 : t_3 < t_1 \text{ and } \mathbf{M}, [t_3, t_2] \models \phi
\end{array}
$$

A wff ϕ is *globally true* in $\mathbf{M}$ iff $\mathbf{M}, [t_1, t_2] \models \phi$ for all $[t_1, t_2] \in I(\mathbf{T})$, and in such a case we write $\mathbf{M} \models \phi$. A wff ϕ is *valid on a frame* $\mathbf{T}$ iff for all valuations V on $\mathbf{T}$, $\langle \mathbf{T}, V\rangle \models \phi$, and in such a case write $\mathbf{T} \models \phi$. If a wff ϕ is valid on all (STOed) frames we say it's *valid* and write $\models \phi$. If ϕ and ψ are wffs such that

[24] They're in 1-1 correspondence with the points of the underlying frame, and when $P(\mathbf{T})$ is equipped with the natural ordering $\prec$ defined by $[t, t] \prec [t', t']$ iff $t < t'$, the resulting frame is isomorphic to the original.

[25] Note that we're handling the distinction between interval nominals and point nominals slightly differently from the way did in referential tense logic. In referential tense logic interval nominals could name points, for singleton subsets of STOs are convex, and hence, under our previous definition, are intervals. However, in referential *interval* logic, interval nominals cannot name points, for $S(\mathbf{T})$ and $P(\mathbf{T})$ are disjoint. If desired, we could add a third referential sort to the language — call it INOM — whose members could refer to any interval whatsoever in $I(\mathbf{T})$. Such a sort would be analogous to the interval nominals of referential tense logic. However we'll stick with SNOM and PNOM in this paper.

$\models \phi \leftrightarrow \psi$ then we say that ϕ and ψ are *logically equivalent.*

Let's consider the language more closely. First note that we can define interval analogs of the Priorean operators: for example, stipulating that $F\phi =_{def} \langle A\rangle\phi \vee \langle A\rangle\langle A\rangle\phi$, yields a future tense operator. Next, note that because we're working with a linear conception of time the language is strong enough to define the universal modality. We first define its dual:

$$\begin{aligned} \Diamond\phi \quad =_{def} \quad & \langle A\rangle\phi \vee \langle \overline{A}\rangle\phi \vee \langle B\rangle\phi \vee \langle \overline{B}\rangle\phi \vee \langle E\rangle\phi \vee \langle \overline{E}\rangle\phi \vee \\ & \langle L\rangle\phi \vee \langle \overline{L}\rangle\phi \vee \langle D\rangle\phi \vee \langle \overline{D}\rangle\phi \vee \langle O\rangle\phi \vee \langle \overline{O}\rangle\phi \vee \phi. \end{aligned}$$

That is, a wff $\Diamond\phi$ is true iff it is true at an interval related in one of the thirteen fundamental ways to the interval of evaluation. As any two intervals on an STOed frame must be related in one of these ways, we are entitled to read $\Diamond$ as 'at some interval'. We then define $\Box\phi$ to be $\neg\Diamond\neg\phi$, and read $\Box$ as 'at all intervals'. $\Box$ and $\Diamond$ co-operate with interval nominals and point nominals in the interval-based semantics just as well as they did in the point-based setting, and if we were working with intervals over non-linear time, or with a weaker choice of interval operators in which $\Box$ and $\Diamond$ were not definable, it would be a excellent idea to introduce them as primitives.

We can also define the D operator: we only need to drop that last disjunct from the definition of $\Diamond$:

$$\begin{aligned} D\phi \quad =_{def} \quad & \langle A\rangle\phi \vee \langle \overline{A}\rangle\phi \vee \langle B\rangle\phi \vee \langle \overline{B}\rangle\phi \vee \langle E\rangle\phi \vee \langle \overline{E}\rangle\phi \vee \\ & \langle L\rangle\phi \vee \langle \overline{L}\rangle\phi \vee \langle D\rangle\phi \vee \langle \overline{D}\rangle\phi \vee \langle O\rangle\phi \vee \langle \overline{O}\rangle\phi. \end{aligned}$$

Clearly $D\phi$ holds at an interval iff ϕ holds at some other interval.

As with referential tense logic, the definability of D gives us some information about the complexity induced by our sorting. As before, we first use $\Diamond$ and D to define an operator U that insists that ϕ holds at a unique interval: $\Diamond(\phi \wedge \neg D\phi)$ suffices. Next we must simulate the point and the interval nominals. Observe that for any frame $\mathbf{T}$, $[B]\bot$ is true on precisely the elements of $P(\mathbf{T})$, while $\langle B\rangle\top$ is true on precisely the elements of ST. So, define $U^p\phi$ to be of $U(\phi\wedge[B]\bot)$. $U^p\phi$ insists that ϕ is true at a unique *point* interval, and it enables us to simulate the point nominals. On the other hand, if we define $U^s\phi$ to be $U(\phi \wedge \langle B\rangle\top)$, we have a way of insisting that ϕ is true at a unique stretched interval, and this enables us to simulate interval nominals. So, by making use of U^p and U^s we can prove an interval-based analog of Theorem 1.2.4. We proceed pretty much as in our discussion of the complexity of referential tense logic. Define β to be a bijection from VAR $\cup$ SNOM $\cup$ INOM to VAR, and extend this to a substitution translation σ which commutes with all the operators. Then, for any wff ϕ, define ϕ^b to be:

$$U^p(\sigma(i_1)) \wedge \cdots \wedge U^p(\sigma(i_n)) \wedge U^s(\sigma(e_1)) \wedge \cdots \wedge U^s(\sigma(e_m)) \wedge \sigma(\phi),$$

where $i_1, \ldots, i_n$ and $e_1, \ldots, e_m$ are all the pointminals and interval nominals that occur in ϕ. Analogs of Lemma 1.2.2 and Lemma 1.2.3 are easily proved, and this leads to:

Theorem 1.4.1 *Let $\mathcal{S}$ be a class of* STOs. *Determining whether an arbitrary wff of referential interval logic is satisfiable in a model based on a frame in $\mathcal{S}$, is linear time reducible to the satisfiability problem for the system of Halpern and Shoham on $\mathcal{S}$.*[26] □

Unsurprisingly, our language is strong enough to support analogs of Allen's favored vocabulary. In fact, as Halpern and Shoham's operators are tailored to express the relationships Allen wants, we can simulate Allen's system far more naturally than in referential tense logic. In the following definitions r and r' are metavariables over both interval nominals and point nominals:

$$
\begin{array}{lll}
\mathbf{Equals}(r,r') & =_{def} & \Box(r \leftrightarrow r') \\
\mathbf{Before}(r,r') & =_{def} & \Box(r \rightarrow \langle L\rangle r') \\
\mathbf{After}(r,r') & =_{def} & \Box(r \rightarrow \langle \overline{L}\rangle r') \\
\mathbf{Meets}(r,r') & =_{def} & \Box(r \rightarrow \langle A\rangle r') \\
\overline{\mathbf{Meets}}(r,r') & =_{def} & \Box(r \rightarrow \langle \overline{A}\rangle r') \\
\mathbf{Overlaps}(r,r') & =_{def} & \Box(r \rightarrow \langle O\rangle r') \\
\overline{\mathbf{Overlaps}}(r,r') & =_{def} & \Box(r \rightarrow \langle \overline{O}\rangle r') \\
\mathbf{Starts}(r,r') & =_{def} & \Box(r \rightarrow \langle \overline{B}\rangle r') \\
\mathbf{Co\text{-}starts}(r,r') & =_{def} & \Box(r \rightarrow \langle B\rangle r') \\
\mathbf{During}(r,r') & =_{def} & \Box(r \rightarrow \langle \overline{D}\rangle r') \\
\mathbf{Contains}(r,r') & =_{def} & \Box(r \rightarrow \langle D\rangle r') \\
\mathbf{Finishes}(r,r') & =_{def} & \Box(r \rightarrow \langle \overline{E}\rangle r') \\
\mathbf{Co\text{-}finishes}(r,r') & =_{def} & \Box(r \rightarrow \langle E\rangle r')
\end{array}
$$

The effect of these definitions should be clear: if both r and r' are instantiated in interval nominals, the resulting expression makes the same assertion about the two named intervals as does the use of Allen's corresponding predicate. For example, **Before**(e,d) is true in any model **M** iff the unique stretched interval denoted by e properly precedes that denoted by d. Note that if we instantiate at least one of r and r' in point nominals, the macros extend Allen's terminology to express relationships between a point and an interval, or between two points. Of course, not all of the expressions are meaningful in such cases, but all the

[26] As Halpern and Shoham[48] show, this can be very hard problem indeed (for example, validity over $\mathbf{R}$, the real numbers in their usual order, is not recursively axiomatizable). Interval logic is vastly more expressive than point-based logic, and we pay a price for this. But if we decide this is a price worth paying, sorting doesn't make matters worse.

incorrect uses are weeded out by the semantics. For example, $\mathbf{Overlaps}(i, j)$ is logically equivalent to $\bot$; our semantics (quite correctly) insists that we are talking nonsense.

Just as with referential tense logic, the force of Allen's axioms is captured by the semantics of our language. For example, corresponding to Allen's axiom:

$$\begin{aligned}&\mathrm{MEETS}(t_1, t_2) \wedge \mathrm{DURING}(t_2, t_3) \rightarrow \\ &\qquad \mathrm{OVERLAPS}(t_1, t_3) \vee \mathrm{DURING}(t_1, t_3) \vee \mathrm{STARTS}(t_1, t_3),\end{aligned}$$

we can write down macros of the form

$$\mathbf{Meets}(e, d) \wedge \mathbf{During}(d, c) \rightarrow \mathbf{Overlaps}(e, c) \vee \mathbf{During}(e, c) \vee \mathbf{Starts}(e, c).$$

Expanding such a macro yields:

$$\Box(e \rightarrow \langle A \rangle d) \wedge \Box(d \rightarrow \langle \overline{D} \rangle c) \rightarrow \Box(e \rightarrow \langle O \rangle c) \vee \Box(e \rightarrow \langle \overline{D} \rangle c) \vee \Box(e \rightarrow \langle \overline{B} \rangle c),$$

which is easily seen to be valid.

Let's consider the HOLDS predicate. This can be mimicked as follows:

$$\mathbf{Holds}(\phi, e) =_{def} \Box(e \rightarrow \phi \wedge [D]\phi \wedge [B]\phi \wedge [E]\phi).$$

That is, just an in referential tense logic the definition of **Holds** hinges on the universal modality cooperating with the referential sorts. But note the crucial difference. In the point-based setting, information that holds over an interval *automatically* trickles down to sub-intervals (this is what blocked a treatment of occurrences). In the interval-based setting this doesn't happen, and if we want **Holds** to enforce information percolation down to sub-intervals, we have to spell out this requirement explicitly — hence the last three conjuncts in the definition's consequent.

Actually, we can do better than this. Galton [25] argues that Allen really requires not one but *three* variants of the HOLDS predicate: HOLDS-AT(P, I), which asserts that the property P holds at the instant I, HOLDS-IN(P, T), which asserts that the property P holds at some instant during the interval T, and HOLDS-ON(P, T), which asserts that the property P holds at every instant during the interval T. Discussing Galton's reasons for this claim would take us too far afield, but it's worth pointing out that referential interval logic can cope with Galton's extensions. For a start, it's clear how to simulate the HOLDS-AT operator: $\mathbf{Holds\text{-}at}(\phi, i) =_{def} \Box(i \rightarrow \phi)$. What about HOLDS-IN and HOLDS-ON? Suppose we had the following 'point finding' operator $\langle \dagger \rangle$ at our disposal:

$$\langle \mathbf{T}, V \rangle, [t', t''] \models \langle \dagger \rangle \phi \text{ iff } (\exists [t, t] \in P(\mathbf{T}))([t, t] \subseteq [t', t''] \ \& \ \langle \mathbf{T}, V \rangle, [t, t] \models \phi).$$

We could then simulate the HOLDS-IN predicate as follows:

$$\textbf{Holds-in}(\phi, e) =_{def} \Box(e \rightarrow \langle\dagger\rangle\phi),$$

and, using the dual operator $[\dagger]$ of $\langle\dagger\rangle$, we could mimic HOLDS-ON:

$$\textbf{Holds-on}(\phi, e) =_{def} \Box(e \rightarrow [\dagger]\phi).$$

And in fact, $\langle\dagger\rangle$ *is* available as a defined operator. First (as Halpern and Shoham observe), we can define a 'beginning point' operator $[\![BP]\!]$ as follows:

$$[\![BP]\!]\phi =_{def} ([B]\bot \wedge \phi) \vee \langle B\rangle([B]\bot \wedge \phi).$$

That is, $[\![BP]\!]\phi$ is true at an interval t iff ϕ is true at the point that begins t. In similar fashion, we can define an 'end point' operator:

$$[\![EP]\!]\phi =_{def} ([E]\bot \wedge \phi) \vee \langle E\rangle([E]\bot \wedge \phi).$$

Using these we can define $\langle\dagger\rangle\phi$ as follows:

$$\langle\dagger\rangle\phi =_{def} [\![BP]\!]\phi \vee [\![EP]\!]\phi \vee \langle D\rangle[\![BP]\!]\phi.$$

Let's turn to what defeated us in the point-based setting: occurrences, and in particular, events. As a first step, let's define an analog of Allen's OCCUR. This is straightforward:

$$\textbf{Occur}(\phi, e) =_{def} \Box(e \rightarrow \phi \wedge [D]\neg\phi \wedge [B]\neg\phi \wedge [E]\neg\phi).$$

This is simply a variant of HOLDS in which percolation of information down to proper sub-intervals is explicitly *forbidden.*

There is one other thing that really should be done — and this concerns not merely occurrences, but properties as well. In the previous section we suggested imposing sortal constraints on the propositional variables to mirror the difference between properties and events. We couldn't do this, however, because the point-based semantics automatically enforced property-like behavior. Not only *can* we now do this, it is practically forced on us: without some constraints on valuations we have no guarantee that *any* of our propositional variables behave like properties or events! The information distributions possible in interval-based semantics are truly wild, and if we don't want the blooming buzzing confusion of a Humean universe we must impose order ourselves.

So let's do this. Subdivide VAR into two mutually disjoint and denumerably infinite sets, PVAR and EVAR. We call the elements of PVAR *property variables* and we'll represent its elements by p, p_1, p_2, p_3 and so on, and we'll call the elements of EVAR *event variables* and represent them by q, q_1, q_2, q_3 and so on. The definition of our language is unchanged: we have precisely the same atoms as before — VAR∪INOM∪SNOM — and we build the wffs out of them just as we used to.

Now for the semantics. Given an STOed frame $\mathbf{T}$, by a *PE-sorted valuation* V on $\mathbf{T}$ is meant a valuation that satisfies two further constraints.

$$(\forall p \in \text{PVAR})(\forall \mathbf{i} \in I(\mathbf{T}))(\mathbf{i} \in V(p) \Leftrightarrow (\forall \mathbf{i}' \in I(\mathbf{T})(\mathbf{i}' \subset \mathbf{i} \Rightarrow \mathbf{i}' \in V(p))))$$

$$(\forall q \in \text{EVAR})(\forall \mathbf{i}, \mathbf{i}' \in I(\mathbf{T}))(\mathbf{i} \in V(q) \ \&\ \mathbf{i}' \in V(q) \ \&\ \mathbf{i} \neq \mathbf{i}' \Rightarrow \mathbf{i} \not\subset \mathbf{i}'))$$

We then define *PE-sorted models* to be models whose valuations are PE-sorted. The satisfaction definition, and all the usual semantic definitions are exactly as before. This sorted version of Halpern and Shoham's logic captures the major ideas underlying Allen's framework: it can refer to times, reflects Allen's major ontological division (between properties and events), and is strong enough to deal with the refinements of HOLDS suggested by Galton.

1.5 Concluding Remarks

In this paper I have argued that the gap between temporal logic in AI and philosophical logic is not as wide as at first appears, and that natural language provides an interesting bridge between the two traditions. Underpinning our discussion was the idea of sorted modal languages, or hybrid languages, as they are usually called.

Hybrid languages are based on a deceptively simple insight due to Arthur Prior: *many types of information can be viewed as propositions and manipulated using Boolean operators and modalities.* Not only does this enable us to draw some useful sortal distinctions (such as the distinction between properties and events) it also enables us to handle certain intrinsically *logical* ideas, notably those concerning temporal reference and the identity of times, which at first seem to lie beyond the reach of propositional formalisms. Moreover, the "democratic" treatment of information underlying Prior's approach enables us to treat temporal representation in a very straightforward way. When we discussed Allen's account of properties, it was clear that Allen wanted to treat properties as term-like entities that behaved in a formula-like manner. This is a powerful intuition — after all, it's all just information, and it seems we *should* be able to use it as we see fit. But Allen's first-order syntax with its formula/term distinction is a straitjacket that blocks the natural expression of this idea, and he was forced to introduce 'logical functions' to try and capture it. Prior's approach zeroes in on the crucial point: all there is is different sorts of temporal information, just waiting to be combined, and information can be viewed propositionally. There's simply no need to construct a second level of logic: right from the start, all types of information, referential and otherwise, play a first-class role in the logical economy.

Prior's idea meshes neatly with contemporary perspectives on modal logic. If you ask a modal logician why modal logic is interesting, it's unlikely that he or she will appeal to a particular application (such as reasoning about knowledge) to justify it. Rather, much interest in modal logic now centers on the fact that (propositional) modal languages are simple systems which correspond to interesting fragments of classical logic: first-order logic when talking about models, and second-order logic when talking about frames.[27] Effort is devoted to developing well behaved formalisms that offer interesting expressive power; work on the difference operator, for example, falls into this tradition. Hybrid languages are part of this general research program — but instead of focusing on new operators (such as D) the idea is to investigate what happens when the atomic propositions encode semantic distinctions. As we have seen, hybridization can lead to new expressive possibilities, and enables us to do interesting temporal modeling in a propositional language.

Sometimes, of course, we want something more powerful: in particular, we want to *quantify* across temporal entities. Certainly Allen wanted to be able to this; indeed (as we mentioned earlier) he even introduced a 'logical function' *exists* so that his internal logic could do this too. But once again, matters are simpler in hybrid languages. It is straightforward to bind nominals classically with $\exists$ and $\forall$.[28] Moreover, recent work on analytic proofs systems for hybrid languages shows that once the underlying propositional systems have been properly handled (the tricky part is devising decent mechanisms for the modalities) the mechanisms for the binders can be bolted on afterwards in a modular way.[29] Moreover, we don't need to jump all the way up to the full first-order quantification offered by $\forall$ and $\exists$; there are interesting intermediate systems (notably those using the $\downarrow$ binder which binds a nominal to the point of evaluation) and these have also turned out to be logically natural (see Areces, Blackburn and Marx [2]).

[27]This *correspondence-theoretic* perspective is strongly emphasized in the work of Johan van Benthem and other Amsterdam logicians, and traces back to van Benthem [4]. For an up-do-date textbook treatment of modal logic which takes this perspective as its starting point, see Blackburn, de Rijke and Venema [11].

[28]Robert Bull did so in his 1970 paper (see Bull [18]), the Sofia School looked at such languages in the mid 1980s (see Passy and Tinchev [40]) and there are a number of recent papers on the topic (for example Blackburn and Tzakova [15]).

[29]This certainly is true of the sequent, tableau, and natural deduction systems discussed in Seligman [47], Blackburn [10], and Tzakova [53].

In short, hybrid languages offer a framework which takes us slowly up an expressivity hierarchy from simple propositional systems up to rich languages offering full quantification, always treating different types of information in an even-handed way: all in all, a natural setting for developing fine grained theories of time.

PATRICK BLACKBURN
INRIA, Lorraine
54602 Villers lès Nancy Cedex, France
E-mail: patrick@aplog.org

Bibliography

[1] J. Allen. Towards a general theory of action and time. *Artificial Intelligence*, 23:123–154, 1984.

[2] C. Areces, P. Blackburn, and M. Marx. Hybrid logics. Characterization, Interpolation and Complexity. To appear in *Journal of Symbol Logic*. `http://www.hylo.net`.

[3] C. Areces. Logic Engineering. The Case of Description and Hybrid Logics. PhD Thesis, ILLC, University of Amsterdam, October 2000. Available at `http://www.hylo.net`

[4] J. van Benthem. *Modal Logic and Classical Logic*. Bibliopolis, Napoli, 1983.

[5] J. van Benthem. *The Logic of Time*. Reidel: Dordrecht, 1983.

[6] P. Blackburn. *Nominal Tense Logic and other Sorted Intensional Frameworks*. PhD Thesis, Centre for Cognitive Science, University of Edinburgh, Scotland, 1990.

[7] P. Blackburn. Nominal tense logic. *Notre Dame Journal of Formal Logic*, 14:56–83, 1993.

[8] P. Blackburn. Modal logic and attribute value structures. In de Rijke, editor, *Diamonds and Defaults*, pages 19-65, Synthese Language Library vol 229, Dordrecht, 1993.

[9] P. Blackburn. Tense, temporal reference, and tense logic. *Journal of Semantics*, 11:83–101, 1994.

[10] P. Blackburn. Internalizing labelled Deduction. *Journal of Logic and Computation*, 10: 137–168, 2000.

[11] P. Blackburn, M. de Rijke, and Y. Venema. *Modal Logic*. Cambridge University Press, 2001.

[12] P. Blackburn and J. Seligman. Hybrid languages. *Journal of Logic, Language and Information*, 4:251–272, 1995.

[13] P. Blackburn and J. Seligman. What are hybrid languages? In M. Kracht, M. de Rijke, H. Wansing, and M. Zakharyaschev, editors, *Advances in Modal Logic, Volume 1*, pages 41–62. CSLI Publications, Stanford University, 1998.

[14] P. Blackburn and E. Spaan. A modal perspective on the computational complexity of attribute value grammar. *Journal of Logic, Language and Information*, 2:129–169, 1993.

[15] P. Blackburn and M. Tzakova. Hybrid completeness. *Logic Journal of the IGPL*, 4:625–650, 1998. `http://www.oup.co.uk/igpl`.

[16] P. Blackburn and M. Tzakova. Hybridizing concept languages. *Annals of Mathematics and Artificial Intelligence*, 24:23–49, 1998.

[17] P. Blackburn and M. Tzakova. Hybrid languages and temporal logic. *Logic Journal of the IGPL*, 7(1):27–54, 1999. `http://www.oup.co.uk/igpl`.

[18] R. Bull. An approach to tense logic. *Theoria*, 36:282–300, 1970.

[19] B. Comrie. *Tense*. Cambridge Textbooks in Linguistics, Cambridge University Press, 1985.

[20] S. Demri. Sequent calculi for nominal tense logics: a step towards mechanization? In N. Murray (ed.), *Conference on Tableaux Calculi and Related Methods (TABLEAUX), Saratoga Springs, USA*, Springer Verlag, LNAI 1617, pages 140–154, 1999.

[21] S. Demri and R. Goré. Cut-free display calculi for nominal tense logics. In N. Murray (ed.), *Conference on Tableaux Calculi and Related Methods (TABLEAUX), Saratoga Springs, USA*, Springer Verlag, LNAI 1617, pages 155–170, 1999.

[22] D. Dowty. *Word Meaning and Montague Grammar*. Reidel, 1979.

[23] H. Enderton. *A Mathematical Introduction to Logic*. Academic Press, 1972.

[24] K. Fine. An Incomplete Logic Containing S4. *Theoria*, 40:23–28, 1974.

[25] A Galton. A Critical Examination of Allen's Theory of Action and Time. *Artificial Intelligence*, 42:159–188, 1990.

[26] G. Gargov and S. Passy. Determinism and Looping in Combinatory PDL. *Theoretical Computer Science*, 61:259–277, 1988.

[27] G. Gargov, G. and V. Goranko. Modal logic with names. *Journal of Philosophical Logic*, 22:607–636, 1993.

[28] V. Goranko. Temporal logic with reference pointers. In *Temporal Logic. First International Conference, ICTL '94 Bonn, Germany*, D. Gabbay and H. Ohlbach, ed., pp. 133–164, Springer-Verlag, 1994.

[29] V. Goranko. Hierarchies of modal and temporal logics with reference pointers. *Journal of Logic, Language and Information*, 5:1–24, 1996.

[30] V. Goranko. An interpretation of computational tree logics into temporal logics with reference pointers. Verslagreeks van die Department Wiskunde, RAU, Nommer 2/96, Department of Mathematics, Rand Afrikaans University, Johannesburg, South Africa, 1996.

[31] R. Goldblatt. The Metamathematics of Modal Logic, Parts 1 and 2. *Reports on Mathematical Logic*, 6:41–77 and 7:21–52, 1976.

[32] V. Goranko, and S. Passy. Using the universal modality. *Journal of Logic and Computation*, 2:5–20, 1992.

[33] J. Halpern and Y. Shoham. A Propositional Modal Logic of Time Intervals. In *Proceedings of the First IEEE Symposium on Logic in Computer Science, Cambridge, Massachusetts*, Computer Society Press: Washington.

[34] D. McDermott. A Temporal Logic for Reasoning about Plans and Actions. *Cognitive Science*, 6:101–155, 1982.

[35] M Moens and M. Steedman Temporal Ontology and Temporal Reference. *Computational Linguistics*, 14:15–28, 1988.

[36] P Ohrstrom and P. Hasle A. N. Prior's rediscovery of tense logic. *Erkenntnis*, 39:23–50, 1993.

[37] H. Kamp and U. Reyle. *From Discourse to Logic.* Kluwer Academic Publishers, 1993.

[38] B. Konikowska. A logic for reasoning about relative similarity. *Studia Logica*, 58:185–226, 1997.

[39] H. Ono and A. Nakamura. On the size of refutation Kripke models for some linear modal and tense Logics. *Studia Logica*, 34:325–333, 1980.

[40] S. Passy and T. Tinchev. An essay in combinatory dynamic logic. *Information and Computation*, 93:263–332, 1989.

[41] A. Prior. *Past, Present and Future.* Oxford University Press, 1967.

[42] A. Prior. "Now". *Nous*, pages 101–119, 1968.

[43] W. Quine. *Philosophy of Logic.* Prentice-Hall: Englewood Cliffs, 1970.

[44] M. Reape. A feature value logic. In Rupp, Rosner and Johnson, editors, *Constraints, Language and Computation*, pages 77–110. Academic Press, 1994.

[45] M. de Rijke. The modal logic of inequality. *Journal of Symbolic Logic*, 57:566–584, 1992.

[46] S. Russell and P. Norvig. *Artificial Intelligence. A Modern Approach.* Prentice-Hall, 1995.

[47] J. Seligman. The logic of correct description. In de Rijke, editor, *Advances in Intensional Logic*, Kluwer, 107–135,1997.

[48] Y. Shoham. *Reasoning about Change.* The MIT Press: Cambridge, Massachusetts, 1988.

[49] S. Thomason. Semantic analysis of tense logic. *Journal of Symbolic Logic*, 37:50–158, 1972.

[50] S. Thomason. An incompleteness theorem in modal logic. *Theoria*, 40:30–34, 1974.

[51] S. Thomason. Reduction of second-order logic to modal logic. *Zeitschrift für mathematische Logik und Grundlagen ser Mathematik*, 21:107–114, 1975.

[52] R. Turner. *Logics for Artificial Intelligence.* Ellis Horwood: Chichester, 1984.

[53] M. Tzakova. Tableaux calculi for hybrid logics. In N. Murray (ed.), *Conference on Tableaux Calculi and Related Methods (TABLEAUX), Saratoga Springs, USA*, Springer Verlag, LNAI 1617, pages 278–292, 1999.

[54] Z. Vendler. *Linguistics in Philosophy*, Cornell University Press, 1967.

[55] Y. Venema. Expressiveness and completeness of an interval tense logic. *Notre Dame Journal of Formal Logic*, 31:529–547, 1990.

Chapter 2

Revision Sequences and Computers With an Infinite Amount of Time

BENEDIKT LÖWE

2.1 Introduction

First–order definitions and even inductive definitions using the second–order induction scheme are neither sufficient for scientific discourse in general nor for the technical applications using computers to check properties which seem to be simple from a heuristic standpoint[1]. Many natural–language notions use some degree of circularity or impredicativity in their definitions. One of these notions is the notion of truth, if you consider TRUE to be a predicate of sentences (*i.e.*, natural numbers via Gödelization): If your language contains a truth predicate you will necessarily run into sentences asserting truth of sentences, so to determine their truth values you have to already know the extension of the truth predicate.

Consequently, building on the theory of inductive definitions and work of Mar-

[1] *Cf.*, *e.g.*, the Ehrenfeucht–Fraïssé proof that the notion of connectedness for finite graphs is not first–order definable, *cf.* [6, §1].

tin, Woodruff and Kripke[2], Herzberger developed a theory called "Naive Semantics" that went beyond inductive definitions.[3] This theory was further refined by Gupta an Belnap in [7], [3], and [8], where they call the system "Revision Theory of Truth" and develop their semantic systems $\mathbf{S}^*$ and $\mathbf{S}^\#$ that allow an analysis of definitions that would be logically illicit in classical definability theory. In fact, the aim of this enterprise is even more aspiring:

> "The key to the proper resolution of the problem of truth and paradox lies, in our view, in the theory of definitions. [8, p. 113]."

Their focus on the question of truth leads to a certain disrespect towards the definability aspect of their work, although the definability aspect is a natural feature of the theory (being a generalization of inductive definability with its extensive literature on definability and complexity questions). In this paper we shall stress the question "Which sets of natural numbers can be defined using a Gupta–Belnap definition?" (as opposed to the question "Which sentences are true in a Gupta–Belnap semantic system?").

Roughly speaking (we shall make this more precise in Subsection 2.2.2) a property P of natural numbers is said to be **revision theoretically definable** if there is a formula Φ (possibly containing a symbol for P) such that a natural number n has the property P if and only if n is in every reasonable approximation for the extension of Φ, where "reasonable" means that the approximation h reoccurs in a transfinite sequence of iterated applications of Φ starting from h.

We will show that the Gupta–Belnap revision sequences are deeply connected with the Infinite Time Turing Machines defined by Hamkins and Kidder[4]. This fact is intuitively plausible: With Turing machines consisting of a finite program (corresponding to the formula Φ in the description of revision theoretic definability) being applied iteratively, their generalization to transfinite computation sequences of ordinal length looks just like the "transfinite sequence of iterated applications of Φ" in Revision Theory. We will add some substance to this intuition in Section 2.4.

This connection and the fact that there is a nice structure theory of Infinite Time Turing Computability give rise to possible applications:

---

[2] *Cf.* [17] and [15].

[3] *Cf.* [11] and [12], especially [11, p. 485 & 489] where the reader can find pictures of what was to become the Revision Sequences of [8] and Definition 2.2.3.

[4] *Cf.* [9].

The profound analysis of the lengths of Infinite Time Turing Computation gives hopes that the lengths of (the relevant part of) revision sequences can also be understood.

Even more so, Welch's theorem that Infinite Time Turing machine architecture is somewhat robust with respect to changing the limit rule (Theorem 2.3.7) seems to point into the direction of the limit rule problem of Revision Theory: There has been a discussion[5] whether changing the limit rule for revision sequences might change the semantic content of the definability notions in a relevant manner.

When Sections 1 to 5 of this paper were prepared (Spring 1999), the author already suspected that a refinement of the methods of Section 4 might lead to a solution of the limit rule problem. When the paper was presented as a talk at the workshop "Nicht-klassische Formen der Logik" at the XVIII. Deutscher Kongreß für Philosophie in Konstanz (October 1999), the problem had been solved by Philip Welch. These results are briefly mentioned in Section 6 which was prepared after the rest of the paper.

For the paper to be understandable to readers from both Revision Theory and Computability Theory we try and give a rather long introduction to both areas omitting almost all proofs.

The main part of the paper is the construction of the Turing machine $M_{\Phi,\alpha}$ in Section 2.4 in which we tried to suppress most of the tedious details of storing and copying information.

2.2 The Gupta–Belnap Systems

2.2.1 Revision Sequences

The Revision Theory of Truth as laid out in [8] is very general as it allows definitions of the extensions of arbitrary predicates over arbitrary models (of arbitrary languages), and uses arbitrary many-valued logics. To simplify notation (and to stress the similarity to Turing machines which are normally used to compute subsets of the natural numbers), we shall restrict ourselves to the most basic case throughout this paper; the ground model will be $\mathbb{N}$, the set of natural numbers, our predicate $\dot{x}$ will be unary, and the logic will be classical two-valued logic. Thus the extension we want to define will be a subset of $\mathbb{N}$. As usual in set theory, we call these objects "real numbers", although they are

[5] *Cf.* [4] and [23].

not exactly real numbers in the sense of real analysis (but rather elements of the Cantor space).

We fix a base language $\mathcal{L}$, and let $\mathcal{L}^*$ be the language $\mathcal{L}$ augmented by the additional unary predicate symbol $\dot{x}$ whose extension we want to define.

Gupta–Belnap definitions can be seen as a generalization of inductive definitions; in an inductive definition[6] we construct a monotone operator $M : \mathbb{R} \to \mathbb{R}$ derived from a formula in the augmented language $\mathcal{L}^*$ and define the extension of $\dot{x}$ to be the least fixed point of M (starting with the empty extension) which must exist since M was monotone.

In the Gupta–Belnap approach we discard the assumption of monotonicity and have to replace it by a closer analysis of the starting extensions:

As in the inductive case, let $\Phi(v_0)$ be a formula of $\mathcal{L}^*$. Then we shall say that a function $\delta_\Phi : \mathbb{R} \to \mathbb{R}$ is the **revision operation determined by Φ** if

$$k \in \delta_\Phi(z) \iff \langle \mathbb{N}, z \rangle \models \Phi[k]$$

for all real numbers z. (Again, note that elements of $\mathbb{R}$ are identified with subsets of $\mathbb{N}$.)

For revision operations $\delta : \mathbb{R} \to \mathbb{R}$ we use the obvious notation for the iterated application of δ. In the following we will consider sequences of real numbers $\vec{s} = \langle s_\alpha ; \alpha \in \eta \rangle$ where η is either a limit ordinal or the class of all ordinals.[7] These sequences are interpreted as approximations to our final interpretation of the predicate $\dot{x}$.

Definition 2.2.1 *Let $\vec{s}$ be a sequence of real numbers of length η (η might be the class of all ordinals), and let d be a natural number. We shall say that "$d \in \dot{x}$" is* **$\vec{s}$–stably true** *if there is a β such that for all $\alpha \geq \beta$ we have $d \in s_\alpha$.*
Likewise, we shall say that "$d \in \dot{x}$" is **$\vec{s}$–stably false** *if there is a β such that for all $\alpha \geq \beta$ we have $d \notin s_\alpha$.*

Definition 2.2.2 *Let $\vec{s}$ be a sequence of reals. Then a real h is said to be* **$\vec{s}$–coherent** *(in symbols: $\mathrm{Coh}(h, \vec{s})$) if for all natural numbers d the following hold:*

[6] *Cf.* [18].

[7] Of course, revision sequences of successor length can be easily extended to revision sequences of limit length, so these are the only ones we have to think about.

(i) If "$d \in \dot{x}$" is $\vec{s}$–stably true, then $d \in h$.

(ii) If "$d \in \dot{x}$" is $\vec{s}$–stably false, then $d \notin h$.

Definition 2.2.3 *Let $\vec{s}$ be a sequence of reals and Φ a formula of $\mathcal{L}^*$. We shall call $\vec{s}$ a* **Φ–revision sequence** *if*

(i) For all ordinals α, we have $s_{\alpha+1} = \delta_\Phi(s_\alpha)$.

(ii) For every limit ordinal λ, we have that s_λ is $\vec{s}{\restriction}\lambda$–coherent.

In light of the later discussed question of the limit rule, a revision sequence of the defined kind might be called an **unrestricted revision sequence**. To prepare for the limit rule problem, we introduce restricted revision sequences:

Following [4, p. 400], we shall call a function γ assigning to a sequence of reals $\vec{s}$ of limit length λ a real $\gamma(\vec{s})$ that is $\vec{s}$–coherent a **bootstrapping policy**. If Γ is a class of bootstrapping policies, then we shall say that $\vec{s}$ is a **$\langle\Phi,\Gamma\rangle$–revision sequence** if it's a Φ–revision sequence and there is a $\gamma \in \Gamma$ such that for each limit ordinal λ we hae $s_\lambda = \gamma(\vec{s}{\restriction}\lambda)$.

The most interesting cases are the class Γ_∞ of all bootstrapping policies (being a Φ–revision sequence and being a $\langle\Phi,\Gamma_\infty\rangle$–revision sequence are the same), and the one–element classes where we have one particular limit rule applied in all limit stages.

At this point we single out the class $\Gamma_0 := \{\gamma_0\}$ where γ_0 is the liminf rule (*i.e.*, exactly the stably true formulae hold in the limit stage). The limit rule γ_0 is the minimal bootstrapping policy in the sense that all others let more formulae be true in the limit. Γ_0 will play a decisive rôle in the construction of Section 2.4.[8]

Definition 2.2.4 *Let Φ be a formula of $\mathcal{L}^*$.*

(i) We shall call a real h **$\langle\Phi,\Gamma\rangle$–recurring** *if h occurs cofinally often in some $\langle\Phi,\Gamma\rangle$–revision sequence $\vec{s}$ of length* Ord. *The set of $\langle\Phi,\Gamma\rangle$–recurring reals will be denoted by* $\mathrm{Rec}_\Gamma(\Phi)$.

[8]The rule Γ_∞ was the original rule used in [8], and it is called the **Belnap rule**. Herzberger in his [11] used the rule Γ_0 whence we call it the **Herzberger rule**. In [11, p. 487], Herzberger compares his liminf rule to Kripke's limsup rule of inductive definitions from [15].

*(ii) A real h is called $\langle\Phi,\Gamma\rangle$–**reflexive** if there is some ordinal $\alpha > 0$ and some $\langle\Phi,\Gamma\rangle$–revision sequence $\vec{s}$ such that $s_0 = s_\alpha = h$. We shall call the least such α the $\langle\Phi,\Gamma\rangle$–**reflexivity** of h, in symbols* $\mathrm{refl}_{\Phi,\Gamma}(h)$.

In the following we state a couple of simple consequences of the basic definitions. Proofs of these easy facts can be found in [8]:

Proposition 2.2.5 *Let $\vec{s}$ be a sequence of real numbers. Then the following are equivalent:*

(i) "$d \in \dot{x}$" is $\vec{s}$–stably true,

(ii) for all h occurring cofinally often in $\vec{s}$ we have $d \in h$.

Proposition 2.2.6 *For any real h the following are equivalent:*

(i) h is $\langle\Phi,\Gamma_\infty\rangle$–recurring,

(ii) h is $\langle\Phi,\Gamma_\infty\rangle$–reflexive.

The use of the Belnap rule Γ_∞ in Proposition 2.2.6 is important. The conclusion is provably false for some other rules, including the Herzberger rule Γ_0.[9]

Proposition 2.2.7 *If h is $\langle\Phi,\Gamma\rangle$–reflexive then* $\mathrm{refl}_{\Phi,\Gamma}(h) < \omega_1$.

2.2.2 The Systems $\mathbf{S}^\#$ and $\mathbf{S}^*$

Now we define the semantic relation for the Gupta–Belnap systems $\mathbf{S}^\#$ and $\mathbf{S}^*$:

$$\mathbb{N} \models^{\mathbf{S}^\#}_{\Phi,\Gamma} \varphi \iff \forall h \in \mathrm{Rec}_\Gamma(\Phi)\exists n\forall p \geq n(\langle\mathbb{N}, \delta^p_\Phi(h)\rangle \models \varphi),$$

and

$$\mathbb{N} \models^{\mathbf{S}^*}_{\Phi,\Gamma} \varphi \iff \forall h \in \mathrm{Rec}_\Gamma(\Phi)(\langle\mathbb{N}, h\rangle \models \varphi).$$

We shall say that a real number z is $\mathbf{S}^\#_\Gamma$–definable ($\mathbf{S}^*_\Gamma$–definable) if there is a formula of $\mathcal{L}^*$ such that for all natural numbers n the following holds:

$$n \in z \iff \mathbb{N} \models^{\mathbf{S}^\#}_{\Phi,\Gamma} \text{“}n \in \dot{x}\text{”}$$

[9] *Cf.* [8, p. 175].

$$\left(n \in z \iff \mathbb{N} \models^{\mathbf{S}^*}_{\Phi,\Gamma} \text{“}n \in \dot{x}\text{”}\right).$$

In the following, we shall omit Γ in the notation if $\Gamma = \Gamma_\infty$.

Of course, if φ is a sentence not containing $\dot{x}$ (*i.e.*, a sentence of $\mathcal{L}$), then $\mathbb{N} \models^{\mathbf{S}^\#}_{\Phi,\Gamma} \varphi$ if and only if $\mathbb{N} \models \varphi$, so $\{\varphi\,;\, \mathbb{N} \models^{\mathbf{S}^\#}_{\Phi,\Gamma} \varphi\}$ does contain the true sentences of arithmetic. Thus, by Gödel's Incompleteness Theorem it can't be first order definable.

Kremer and Antonelli in [14], [1] and [2] progressed further along this line and showed that $\{\varphi\,;\, \mathbb{N} \models^{\mathbf{S}^\#}_{\Phi} \varphi\}$ is Π^1_2–complete.[10]

From our definability standpoint, the most interesting open question about the complexity of revision theory is: "What reals are $\mathbf{S}^\#_\Gamma$– ($\mathbf{S}^*_\Gamma$–)definable?" More precisely, this innocuous question is a vast array of questions. Not only can we try and compute the set of $\mathbf{S}^\#_\Gamma$–definable reals for all sorts of Γ, but we can ask the question

> Under what circumstances (*i.e.*, what conditions do we have to impose on Γ) is $\mathbf{S}^\#_\Gamma$–definability equivalent to $\mathbf{S}^\#$–definability?

This question keeps us very close to the limit rule question: There have been various proposals for the most natural choice of Γ, and it is still under discussion for which Γ the system $\mathbf{S}^\#_\Gamma$ is most natural.[11]

If we fix $\Gamma := \Gamma_\infty$, we can (just by counting quantifiers) make the following immediate observation:[12]

Proposition 2.2.8 *The sets* $\{\varphi\,;\, \mathbb{N} \models^{\mathbf{S}^\#}_{\Phi,\Gamma_\infty} \varphi\}$ *and* $\{\varphi\,;\, \mathbb{N} \models^{\mathbf{S}^*}_{\Phi,\Gamma_\infty} \varphi\}$ *are* Π^1_2.

Proof : Using Proposition 2.2.7 and Proposition 2.2.6 we can transform the

[10] For a weaker result with proof, *cf.* Proposition 2.2.8. The Kremer-Antonelli result is not only stronger but also much more general since they do not restrict their attention to the standard model $\mathbb{N}$.

Furthermore, Kremer's completeness result extends to a broader class of revision theories he calls **plausible revision theories**, *cf.* [14, p.590*sqq*]. $\mathbb{N} \models^{\mathbf{S}^\#}_{\Phi,\Gamma}$ is a plausible revision theory for arbitary Γ, hence these relations constitute Π^1_2–complete sets.

[11] *Cf.* [4].

[12] The corresponding computation for $\Gamma := \Gamma_0$ can be found in [16, Proposition 4.1].

definition equivalently to the form

$$\begin{array}{lll}\forall h((\exists\alpha<\omega_1(\exists\vec{s}\in(\mathbb{R})^{\alpha+1} & (& \forall\beta<\alpha(s_{\beta+1}=\delta_\Phi(s_\beta)) \\ & \wedge & \forall\lambda<\alpha(\mathrm{Lim}(\lambda)\to\mathrm{Coh}(s_\lambda,\vec{s}\restriction\lambda)) \\ & \wedge & s_0=s_\alpha=h)) \quad) \\ & \to & (\exists n\forall p\geq n(\langle\mathbb{N},\delta_\Phi^p(h)\rangle\models\varphi))\ )\end{array}$$

for $\mathbf{S}^\#$ and

$$\begin{array}{lll}\forall h((\exists\alpha<\omega_1(\exists\vec{s}\in(\mathbb{R})^{\alpha+1} & (& \forall\beta<\alpha(s_{\beta+1}=\delta_\Phi(s_\beta)) \\ & \wedge & \forall\lambda<\alpha(\mathrm{Lim}(\lambda)\to\mathrm{Coh}(s_\lambda,\vec{s}\restriction\lambda)) \\ & \wedge & s_0=s_\alpha=h)) \quad) \\ & \to & \langle\mathbb{N},h\rangle\models\varphi\ )\end{array}$$

for $\mathbf{S}^*$.

To compute the complexity of these formulae, first note that the function δ_Φ doesn't add complexity since it is first–order definable (via Φ).

Now both formulae are of the form

$$\forall h\Big(\ (\exists\alpha<\omega_1\exists\vec{s}\,\Psi(\alpha,\vec{s},h))\to\Psi^*(h)\Big),$$

where Ψ is arithmetic in its arguments (already assuming that ordinal quantifiers bounded by α will be natural number quantifiers after coding $\langle\alpha,\in\rangle$ as a real). Note that the satisfaction relation in $\langle\mathbb{N},h\rangle$ is $\Delta^1_1(h)$, so the Ψ^*–part doesn't add complexity either.

Now we code the countable ordinal by a real and receive

$$\forall h\Big(\ (\exists y(\mathrm{WO}(y)\wedge\exists\vec{s}\,\Psi(\alpha,\vec{s},h)))\to\Psi^*(h)\Big).$$

Thus the premiss of the implication is $\exists(\Pi^1_1\wedge\Sigma^1_1)$ which is Σ^1_2, and hence the whole formula is Π^1_2. q.e.d.

This computation gives an upper bound for the complexity of any given $\mathbf{S}^\#$–definable real:

Corollary 2.2.9 *Every $\mathbf{S}^\#_{\Gamma_\infty}$–definable real (and every $\mathbf{S}^*_{\Gamma_\infty}$–definable real) is a Π^1_2 real.*

Proof: By definition, a real x is $\mathbf{S}^{\#}_{\Gamma_\infty}$–definable if and only if there is a formula Φ of $\mathcal{L}^*$ such that for all n

$$n \in x \iff \mathbb{N} \models^{\mathbf{S}^{\#}}_{\Phi,\Gamma_\infty} \text{“}n \in \dot{x}\text{”}.$$

But by Proposition 2.2.8, the right–hand side is Π^1_2. q.e.d.

What is to be said about lower bounds? Using an idea of Gupta, Kremer has proved that every inductively definable real is $\mathbf{S}^{\#}$–definable.[13] Since inductive definability over $\mathbb{N}$ and being Π^1_1 coincide,[14] we have a lower bound for the complexity of $\mathbf{S}^{\#}$–definability. It was unknown until very recently[15] whether there were more complicated $\mathbf{S}^{\#}$–definable sets (see Section 2.6).

2.3 Infinite Time Turing Machines

The notion of an Infinite Time Turing Machine is a natural generalization of the ordinary Turing machines that constitute our basic model of computation. Jeffrey Kidder and Joel Hamkins blended the fields of Recursion Theory (Computability Theory) and Set Theory by allowing their Turing machines to resume their computations after infinitely many steps and start at limit steps in a specified limit stage.[16]

Although probably technically of no importance,[17] the investigation of Infinite Time Turing Machines is motivated by certain philosophical thought–experiments using the Lorentz contraction of spacetime to fit a countable sequence of time intervals into a finite time interval (according to the timeline of a different observer), or, more in the language of general relativity, to fit the entire future time cone of one observer into the past time cone of a second observer.

Readers interested in this basic background are referred to the introduction of [9], and the papers [5] and [13].

---

[13] *Cf.* [14, p. 590*sqq.*].
[14] *Cf.* [18, p. 20 & p. 24*sq.*].
[15] *Cf.* [22].
[16] *Cf.* [9].
[17] “Thompson lamps, super π machines, and Platonist computers are playthings of philosophers; they are able to survive only in the hothouse atmosphere of philosophy journals. In the end, [Malament–Hogarth] spacetimes and the supertasks they underwrite may similarly prove to be recreational fictions for general relativists with nothing better to do. [5, p.40]”

In the following, we shall assume that the reader is familiar with the basic theory of ordinary Turing machines.[18]

An Infinite Time Turing Machine works like an ordinary Turing machine — it has a finite program including a specified finite set of states, one of these states is a Halt state telling the program to stop, and in addition to that, it has an infinite tape for output.

The content of the infinite tape of a Turing machine can be seen as a real number. We shall identify the tape with this real number at numerous points in the construction of Section 2.4. If we have an Infinite Turing Machine Computation of ordinal length α with a tape labeled x, and $\beta < \alpha$ then we shall denote the snapshot real at time β with x^β. We can (and shall) go even further: If we have an Infinite Time Turing Machine with a tape that is split into countably many infinite components $\langle x_i; i \in I\rangle$, then we shall denote with x_i^β the real that constitutes the snapshot of tape x_i at the time β.

There is no difference between Infinite Time Turing machines and ordinary Turing machines in the part of the Infinite Time Turing machines described up to now. The only difference from ordinary Turing machines is the Infinite Time Turing machine's Limit state, and the fact that if the computation doesn't reach the Halt state at any given $\beta < \lambda$ for a limit ordinal λ, then it will go into the Limit state and set all cells according to the limsup rule: Every cell gets the *limes superior* of the cell values at the stages below λ; in other words: If a cell contains a 1 cofinally often, it has 1 in the limit.

As in the standard case we can define Infinite Time Turing Computability as follows:

Definition 2.3.1 *A real x is* **Infinite Time Turing Computable** *if there is an Infinite Time Turing Machine that produces, starting from the empty input, the real x on the tape at the time it reaches the* Halt *state.*

This definition immediately leads to Relative Infinite Time Turing Computability (denoted by $\leq_T^\infty$) and a degree structure as for the ordinary Turing degrees.

At present, the structure theory of Infinite Time Turing degrees is only of marginal importance to the results of Section 2.4. But since the main aim of this paper is to open up a possible area of applications of the field of Infinite Time Computability theory to Revision Theory, it seems reasonable to give the reader a faint idea about what is known in the former area. Thus we briefly

[18] As it is to be found in any good textbook of Recursion Theory; *e.g.*, [19].

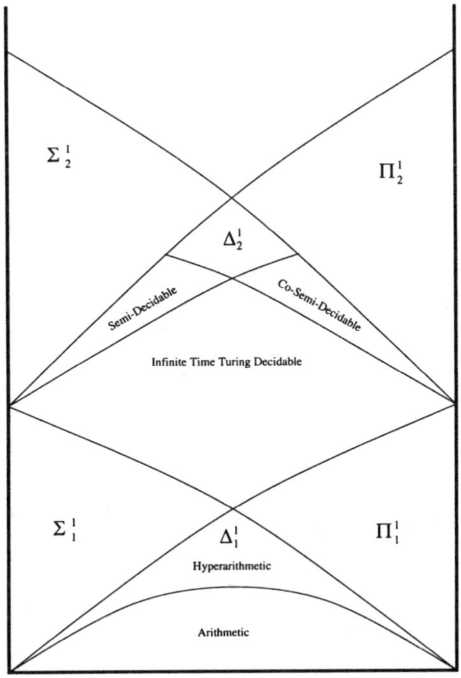

Figure 2.1: The extend of infinite time turing computation

describe what is known without any proofs:

Hamkins and Lewis[19] and (following a visit of Joel Hamkins to Kobe in the year 1998) Philip Welch provided us with an abundance of structure theoretic results about Infinite Time Turing Computability and the derived degree structure.

It is easily seen that arithmetic truth is Infinite Time Turing computable, since you can just use ω steps to check every possible witness for an existential quantifier.[20] The class of Infinite Time Turing computable reals forms a subclass of the Δ^1_2–reals as can be seen in Figure 2.1.

The analysis of the Infinite Time Halting problem is an important component of the structure theory of Infinite Time Turing Machines: The Infinite Time Halting Problem (*i.e.*, the set of machines halting given the empty input) is not Infinite Time Turing Computable. The halting problem and its boldface version (the set of reals coding a machine M and a real x such that M halts

[19] [9].
[20] [9, Theorem 2.1 & Theorem 2.6].

given the input x) yield Infinite Time Turing jump operations $x \mapsto x^\triangledown$ and $x \mapsto x^\blacktriangledown$ of which the following can be shown [9, Theorems 5.1 & 5.6]:

Theorem 2.3.2 *(i)* $x <_T^\infty x^\triangledown <_T^\infty x^\blacktriangledown$

(ii) Δ^1_2 *is closed under* $x \mapsto x^\triangledown$ *and* $x \mapsto x^\blacktriangledown$

Hamkins and Lewis[21] have looked much closer at the connections between these jump operations and the Infinite Time degree structure, finding situations both symmetrical and asymmetrical with respect to classical Turing degree theory.

Infinite Time Turing Machines are connected to a couple of interesting classes of ordinals. For the following, we fix a coding of countable ordinals as real numbers.

Definition 2.3.3 *Let α be an ordinal.*

(i) α is called **writable** *if there is a real x coding α such that x is Infinite Time Turing Computable,*

(ii) α is called **clockable** *if there is an Infinite Time Turing Machine which reaches its* HALT *state after exactly α steps of computation, and*

(iii) α is called **eventually writable** *if there is an Infinite Time Turing Machine and an ordinal η such that after step η the machine just has a fixed code for α on the tape.*

We shall write Λ_∞ for the supremum of the writable ordinals, Υ_∞ for the supremum of the clockable ordinals, and Z_∞ for the supremum of the eventually writable ordinals. These ordinals reach quite far into the hierarchy of countable ordinals [9, Corollary 8.2 & Corollary 8.6]:

Theorem 2.3.4 *Λ_∞ and Z_∞ are admissible ordials.*

Philip Welch [21, Theorem 1.1] was able to prove the following connection between the length of Infinite Time Turing Computations and the possible outputs and then to actually compute Z_∞:

Theorem 2.3.5 *(i)* $\Lambda_\infty = \Upsilon_\infty$*, and*

[21] *Cf.* [10].

(ii) $Z_\infty = \min\{\,\xi\,;\ \mathbf{L}_\xi$ *has a transitive* Σ_2*-end extension*$\}$.

The computation of Theorem 2.3.5 gives a very interesting result about the actual power of the Infinite Time Turing machine architecture [20, Theorem 2.6]. At limit stages the original Hamkins–Kidder machine used the limsup rule: if a cell contains the value 1 cofinally often, the limit value is also 1. If we look at machine architectures that use different rules, then the computational power does not change (provided the different rule is simple enough). To make this more precise, let us fix the notation: let $z^\beta_{p,y}$ be the real containing the snapshot of the computation of the Infinite Time Turing Machine with the code p on input y at time β.

Definition 2.3.6 *Let* $\Gamma : (2^{\mathbb{N}})^{<\mathrm{Ord}} \to 2^{\mathbb{N}}$ *be a function. Then* Γ *is called a* **suitable Σ_2 operator** *if for every machine using* Γ *in the limit stages there is a* Σ_2 *formula* $\Psi(v_0, v_1, v_2)$ *such that*

$$\mathbf{L}_\nu[y] \models z^\nu_{p,y}(i) = 0 \leftrightarrow \Psi[i, p, y].$$

Theorem 2.3.7 (Welch) *Let* Γ *be a suitable* Σ_2 *operator. Then a real is computable by a Hamkins–Kidder machine (an Infinite Time Turing machine as described above) if it's computable by a machine using the limit rule* γ.

2.4 Revision Sequences Modeled by Infinite Time Turing Machines

By now, it should be clear to the reader that there is some connection between Infinite Time Turing Machines and revision sequences: Both concepts move stepwise, taking the information given in the previous step and computing the next one with a finite amount of programming; both concepts are about moving on throughout the ordinals and in both cases we can use the fact that we can run for an infinite amount of time to check arithmetic truth. The following two quotes highlight this similarity:

> A central idea in our approach is to view the function $\delta_{D,M}$ that is supplied by a circular definition D as a rule of revision. Its application to a hypothetical extension X results in a set $\delta_{D,M}(X)$ that is a better candidate for the extension of G, according to the definition, than X. [8, p. 121]

> The Infinite Time Turing Machines have something in the nature of a non–monotonic inductive operator: a set of integers may be input, and at various stages there is a set of integers present on the output tape. [20]

In this section, we shall assume that we have a $\langle\Phi, \Gamma_0\rangle$–revision sequence of writable ordinal length α, and construct an Infinite Time Turing Machine that in its course of computation constructs the revision sequence on its tape. Our Infinite Time Turing Machine will not use the limsup rule as the standard Hamkins–Kidder machines did, but it will use the liminf rule. This doesn't change the computational power of the machine by Theorem 2.3.7.

For $\eta < \alpha$ we will denote by ϱ_η the stage of the computation of our machine where s_η appears on the tape for the first time. Our machine will be constructed such that for limit ordinals λ we have $\varrho_\lambda = \bigcup_{\beta<\lambda} \varrho_\beta$.

Now we fix a first–order formula Φ and a writable ordinal α. The Infinite Time Turing Machine we shall construct will have a couple of states that are needed for counting and checking arithmetic truth (we will try and suppress all this detail in the description of the Turing machine architecture), the START, the HALT and the LIMIT state, and three distinguished states COMPUTE, PRED and NOPRED.

We now describe the action of our machine:

Case 1 : If the machine is in the state START, it splits its tape into six countable parts x_0, x_1, x_2 x_3, x_4 and x_5. It copies the previous content of the tape into x_3, then it initializes x_0, x_1, x_4 and x_5 with an infinite sequence of 0s, and x_2 with an infinite sequence of 1s.

The machine will fill x_0 with a code for the ordinal α, x_2 will be an array telling the machine what natural numbers it has already checked, x_3 will be the storage of initial segments of the new real (*i.e.*, the next real in the revision sequence), and x_1 will be the list of ordinals already handled.

The part x_5 will be used by the machine to do its computations and other details like storing the natural number and the ordinal $\beta < \alpha$ it is working on at the moment. This is the part of the action of the machine that we will suppress almost completely in our account. The bits $x_5(0)$ and $x_5(1)$ will have a special significance:

$x_5(0)$ will be called the SEQUENCE bit, it contains the information whether we are done writing the next element of $\vec{s}$ onto x_3.

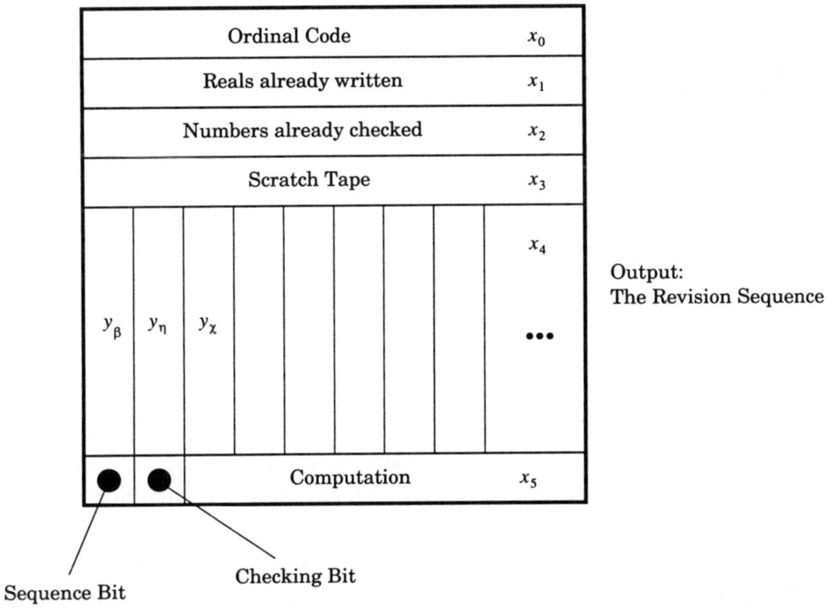

Figure 2.2: The infinite time turing machine $M_{\Phi,\alpha}$ and its partitioned tape

$x_5(1)$ will be called the CHECKING bit, and it contains the information whether we are finished with checking an arithmetic truth for some fixed natural number.

x_4 will be split up into countably many pieces and will contain the whole revision sequence in the end. The partitioning of the tape can be seen in Figure 2.2.

After the initialization, the machine writes the ordinal α (*i.e.*, a code for it) onto the tape x_1. Then it splits up the tape x_4 into a countable sequence of tapes $\langle y_\beta ; \beta < \alpha \rangle$.[22] The content of tape x_1 tells us the order of the countable sequence of tapes. Then it copies the content of x_3 to every tape y_β and goes to the COMPUTE state.

Case 2 : If the machine is in the COMPUTE state, it browses through x_1 in the order given by the code x_0 to find the (in the order of x_0) least β

[22]From this point onwards, we shall confuse α and the ordering of $\mathbb{N}$ isomorphic to α given by x_0. To be exact, we should speak of "$\langle y_n ; n \in \mathbb{N} \rangle$ ordered by $y_n \prec y_m$ if and only if $\pi_{x_0}(n) < \pi_{x_0}(m)$ where π_{x_0} is the bijection between $\mathbb{N}$ and α coded by x_0" instead of "$\langle y_\beta ; \beta < \alpha \rangle$". But we don't.

such that $x_1(\beta) = 0$.

If this β has a predecessor ζ, the machine moves to the PRED state.

If this β has no predecessor, it moves to the NOPRED state.

Case 3 : If the machine is in the NOPRED state, it just sets $x_1(\beta) := 1$ and starts the COMPUTE state case all over again.

Case 4 : If the machine is in the PRED state, the machine sets the CHECKING bit to 1, the SEQUENCE bit to 0, initializes x_3 with an infinite sequence of 0s and starts checking Φ with input y_ζ at the natural number 0.

Case 5 : If the machine is in the LIMIT state, its head moves to the SEQUENCE bit. If this bit contains a 1, the machine writes the content of x_3 to all y_η such that $x_1(\eta) = 0$, afterwards sets $x_1(\beta) := 1$ and moves into the state COMPUTE.

If the SEQUENCE bit contains a 0, the head moves on to the CHECKING bit. If the CHECKING bit is 1, the machine continues with its checking job. If the CHECKING bit is 0, the machine writes 1 into the SEQUENCE bit, runs along x_2 until it meets the first 1 in x_2. At that point it overwrites the SEQUENCE bit with 0 and the CHECKING bit with 1, and starts the checking of Φ at the next natural number (with the same input).

As soon as the machine determines whether Φ holds at that natural number, the machine writes the outcome of the check into x_3 and sets the appropriate bit of x_2 and the CHECKING bit to 0.

This completes the definition of our Infinite Time Turing Machine. We shall denote it by $M_{\Phi,\alpha}$. The working schematics of the machine can be seen in the flow diagram, Figure 2.3.

Note that the construction is somewhat flexible (remember that we are standing on the shoulders of Theorem 2.3.7). If $\Gamma = \{\gamma\}$ is a singleton with a sufficiently simply definable γ and $\vec{s}$ is a $\langle\Phi,\Gamma\rangle$–revision sequence, we could be a little bit more careful in our construction and receive a machine that computes $\vec{s}$.

Theorem 2.4.1 *Let α be a writable ordinal, Φ be any given formula of $\mathcal{L}^*$, and $\vec{s} = \langle s_\beta; \beta < \alpha\rangle$ a sequence of reals. Then the following are equivalent:*

(i) $\vec{s}$ is a $\langle\Phi,\Gamma_0\rangle$–revision sequence, and

(ii) $M_{\Phi,\alpha}$ eventually computes $\vec{s}$ on the x_4 tape, given s_0 as the input.

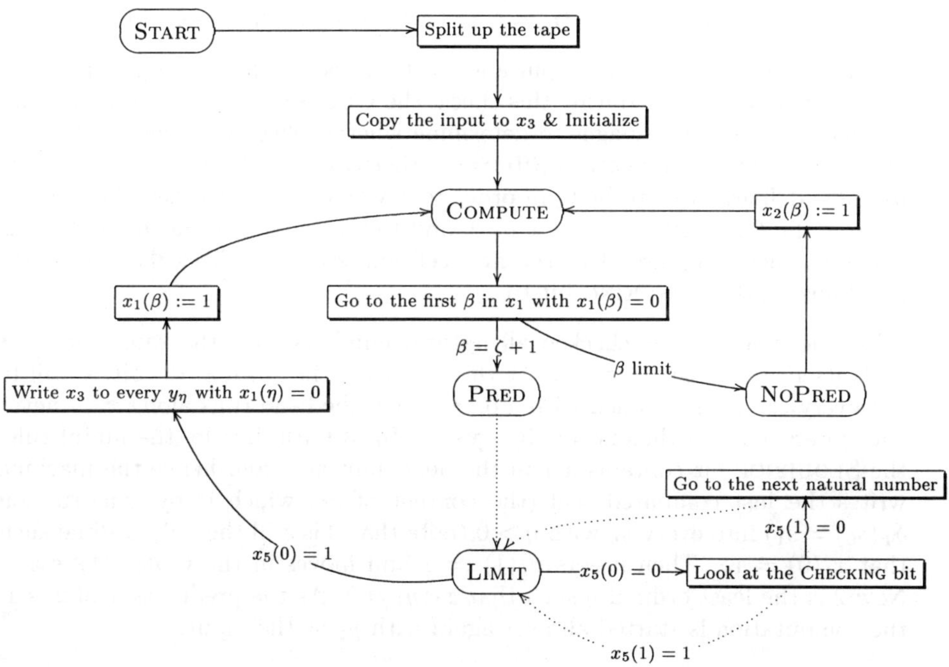

Figure 2.3: Flow Diagram for $M_{\Phi,\alpha}$

Proof : We describe what the machine does to see that it does exactly what it's supposed to do:

We feed s_0 to the machine in the START state. The machine creates six copies of its tape, writing s_0 on x_3 and erasing all information from the other copies.

The machine then writes the ordinal α onto x_0 (which is possible since α was writable). Then it copies the content of x_3 (which is the original input s_0) to every component of y_η of x_4.

In the COMPUTE state, it finds that we have $x_1(\eta) = 0$ for all ordinals η, thus 0 is the least such ordinal. But 0 has no predecessor, so the machine moves to the NOPRED state, writes 1 to $x_1(0)$ and goes back into the COMPUTE state. Now the least η such that $x_1(\eta) = 0$ is 1 which is the successor of 0.

The machine takes y_0 as the input and starts checking whether $\Phi(y_0, 0)$ is true. If it meets a limit stage during this check, the CHECKING bit is 1, so it resumes its checking until it manages to determine whether $\Phi(y_0, 0)$ holds. If $\Phi(y_0, 0)$ holds, then the machine sets $x_3(0) := 1$, otherwise it writes 0. Afterwards the machine defines $x_2(0)$ to be 0, in order to say that it has checked the number 0. Now the CHECKING bit is set to 0, and the machine can move on: It runs along x_2, meets the first 1 at the first cell and starts to check $\Phi(y_0, 1)$ (after reinitializing the CHECKING bit to 1).

After the machine has checked all natural numbers with the same input, it finds itself in the LIMIT state. At this moment, the SEQUENCE bit is still 0, but every cell on x_2 is filled with a 0. So when the head runs along x_2 if never encounters a 1 and thus never changes the SEQUENCE bit; by the liminf rule, the SEQUENCE bit contains a 1 in the next limit step and hence the machine writes the just computed real (the content of x_3, which is by construction $\delta_\Phi(s_0) = s_1$) into every y_η with $\eta > 0$ (note that 0 is still the only ordinal such that $x_1(0) = 1$). Then it sets $x_1(1) := 1$ and moves in the COMPUTE state. Now 2 is the least ordinal η such that $x_1(\eta) = 0$. As the predecessor of 2 is 1, the computation is started all over again with y_1 as the input.

This describes in fact how that machine computes all successor steps of the revision sequence $\vec{s}$.

What about the limit stages in the sequence $\vec{s}$?

Let λ be a limit ordinal and $\varrho := \bigcup_{\eta<\lambda} \varrho_\eta$.

Then ϱ is a limit, since $\langle \varrho_\eta ; \eta < \lambda \rangle$ is a strictly increasing sequence of limit length. But if we look at y_λ in the course of computation up to ϱ, y_λ contains every element of $\vec{s}\upharpoonright\lambda$. So the following holds for all natural numbers n:

$$\exists\zeta < \varrho\forall\xi \geq \zeta\,(y^{\xi}_{\lambda}(n) = 1) \iff \exists\zeta < \lambda\forall\xi \geq \zeta(n \in s_{\xi}).$$

Thus by the liminf rule and by the fact that $s_{\lambda} = \gamma_0(\vec{s}\upharpoonright\lambda)$, we have $y^{\varrho}_{\lambda} = s_{\lambda}$. In fact, this is true for all y^{ϱ}_{χ} with $\chi \geq \lambda$.

Now below ϱ the machine has run through the COMPUTE case cofinally often. Thus, the SEQUENCE bit has been reset to 0 cofinally often and by the liminf rule this means that it is 0 at ϱ.

The CHECKING bit is also 0 since the machine has successfully checked a given natural number cofinally often below ϱ.

With the same argument, x_2 at the stage ϱ is constantly 0 (every natural number has been checked cofinally often), so the machine runs along x_2 and in the step $\varrho + \omega$, the SEQUENCE bit is at 1.

Consequently, the machine moves to the COMPUTE state, realizes that λ is the least ordinal such that $x_1(\lambda) = 0$. Since λ does not have a predecessor, it writes $x_1(\lambda) = 1$ and moves on to compute $y_{\lambda+1}$. q.e.d.

2.5 The Limit Rule and Other Applications

Using the correspondence between revision sequences and Infinite Time Turing Machines we head towards possible applications (and point out possible complications and obstacles):

We mentioned the limit problem of Revision Theory a couple of times before:

"If we let Γ vary, what happens to the notion of $\mathbf{S}^{\#}_{\Gamma}$–definability?[23]"

The apparent freedom of choosing the limit rule for Infinite Time Turing machines should give us some way of tackling the limit problem for Revision Theory. In order to use that, we would have to get a uniform version of Theorem 2.4.1: Suppose that h is $\mathbf{S}^{*}_{\Gamma}$–definable. Then for every natural number n

[23] *Cf.* the analogous question for the context of validity instead of definability in [4, p.403]: "What category a proposition is going to belong to depends on the kinds of bootstrapping policies admitted."

such that $n \notin h$, we have a revision sequence $\vec{s^n}$ witnessing this (*i.e.*, $n \notin s_0^n$ and s_0^n recurs in $\vec{s^n}$). One of the problems applying Theorem 2.4.1 is that we don't know anything about the lengths of the witnessing sequences $\vec{s^n}$, and our theorem works only for sequences of writable ordinal length.

This problem naturally leads us into a second possible field of applications: The fact that we have a good understandin what ordinals are writable and where the boundaries of writability lie, poses several interesting related questions about Revision Theory:

> "What can we say about the length of relevant parts of revision sequences? (*I.e.*, how large can $\mathrm{refl}_{\Phi,\Gamma}(h)$ become?)"

A useful solution of this question would also give us the needed uniform version of Theorem 2.4.1.

In solving the limit rule problem, there are some additional (somewhat deeper) problems with unrestricted revision sequences (*i.e.*, if the class Γ is large), though, since the mere existence of a revision sequence doesn't say anything about the complexity of choices from Γ made on the way to $\mathrm{refl}_{\Phi,\Gamma}(s_0)$.

A third area of possible applications concerns the extent of revision theoretic definability. It might be possible to use the stratification of Δ^1_2 by the relation $\leq_T^\infty$ to get results for the complexity of revision theoretically definable reals.

Concluding, there is a clear connection between Revision Theory and Infinite Time Turing machines, and it seems very promising, but there is still a lot of technical work to be done to get to a point where we can exploit this connection.

2.6 Aftermath

In the months between the preparation of the first version (June 1999) and the submission of the final version of this article (October 1999), Philip Welch has used the methods of this paper in his [22] to solve the questions mentioned, thereby doing the technical work mentioned in Section 2.5 to be necessary to "exploit the connection". These developments are described in the survey article [16].

Theorem 2.6.1 (Welch) *Every Π^1_2 real is $\mathbf{S}^\#_\Gamma$-definable and $\mathbf{S}^*_\Gamma$-definable for a class of Γ including Γ_0 and Γ_∞.*

Theorem 2.6.1 together with Corollary 2.2.9 gives an exact computation of the class of $\mathbf{S}^\#_{\Gamma_\infty}$-definable reals: They are exactly the Π^1_2 reals.

Theorem 2.6.2 (Welch) *For arithmetic formulae Φ, simple classes Γ of bootstrapping policies and any $\langle\Phi,\Gamma\rangle$-reflexive real number h, we have* $\mathrm{refl}_{\Phi,\Gamma}(h) < \Upsilon_\infty(h)$*, where $\Upsilon_\infty(h)$ is the supremum of the ordinals clockable relative to h.*

Acknowledgments. The author is indebted to Kai–Uwe Kühnberger (Bloomington IN & Tübingen) who introduced him to the problem discussed in this paper, to Philip Welch (Kobe, Bristol & Berkeley CA) for discussions and advice, and to the anonymous referee. Part of this work was completed whilst the author held a grant of the Studienstiftung des deutschen Volkes. The author wishes to extend his special gratitude towards the Association of Symbolic Logic for a travel grant to Logic Colloquium 1998 in Prague. A virtually identical version of this paper has appeared in volume 11 (2001) of the **Journal of Logic and Computation**.

BENEDIKT LÖWE
Rheinische Friedrich–Wilhelms–Universität Bonn
Mathematisches Institut
53115 Bonn, Germany
E-email: loewe@math.uni-bonn.de

Bibliography

[1] Gian Aldo Antonelli, The Complexity of Revision, Notre Dame Journal of Formal Logic 35 (1994), p. 67–72

[2] Gian Aldo Antonelli, The Complexity of Revision, revised, *unpublished notes*, 1998

[3] Nuel D. Belnap, Jr., Gupta's rule of revision theory of truth, Journal of Philosophical Logic 11 (1982), p. 103–116

[4] André Chapuis, Alternative Revision Theories of Truth, Journal of Philosophical Logic 25 (1996), pp. 399–423

[5] John Earman, John D. Norton, Forever is a day: Supertasks in Pitowsky and Malament–Hogarth Spacetimes, Philosophy of Science 60 (1993), p. 22–42

[6] Heinz–Dieter Ebbinghaus, Jörg Flum, Finite Model Theory, Berlin 1995 [Perspectives in Mathematical Logic]

[7] Anil Gupta, Truth and Paradox, Journal of Philosophical Logic 11 (1982), p. 1–60

[8] Anil Gupta, Nuel Belnap, The Revision Theory of Truth, Cambridge MA 1993

[9] Joel D. Hamkins, Andy Lewis, Infinite Time Turing Machines, Journal of Symbolic Logic 65 (2000), p. 567–604

[10] Joel D. Hamkins, Andy Lewis, Post's problem for supertasks has both positive and negative solutions, *to appear in :* Archive for Mathematical Logic

[11] Hans G. Herzberger, Naive Semantics and the Liar Paradox, Journal of Philosophy 79 (1982), p. 479–497

[12] Hans G. Herzberger, Notes on Naive Semantics, Journal of Philosophical Logic 11(1982), p. 61–102

[13] M.L. Hogarth, Does general relativity allow an observer to view an eternity in a finite time?, Foundations of Physics Letters 5 (1992), p. 173–181

[14] Philip Kremer, The Gupta–Belnap Systems $\mathbf{S}^{\#}$ and $\mathbf{S}^{*}$ are not Axiomatisable, Notre Dame Journal of Formal Logic 34 (1993), p. 583–596

[15] Saul Kripke, Outline of a theory of truth, Journal of Philosophy 72 (1975), p. 690–716

[16] Benedikt Löwe, Philip D. Welch, Set-Theoretic Absoluteness and the Revision Theory of Truth, *to appear in:* Studia Logica

[17] Robert L. Martin, Peter W. Woodruff, On representing 'true-in-L' in L, Philosophia 5 (1975), p. 217–221

[18] Yiannis N. Moschovakis, Elementary Induction on Abstract Structures, Amsterdam 1974 [Studies in Logic and the Foundations of Mathematics 77]

[19] Hartley Rogers Jr., Theory of Recursive Functions and Effective Computability, Maidenhead 1967

[20] Philip D. Welch, Eventually Infinite Time Turing Machine Degrees: Infinite Time Decidable Reals, Journal of Symbolic Logic 65 (2000), p. 1193–1203

[21] Philip D. Welch, The Length of Infinite Time Turing Machine Computation, *to appear in:* Bulletin of the London Mathematical Society 32 (2000), p. 129–136

[22] Philip D. Welch, On Gupta-Belnap Revision Theories of Truth, *in preparation*

[23] Aladdin M. Yaqūb, The Liar Speaks the Truth. A Defense of the Revision Theory of Truth, Oxford 1993

Chapter 3

On Frege's Nightmare: A Combination of Intuitionistic, Free and Paraconsistent Logics

SHAHID RAHMAN

In this paper I present a dialogical formulation of free logic which allows a straightforward combination of paraconsistent and intuitionistic logic — I call this combination Frege's Nightmare. The ideas behind this combination can be expressed in few words: in an argumentation, it sometimes makes sense to restrict the use and introduction of singular terms in the context of quantification to a formal use of those terms. That is, the Proponent is allowed to use a constant for a defense (of an existential quantifier) or an attack (on a universal quantifier) iff this constant has been explicitly conceded by the Opponent. When the Opponent concedes any constant occurring in an atomic formula he concedes tertium non-datur (for this formula) to. This yield a free logic which combines classical (for propositions with singular terms for realities) with intuitionistic logic (for propositions with singular terms for fictions). This extended free logic can be also combined with paraconsistent logic in such a way that contradictory objects can be included in the domain of fictions. The idea is here to combine the concept of formal use of constants in free logics and that of the formal use of elementary negations in paraconsistent logics.

3.1 Aims of This Paper

Issue of this paper is a dialogical formulation of free logic which allows a straightforward combination of paraconsistent and intuitionistic logic — I call this combination Frege's Nightmare.[1] The ideas behind this combination can be expressed in few words: in an argumentation, it sometimes makes sense to restrict the use and introduction of singular terms in the context of quantification to a formal use of those terms. That is, the Proponent is allowed to use a constant for a defense (of an existential quantifier) or an attack (on a universal quantifier) iff this constant has been already introduced by the Opponent's attack (on a universal quantifier) or the Opponent's defense (of an existential quantifier). When the Opponent concedes any constant occurring in an atomic formula he concedes tertium non-datur (for this formula) to. This yield a free logic which combines classical (for propositions with singular terms for realities) with intuitionistic logic (for propositions with singular terms for fictions). This extended free logic which picks up some suggestions of Francisco Suárez theory of *privatio* can be also combined with paraconsistent logic in such a way that contradictory objects can be included in the domain of fictions. The idea is here to combine the concept of formal use of constants in free logics and that of the formal use of elementary negations in paraconsistent logics.[2]

---

[1]I adopted this name from an ironic remark made by Markus Stepanians (Saarbrücken) who by the way wrote an excellent book on Frege's theory of judgment (Stepanians [30]).

[2]Such a combination of logics may help in the reconstruction of Hugh MacColl's concept of symbolic universe (MacColl [12], p. 74–77):

> "Let e_1, e_2, e_3, etc. (up to any number of individuals mentioned in our argument or investigation) denote our universe of real existences. Let 0_1, 0_2, 0_3, etc., denote our universe of non-existences, that is to say, of unrealities, such as centaurs, nectar, ambrosia, fairies, with self-contradictions, such as round squares, square circles, flat spheres, etc., including, I fear, the non-Euclidean geometry of four dimensions and other hyper-spatial geometries. Finally, let S_1, S_2, S_3, etc., denote our Symbolic Universe, or 'Universe of Discourse', composed of all things real or unreal that are named or expressed by words or other symbols in our argument or investigation [...].
>
> When a class A belongs wholly to the class e, or wholly to the class 0; we may call it a pure class [...].
>
> We may sum up briefly as follows: Firstly, when any symbol A denotes an individual; then any intelligible statement $((A)$, containing the symbol A, implies that the individual represented by A has a symbolic existence; but whether the statement $((A)$ implies that the individual represented by A has real existence depends upon the context. Secondly, when any symbol A denotes a class; then any intelligible statement $((A)$, containing the symbol A implies that the whole class A has a symbolic existence; but whether the statement

3.2 The dialogical approach to free logic

3.2.1 Dialogical Free Logic With and Without *tertium non datur*

Dialogical logic, suggested by Paul Lorenzen in 1958 and developed by Kuno Lorenz in several papers from 1961 onwards[3] was introduced as a pragmatical semantics for both classical and intuitionistic logic.

The dialogical approach studies logic as an inherently pragmatic notion with the help of an overtly externalised argumentation formulated as a *dialogue* between two parties taking up the roles of an *Opponent* (**O** in the following) and a *Proponent* (**P**) of the issue at stake, called the *principal thesis* of the dialogue. **P** has to try to defend the thesis against all possible allowed criticism (*attacks*) by **O**, thereby being allowed to use statements that **O** may have made at the outset of the dialogue. The thesis A is logically valid if and only if **P** can succeed in defending A against all possible allowed criticism by the Opponent. In the jargon of game theory: **P** has a *winning strategy* for A.

The philosophical point of dialogical logic is that this approach does not understand semantics as mapping names and relationships into the real world to obtain an abstract counterpart of it, but as acting upon them in a particular way.

I will now describe an intuitionistic and a classical version of a very basic system called **DFL** (dialogical free logic) introduced by Rahman, Rückert and Fischmann in [13].

Suppose the elements of first-order language are given with small letters $(a, b, c, \dots)$ for elementary formulae, capital italic letters for formulae that might be complex $(A, B, C, \dots)$, capital italic bold letters $(\boldsymbol{A}, \boldsymbol{B}, \boldsymbol{C}, ...)$ for predicators and constants τ_i. A dialogue is a sequence of labelled formulae of this first-order language that are stated by either **P** or **O**.[4] The label of a formula describes its role in the dialogue, whether it is an aggressive or a defensive act. An *attack* is labelled with $?_{n/\dots}$, while $!_{n/\dots}$ tags a *defense*. (n is the number of the formula the attack or defense reacts to, the dots are sometimes completed with more information. The use of indices of labels will be made clear in the following). In dialogical logic the meaning in use of the logical

---

((A) implies that the class A is wholly real, or wholly unreal, or partly real and partly unreal, depends upon the context."

Cf. Rahman [20] for a discussion of Hugh MacColl's ideas on symbolic existence.

[3]Lorenzen and Lorenz [11]. Further work has been done by Rahman [14].

[4]Sometimes, I use **X** and **Y** to denote either **P** or **O**, with $\mathbf{X} \neq \mathbf{Y}$.

particles is given by two types of rules which determine their *local (particle rules)* and their *global (structural rules)* meaning. The particle rules specify for each particle a pair of moves consisting of an attack and (if possible) the corresponding defense. Each such pair is called a *round*. An attack *opens* a round, which in turn is *closed* by a defense if possible. Before presenting a dialogical system **DFL** for free logics, we need the following definition.

- A constant τ is said to be introduced by **X** if (1) **X** states a formula $A[\tau/x]$ to defend $\bigvee_x A$ or (2) **X** attacks a formula $\bigwedge_x A$ with $?_{n/\tau}$, and τ has not been used in the same way before. Moreover, an atomic formula is said to be introduced by **X** if it is stated by **X** and has not been stated before.

DFL is closely related to Lorenz' standard dialogues for both intuitionistic and classical logic. The particle rules are identical, and the sets of structural rules differ in only one point, namely when determining the way constants are dealt with. Before presenting the formal definition of **DFL**, we should have a look at a simple propositional dialogue as an example of notational conventions:

	O	**P**	
		$a \wedge b \to a$	(0)
(1)	$?_0\, a \wedge b$	$!_1\, a$	(4)
(3)	$!_2\, a$	$?_{1/\text{left}}$	(2)

P wins.

Formulae are labelled in (chronological) order of appearance. They are not listed in the order of utterance, but in such a way that every defense appears on the same level as the corresponding attack. Informally, the argument goes like this:

P: "If *a* and *b*, then *a*."

O: "Given *a* and *b*, show me that *a* holds."

P: "If you assume *a* and *b*, you should be able to show me that both hold. Thus show me that the left part holds."

O: "OK, *a*."

P: "If you can say that *a* holds, so can I."

O runs out of arguments, **P** wins.

PARTICLE RULES

Formula	Attack	Defense
$?_{\mathrm{n}}\, \neg A$	$?_{\mathrm{n}}\, A$	$\otimes$ (The symbol "$\otimes$" indicates that no defence, but only a counterattack is allowed.)
$A \wedge B$	$?_{\mathrm{n/left}}$	$!_{\mathrm{m}}\, A$
	$?_{\mathrm{n/right}}$ (The attacker chooses.)	$!_{\mathrm{m}}\, B$
$A \vee B$	$?_{\mathrm{n}}$	$!_{\mathrm{m}}\, A$
		$!_{\mathrm{m}}\, B$ (The defender chooses.)
$A \to B$	$?_{\mathrm{n}}\, A$	$!_{\mathrm{m}}\, B$
$\bigwedge_x A$	$?_{\mathrm{n}/\tau}$ (The attacker chooses.)	$!_{\mathrm{m}}\, A[x/\tau]$
$\bigvee_x A$	$?_{\mathrm{n}}$	$!_{\mathrm{m}/\tau}\, A[x/\tau]$ (The defender chooses.)

The first row contains the form of the formula in question, the second one possible attacks against this formula, and the last one possible defenses against those attacks (the symbol "$\otimes$" indicates that no defense is possible.). Note that $?_{\mathrm{n}/\ldots}$ is a move — more precisely it is an attack — but not a formula. Thus if one partner in the dialogue states a conjunction, the other may initiate the attack by asking either for the left side of the conjunction ("show me that the left side of the conjunction holds", or $?_{\mathrm{n/left}}$ for short) or the right one ("show me that the right side of the conjunction holds", or $?_{\mathrm{n/right}}$). If one partner in the dialogue states a disjunction, the other may initiate the attack by asking to be shown any side of the disjunction ($?_n$). As already mentioned, the number in the index denotes the formula the attack refers to. The notation of defenses is used in analogy to that of attacks. Rules for quantifiers work similarly.

Next, we fix the way formulae are sequenced to form dialogues with a set of structural rules (orig. *Rahmenregeln*).

(DFL0) Formulae are alternately uttered by **P** and **O**. The *initial formula* is uttered by **P**. It does not have a label, but provides the topic of argument. Every formula below the initial formula is either an attack or a defense to an earlier formula of the other player.

(DFL1) Both **P** and **O** may only repeat attacks that change the situation: a situation (allowing the repetition of an attack) is *changed* if and only if **O** introduces a new atomic formula or a new constant (which can now be used by **P**) — the intuitive idea should be clear. The precise formulation of it still need some work.

(DFL2) *(formal rule for atomic formulae)* **P** may not introduce atomic formulae: every atomic formula must be stated by **O** first.

(DFL3) *(formal rule for constants)* Only **O** may introduce constants.

(DFL4) *(winning rule)* **X** wins iff it is **Y**'s turn but he cannot move (either attack or defend).

(DFL_I5) *(intuitionistic rule)* In any move, each player may attack a (complex) formula asserted by his partner or he may defend himself against *the last not already defended* attack. Only the latest open attack may be answered. If it is **X**'s turn at position n and there are two open attacks m, l such that $m < l < n$, then **X** may not defend against m.[5]

DFL is an intuitionistic as well as a classical semantics. To obtain the classical version simply replace (DFL_I5) by the following rule:

(DFL_C5) *(classical rule)* In any move, each player may attack a (complex) formula asserted by his partner or he may defend himself against *any attack* (including those which have already been defended).

If we need to make explicit which system is meant, we write $\mathbf{DFL_I}$ or $\mathbf{DFL_C}$ instead of **DFL**.

[5]Notice that this does not mean that the last attack was the last move.

A **DFL** dialogue is finite, since the particle rules satisfy the subterm property and (DFL1) ensures that no player may enter a loop iterating a finite sequence of arguments infinitely often.

The crucial rule that makes **DFL** behave like a free logic is (DFL3). To see the difference between standard and free dialogues (those with and those without (DFL3)), consider another example. Without (DFL3), we would obtain the following dialogue proving that if nothing is a vampire, Nosferatu is no vampire:

	O	**P**	
		$\bigwedge_x \neg \boldsymbol{A}(x) \rightarrow \neg \boldsymbol{A}(\tau)$	(0)
(1)	$?_0 \bigwedge_x \neg \boldsymbol{A}(x)$	$!_1 \neg \boldsymbol{A}(\tau)$	(2)
(3)	$?_2\, \boldsymbol{A}(\tau)$	$\otimes$	
(5)	$!_4 \neg \boldsymbol{A}(\tau)$	$?_{1/\tau}$	(4)
	$\otimes$	$?_5\, \boldsymbol{A}(\tau)$	(6)

P wins.

If we play the same dialogue again in **DFL**, things look different:

	O	**P**	
		$\bigwedge_x \neg \boldsymbol{A}(x) \rightarrow \neg \boldsymbol{A}(\tau)$	(0)
(1)	$?_0 \bigwedge_x \neg \boldsymbol{A}(x)$	$!_1 \neg \boldsymbol{A}(\tau)$	(2)
(3)	$?_2\, \boldsymbol{A}(\tau)$	$\otimes$	

O wins.

We observe that **P** runs out of arguments. He cannot attack (1) any more, because not a single constant has been introduced so far, and he may not introduce one on its own. Neither can he defend himself against the atomic formula in (3) due to the particle rule for negation.

It is obvious that the (Proponent's) thesis $\boldsymbol{A}(\tau) \rightarrow \bigvee_x \boldsymbol{A}(x)$ cannot be won. This shows that the Opponent may state a proposition about a fictive entity without committing himself to it's existence. MacColl's reflections on non-existence amount to these.[6]

[6] Astroh's thorough discussion of MacColl's conception of existence (Astroh [1], p. 1399–1401) amounts to the failure of this thesis in **DFL**.

3.2.2 Winning Strategies and Dialogical Tableaux for DFL

As already mentioned, validity is defined in dialogical logic via winning strategies of **P**, i.e. the thesis A is logically valid iff **P** can succeed in defending A against all possible allowed criticism by **O**. In this case, **P** has a *winning strategy* for A. It should be clear that the formal rule which elucidates MacColl's understanding of the problematic modality of hypotheticals, does not necessarily imply that winning a dialog with help of this rule yields the validity of the formula involved: the Proponent may win a dialogue, even formally, because the Opponent did not play the best moves. Validity, on the other hand forces the consideration of all possibilities available. A systematic description of the winning strategies available can be obtained from the following considerations:

- If **P** shall win against any choice of **O**, we will have to consider two main different situations, namely the dialogical situations in which **O** has stated a complex formula and those in which **P** has stated a complex formula. We call these main situations the **O**-cases and the **P**-cases, respectively.

In both of these situations another distinction has to be examined:

(i) **P** wins by *choosing* an attack in the **O**-cases or a defense in the **P**-cases, iff he can win *at least one* of the dialogues he has chosen.

(ii) When **O** can *choose* a defense in the **O**-cases or an attack in the **P**-cases, **P** can win iff he can win *all of the* dialogues **O** can choose.

The closing rules for dialogical tableaux are the usual ones: a branch is closed iff it contains two copies of the same formula, one stated by **O** and the other one by **P**. A tree is closed iff each branch is closed.

For the intuitionistic tableaux, the structural rule about the restriction on defenses has to be considered. The idea is quite simple: the tableaux system allows all the possible defenses (even the atomic ones) to be written down, but as soon as determinate formulae (negations, conditionals, universal quantifiers) of **P** are attacked all others will be deleted — this is an implementation of the last attack rule of . Clearly, if an attack on a **P**-statement causes the deletion of the others, then **P** can also answer the last attack. Those formulae which compel the rest of P's formulae to be deleted will be indicated with the expression "$\Sigma_{[\mathbf{O}]}$" which reads *in the set* Σ *save* **O***'s formulae and delete all of* **P***'s formulae stated before.*

To obtain a tableaux system for **DFL** from those described above, add the following restriction to the closing rules and recall the rule (DFL3) for constants:

- *(**DFL**-restriction)* Check that for every step in which **P** chooses a constant (i. e. for every **P**-attack on a universally quantified **O**-formula and for every **P**-defense of an existentially quantified **P**-formula) this constant has been already introduced by **O** (by means of an **O**-attack on a universally quantified **P**-formula or a defense of an existentially quantified **O**-formula).

This restriction can be technically implemented by a device which provides a label (namely an asterisk, "$*$") for each constant introduced by **O**. Thus, the **DFL**-restriction can be simplified in the following way:

- *(**DFL**-restriction with labels)* Check that for every step in which **P** chooses a constant this constant has already been there, labelled with an asterisk.

All these considerations can be expressed by means of the tableaux systems for classical and intuitionistic **DFL**.[7]

Classical Tableaux for DFL

(**O**)-cases	(**P**)-cases
$\dfrac{\Sigma, (\mathbf{O})A \vee B}{\Sigma, \langle(\mathbf{P})?\rangle(\mathbf{O})A \quad \mid \quad \Sigma, \langle(\mathbf{P})?\rangle(\mathbf{O})B}$	$\dfrac{\Sigma, (\mathbf{P})A \vee B}{\begin{array}{l}\Sigma, \langle(\mathbf{O})?\rangle(\mathbf{P})A \\ (\Sigma, \langle(\mathbf{O})?\rangle(\mathbf{P})B)\end{array}}$
$\dfrac{\Sigma, (\mathbf{O})A \wedge B}{\begin{array}{l}\Sigma, \langle(\mathbf{P})_{?/\text{left}}\rangle(\mathbf{O})A \\ (\Sigma, \langle(\mathbf{P})_{?/\text{right}}\rangle(\mathbf{O})B)\end{array}}$	$\dfrac{\Sigma, (\mathbf{P})A \wedge B}{\Sigma, \langle(\mathbf{O})_{?/\text{left}}\rangle(\mathbf{P})A \quad \mid \quad \Sigma, \langle(\mathbf{O})_{?/\text{right}}\rangle(\mathbf{P})B}$

[7] See details on how to build tableaux systems from dialogues in Rahman [14] and Rahman and Rückert [16]. The use of these tableaux systems follows the very well-known analytic trees of Smullyan [29]. Find proofs for correctness and completeness for intuitionistic strategy-tableaux systems in Rahman [14]. Another proof has been given by Walter Felscher in [8].

(O)-cases	(P)-cases
$\dfrac{\Sigma, (\mathbf{O})A \rightarrow B}{\Sigma, (\mathbf{P})A, \ldots \quad \mid \quad \Sigma, \langle(\mathbf{P})A\rangle(\mathbf{O})B}$	$\dfrac{\Sigma, (\mathbf{P})A \rightarrow B}{\Sigma, (\mathbf{O})A;\ (\mathbf{P})B}$
$\dfrac{\Sigma, (\mathbf{O})\neg A}{\Sigma, (\mathbf{P})A; \otimes}$	$\dfrac{\Sigma, (\mathbf{P})\neg A}{\Sigma, (\mathbf{O})A; \otimes}$
$\dfrac{\Sigma, (\mathbf{O}) \bigwedge_x A}{\Sigma, \langle(\mathbf{P})_{?/\tau}\rangle(\mathbf{O})A[\tau^*/x]}$ τ has been labeled with an asterisk before.	$\dfrac{\Sigma, (\mathbf{P}) \bigwedge_x A}{\Sigma, \langle(\mathbf{O})_{?/\tau^*}\rangle(\mathbf{P})A[\tau^*/x]\tau}$ τ is new.
$\dfrac{\Sigma, (\mathbf{O}) \bigvee_x A}{\Sigma, \langle(\mathbf{P})_?\rangle(\mathbf{O})A[\tau^*/x]}$ τ is new.	$\dfrac{\Sigma, (\mathbf{P}) \bigvee_x A}{\Sigma, \langle(\mathbf{O})_?\rangle(\mathbf{P})A[\tau/x]}$ τ has been labeled with an asterisk before.

By a dialogically signed formula I mean $(\mathbf{P})A$ or $(\mathbf{O})A$, where A is a formula. If Σ is a set of dialogically signed formulae and X is a single dialogically signed formula, I will write $\Sigma \cup \{X\}$ as Σ, X.
The exterior brackets occurring in an expression of the Form (for example) $(\Sigma, \langle(\mathbf{P})\rangle(\mathbf{O})B)$ signalize that if there is a winning strategy for B, then an argumentation for A will be redundant and vice versa.
Observe that the formulae below the line represent pairs of attack/defense moves. In other words, they represent rounds.
Note that the expressions between the symbols "$\langle$" and "$\rangle$", such as $\langle(\mathbf{P})_?\rangle$, $\langle(\mathbf{O})_?\rangle$ or $\langle(\mathbf{P})A\rangle$ are moves — more precisely they are attacks — but not statements.

Some definitions:

a) If Ψ is a set of dialogically signed formulae, we say one of the above rules, call it rule R, *applies* to Δ if by appropriate substitution of Σ, A [and B]

the collection of signed formulae above the line in the rule R becomes Δ.

b) By *an application of rule* R *to the set* Δ we mean the replacement of Ψ by Ψ_1 (or by Ψ_1 and Ψ_2 — in the case that R is a branching rule of the form $\Sigma, \ldots \mid \Sigma, \ldots$), where Ψ is the set of formulae above the line in rule R (after suitable substitution of Σ, A [and B]) and Ψ_1 (or Ψ_1 and Ψ_2) is (are) the set of formulae below.

c) By a *strategy-tree* I mean a finite collection $\{\Sigma_1, \Sigma_2, \ldots, \Sigma_n\}$ of sets of dialogically signed formulae.

d) By *an application of the rule* R *to the strategy-tree* $\{\Sigma_1, \Sigma_2, \ldots, \Sigma_n\}$ I mean the replacement of this strategy-tree with a new one which is like the first except for containing instead of some Σ_i the result (or results) of applying rule R to Σ_i.

e) By a *strategy-tableau* I mean a finite sequence of strategy-trees $\Omega_1, \Omega_2, \ldots$ $\ldots, \Omega_n$ in which each strategy-tree except the first is the result of applying one of the above rules to the preceding strategy-tree.

f) A set Σ of dialogically signed formulae is *closed* if it contains both $\mathbf{O}X$ and $\mathbf{P}X$ for some formula X.

g) A strategy-tree $\{\Sigma_1, \Sigma_2, \ldots, \Sigma_n\}$ is *closed* if each Σ_i in it is closed.

h) A strategy-tableau $\Omega_1, \Omega_2, \ldots, \Omega_n$ is closed if some strategy-tree Ω_i in it is closed.

i) By a *tableau for a set* Σ *of dialogically signed formulae* I mean a tableau $\Omega_1, \Omega_2, \ldots, \Omega_n$ in which Ω_1 is $\{\Sigma\}$.

j) The formula A is winnable if there is a closed tableau for $\{\mathbf{P}A\}$.

Intuitionistic Tableaux for DFL

(O)-cases	(P)-cases
$\dfrac{\Sigma, (\mathbf{O})A \vee B}{\Sigma, \langle(\mathbf{P})_?\rangle(\mathbf{O})A \quad \mid \quad \Sigma, \langle(\mathbf{P})_?\rangle(\mathbf{O})B}$	$\dfrac{\Sigma, (\mathbf{P})A \vee B}{\Sigma, \langle(\mathbf{O})_?\rangle(\mathbf{P})A}$ $(\Sigma, \langle(\mathbf{O})_?\rangle(\mathbf{P})B)$
$\dfrac{\Sigma, (\mathbf{O})A \wedge B}{\Sigma, \langle(\mathbf{P})_{?/\text{left}}\rangle(\mathbf{O})A}$ $(\Sigma, \langle(\mathbf{P})_{?/\text{right}}\rangle(\mathbf{O})B)$	$\dfrac{\Sigma, (\mathbf{P})A \wedge B}{\Sigma, \langle(\mathbf{O})_{?/\text{left}}\rangle(\mathbf{P})A \quad \mid \quad \Sigma, \langle(\mathbf{O})_{?/\text{right}}\rangle(\mathbf{P})B}$
$\dfrac{\Sigma, (\mathbf{O})A \to B}{\Sigma, (\mathbf{P})A, \ldots \quad \mid \quad \Sigma, \langle(\mathbf{P})A\rangle(\mathbf{O})B}$	$\dfrac{\Sigma, (\mathbf{P})A \to B}{\Sigma_{[\mathbf{O}]}, (\mathbf{O})A;\ (\mathbf{P})B}$
$\dfrac{\Sigma, (\mathbf{O})\neg A}{\Sigma, (\mathbf{P})A; \otimes}$	$\dfrac{\Sigma, (\mathbf{P})\neg A}{\Sigma_{[\mathbf{O}]}, (\mathbf{O})A; \otimes}$
$\dfrac{\Sigma, (\mathbf{O}) \bigwedge_x A}{\Sigma, \langle(\mathbf{P})_{?/\tau}\rangle(\mathbf{O})A[\tau^*/x]}$ τ has been labeled with an asterisk before.	$\dfrac{\Sigma, (\mathbf{P}) \bigwedge_x A}{\Sigma_{[\mathbf{O}]}, \langle(\mathbf{O})_{?/\tau^*}\rangle(\mathbf{P})A[\tau^*/x]\tau}$ τ is new.
$\dfrac{\Sigma, (\mathbf{O}) \bigvee_x A}{\Sigma, \langle(\mathbf{P})_?\rangle(\mathbf{O})A[\tau^*/x]}$ τ is new.	$\dfrac{\Sigma, (\mathbf{P}) \bigvee_x A}{\Sigma, \langle(\mathbf{O})_?\rangle(\mathbf{P})A[\tau/x]}$ τ has been labeled with an asterisk before.

Definitions:

a) The expressions "$\Sigma, (\mathbf{O})A$", "$\Sigma_{(\mathbf{O})}, (\mathbf{O})A$", "$\Sigma_{(\mathbf{O})}, (\mathbf{P})A$", stand for the sets $\Sigma \cup \{(\mathbf{O})A\}$, $\Sigma_{(\mathbf{O})} \cup \{(\mathbf{O})A\}$, and $\Sigma_{(\mathbf{O})} \cup \{(\mathbf{P})A\}$, respectively.

Let us look at two examples, namely one for classical **DFL** and one for intuitionistic **DFL**:

$$\begin{array}{ll} (\mathbf{P}) & \bigwedge_x \neg \boldsymbol{A}(x) \to \neg \boldsymbol{A}(\tau) \\ (\mathbf{O}) & \bigwedge_x \neg \boldsymbol{A}(x) \\ (\mathbf{P}) & \neg \boldsymbol{A}(\tau) \\ (\mathbf{O}) & \boldsymbol{A}(\tau) \end{array}$$

The tableau remains open as **P** cannot choose τ to attack the universal quantifier of **O**. The following intuitionistic tableau is slightly more complex:

~~$(\mathbf{P})$~~	~~$\bigwedge_x \boldsymbol{A}(x) \to \neg \bigvee_x \neg \boldsymbol{A}(x)$~~
$(\mathbf{O})_{[\mathbf{O}]}$	$\bigwedge_x \boldsymbol{A}(x)$
~~$(\mathbf{P})$~~	~~$\neg \bigvee_x \neg \boldsymbol{A}(x)$~~
$(\mathbf{O})_{[\mathbf{O}]}$	$\bigvee_x \neg \boldsymbol{A}(x)$
$\langle(\mathbf{P})_?\rangle(\mathbf{O})$	$\neg \boldsymbol{A}(\tau^*)$
$\langle(\mathbf{P})_{?\tau}\rangle(\mathbf{O})$	$\neg \boldsymbol{A}(\tau)$
$(\mathbf{P})$	$\boldsymbol{A}(\tau)$

The tree closes.

3.2.3 Many Quantifiers and Sorts of Objects — The Systems $\mathbf{DFL}^n$ and $\mathbf{DFL}^{\langle n \rangle}$

Consider the situation expressed by the following proposition:

> The novel contains a passage in which Sherlock Holmes dreams that he shot Dr. Watson.

There is an underlying reality that the novel is part of, the outer reality of the story told in the novel and an even further outer reality of the dream of the protagonist. To distinguish between the reality of Conan Doyle writing stories, Holmes' reality and the reality of Holmes' dream, we need three pairs of quantifiers expressing the three sorts of reality (or fiction), for which in a first step we do not need to assume that they introduce a order of levels of fiction or (reality). Actually MacColl, as can be read in the text quoted on page 62, formulated a system in which different sorts of elements of the (in MacColl's words) symbolic universe are considered. Now, if the motivation of introducing a formal use of constants is, as already mentioned, an ontologically neutral treatment of these constants, it is not very clear why levels of reality should be considered at all. Narahari Rao, for example, thinks that such a graduation is incompatible with the very idea of logic with singular terms for fictions [24]. Formally, the introduction of sorts of elements is very simple: think of the pair of quantifiers of **DFL** as having the upper index 0 and add new pairs of quantifiers with higher indices, as many as we need to express every sort of reality (or fiction) that could possibly appear. We call the dialogical logic thus derived $\mathbf{DFL}^n$. The new particle rules to be added to **DFL** are:

Formula	Attack	Defense
$\bigwedge_x^i A$	$?_{\mathrm{n}/\tau}$ (The attacker chooses.)	$!_{\mathrm{m}}\ A[\tau/x]$
$\bigvee_x^i A$	$?_{\mathrm{n}}$	$!_{\mathrm{m}/\tau}\ A[x/\tau]$ (The defender chooses.)

The extended set of quantifiers requires a new notion of introduction:

- A constant τ is said to be *introduced as belonging to the sort* i iff it is used to attack a universal quantifier of sort i or to defend an existential quantifier of sort i and has not been used in the same way before.

I adapt (DFL3) to $\mathbf{DFL}^n$:

(DFL^{n}3) *(First extended formal rule for constants)* For each sort of quantification the following rule holds: constants may only be introduced by **O**.

These formulations yield a logic containing an arbitrary number of disjunct pairs of quantifiers dealing with different sorts of reality and fiction — this logic contains also the quantifiers $\exists$ and $\forall$ for which neither (DFL3) nor (DFL^{n}3) hold. Because of the particle and structural rules for $\exists$ and $\forall$ it looks like these quantifiers work as in the standard logic. Actually they are very different: here they work as quantifiers *without any ontological commitment at all*. In the standard logic the ontological commitment is presupposed by the use of these quantifiers. Here not. In other words, the addition of the quantifiers $\exists$ and $\forall$ to **DFL** produces a logic where quantification over fictional entities is possible.

In some contexts, it might be useful to have a logic where these different realities are ordered in a hierarchy. We call the system that establishes this ordering $\mathbf{DFL}^{\langle n \rangle}$; it results from modifying (DFL3) again:

(DFL$^{\langle n \rangle}$3) *(Second extended formal rule for constants)* **P** may introduce a constant τ on a level m iff **O** has introduced τ on some level n with $n < m$ before.

I leave as an exercise for the reader two examples. The first states that in $\mathbf{DFL}^n$, whenever A has an instance in the scope of one or another $\bigvee$-quantifier, it has an instance in the scope of $\exists$; the second makes use of the ordering in $\mathbf{DFL}^{\langle n \rangle}$:

(i) $(\bigvee_x^1 \boldsymbol{A}(x) \vee \bigvee_x^2 \boldsymbol{A}(x)) \rightarrow \exists_x \boldsymbol{A}(x)$ (to be solved with $\mathbf{DFL}^n$)

(ii) $(\bigvee_x^1 \boldsymbol{A}(x) \wedge \bigwedge_x^2 (\boldsymbol{A}(x) \rightarrow \boldsymbol{B}(x))) \rightarrow \bigvee_x^1 \boldsymbol{B}(x)$ (to be solved with $\mathbf{DFL}^{\langle n \rangle}$)

3.2.4 Combining DFLI and DFLC

Suárez' free logic

The Logics $\mathbf{DFL_I}$ and $\mathbf{DFL_C}$ and have the awkward effect that we have to decide between them. Now as Stephen Read remarked in his book "Thinking about Logic" the realist position in classical logic has some plausibility for existents which it definitively lacks for non-existents, fictional and beyond. Consider the proposition *Don Quixote could whistle very loudly*. Is this proposition the case or not? If one seriously believes Don Quixote is a fictional creature, one must prepared for there being no answer to this question.[8] Why should we presuppose tertium non datur for non-existents? One possible way of handling this problem was already mentioned in the introduction: the classical rule applies to existents and the non classical to non-existents. But how to implement this in the dialogical formulation of free logic? In answering this question I will follow an idea of the Spanish philosopher Francisco Suárez (1548–1647) about the non applicability of the tertium non datur to propositions containing privative predicators. That is, Suárez distinguishes — as Aristoteles did before — predicators which can naturally be said or not of an subject from those that can not be naturally applied to this subject. The predicator "blind" for example can be said of Oedipus but not of a stone: You can say of a man that he is blind because the contrary is normally the case.

[8]Cf. Read [25], p. 137.

Suárez followed from this understanding of privative predicators that tertium non datur does not apply in those propositions containing such predicators. Thus, some predicators apply and it can be decided if a given proposition built up from these predicators is the case or not. But some other predicators do not apply for example it does not make any sense to say of Oedipus that he is a even number or not. In other words, if you are allowed to use arbitrary predicators tertium non datur applies, if not (as in the case of propositions with privative predicators) it doesn't.[9] Suárez used his theory of *privationes* for existents. I do not. Nevertheless I will take his advice and will not presuppose in the context of dialogical free logic that any predicator can be applied to any *existent* object. I will presuppose only that any predicator can be applied of any existent object. In the language of dialogical logic: if the Opponent conceded the existence of a given object by introducing a singular term he conceded also that any predicator or its negation can be said of this object.

One way to implement this is to add to the dialogical intuitionistic free logic $\mathbf{DFL_I}$ the following structural rule:

(DFL6) *(Tertium non datur for constants which have been already introduced)* Once the Opponent has introduced a constant he conceded also that tertium non datur holds for any predicator for this constant (we express this concession for an introduced constant τ with the disjunction $\Re_\tau \vee \neg\Re_\tau$, where $\Re$ works as a variable for a predicator which the Proponent can substitute for any suitable predicator).

This rule allows the proponent to choose any predicator at his convenience for the attack on the conceded tertium non datur. This can be made clear with an example (recall that we are playing with the intuitionistic rule ($\text{DFL}_\text{I}5$):

	O	**P**	
		$\bigwedge_x(\boldsymbol{A}(x) \vee \neg\boldsymbol{A}(x))$	(0)
(1)	$?_{0/\tau}\ [\Re_\tau \vee \neg\Re_\tau]$	$!_1\ \boldsymbol{A}(\tau) \vee \neg\boldsymbol{A}(\tau)$	(2)
(3)	$!_2$	$?_1\ \boldsymbol{A}(\tau)$	(6)
(5)	$!_4\ \boldsymbol{A}(\tau)$	$?_{1/\boldsymbol{A}}$	(4)

P wins.

In move (1) the Opponent introduced the constant τ and conceded with this introduction the disjunction $\Re_\tau \vee \neg\Re_\tau$. In move (4) the Proponent attacks

[9]Suárez [31], Disputatio LIV, Sectio IV, vol. VII, p. 432–438.

this disjunction choosing the predicator $\boldsymbol{A}$ as substitution for the predicator-variable $\Re$ and wins — the reader can easily verify that if in move (5) the Opponent chooses to defend $\neg\boldsymbol{A}(\tau)$ he looses, too.

Strategies for Suárez' free logic

The fulation of strategies is straightforward:

(**O**)-cases	(**P**)-cases
$\dfrac{\Sigma, (\mathbf{O}) \bigwedge_x A}{\Sigma, \langle(\mathbf{P})_{?/\tau}\rangle(\mathbf{O})A[\tau^*/x]}$ τ has been labeled with an asterisk before.	$\dfrac{\Sigma, (\mathbf{P}) \bigwedge_x A}{\Sigma_{[\mathbf{O}]}[\Re_\tau \vee \neg\Re_\tau], \langle(\mathbf{O})_{?/\tau^*}\rangle(\mathbf{P})A[\tau^*/x]\tau}$ τ is new. (The disjunction $\Re_\tau \vee \neg\Re_\tau$ occurs in Σ.)
$\dfrac{\Sigma, (\mathbf{O}) \bigvee_x A}{\Sigma[\Re_\tau \vee \neg\Re_\tau], \langle(\mathbf{P})_?\rangle(\mathbf{O})A[\tau^*/x]}$ τ is new. (The disjunction $\Re_\tau \vee \neg\Re_\tau$ occurs in $\Sigma_{[\mathbf{O}]}$.)	$\dfrac{\Sigma, (\mathbf{P}) \bigvee_x A}{\Sigma, \langle(\mathbf{O})_?\rangle(\mathbf{P})A[\tau/x]}$ τ has been labeled with an asterisk before.

I call this logic *Suárez' free logic*. It is not Frege's Nightmare yet but we are near. The next step is to include contradictory objects: I will do this now.

3.3 Inconsistent Objects

3.3.1 Paraconsistency

MacColl's text quoted before describes a logic containing inconsistent objects like round squares, flat spheres and so on. Suárez' logic can deal with this objects as fictional elements. Another way of dealing with this situation is to understand arguments containing propositions about inconsistent objects as arguments in which inconsistent elementary propositions about given elements of the universe of discourse are allowed. That is, instead of allowing the use of constants which name inconsistent objects, you have arguments in which two contradictory elementary propositions are allowed — this way of thinking about inconsistent objects was posed by Richard Routley [26] in his interpretation of Felix Meinong (for a brief exposition of the main ideas of Richard Routley's monumental work see Manuel Bremer [2]). This requires a logic in which such contradictions are allowed. Such a logic was the aim of the founders of paraconsistent logic, namely the Polish logician Stanislaw Jaskowski [9][10] and the Brazilian logician Newton C. A. da Costa [3].

The work of da Costa takes the assumption that contradictions can appear in a logical system without making this system trivial. Actually this leads to the standard definition of paraconsistent logics:

- **(Paraconsistency)** Let us consider a theory $\mathcal{T}$ as a triple $\langle \mathcal{L}, \mathcal{A}, \mathcal{G} \rangle$, where $\mathcal{L}$ is a language, $\mathcal{A}$ is a set of propositions (closed formulae) of $\mathcal{L}$, called the axioms of $\mathcal{T}$, and $\mathcal{G}$ is the underlying logic of $\mathcal{T}$. We suppose that $\mathcal{L}$ has a negation symbol, and that, as usual, the theorems of $\mathcal{T}$ are derived from $\mathcal{A}$ by the rules of $\mathcal{G}$ (cf. da Costa / Bueno / French [5], p. 46).

  In such a context, $\mathcal{T}$ is said to be *inconsistent* if it has two theorems A and $\neg A$, where A is a formula of $\mathcal{L}$. $\mathcal{T}$ is called *trivial* if any formula of $\mathcal{L}$ is a theorem of $\mathcal{T}$. $\mathcal{T}$ is called *paraconsistent* if it can be inconsistent without being trivial. Equivalently $\mathcal{T}$ is paraconsistent if it is not the case that when A and $\neg A$ hold in $\mathcal{T}$, any B (from $\mathcal{L}$) also holds in $\mathcal{T}$.

Thus, if $\mathcal{T}$ is a paraconsistent theory it is not the case that any formula of $\mathcal{L}$ and its negation are theorems of $\mathcal{T}$. Typically, in a paraconsistent theory $\mathcal{T}$, there are theorems whose negations are not theorems of $\mathcal{T}$. Nonetheless, there are formulae which are theorems of $\mathcal{T}$ and whose negations are also theorems (da Costa / Bueno / French [5], p. 46).

Actually there are two main interpretations possible. The one, which I will call the *compelling interpretation*, based on a naive correspondence theory, stresses that paraconsistent theories are ontologically committed to inconsistent objects. The other, which I call the *permissive interpretation*, does not assume this ontological commitment of paraconsistent theories. The usual referential semantics for paraconsistent logics is not really compatible with the idea of a permissive interpretation of paraconsistency. Rahman and Carnielli [22] developed a dialogical approach to paraconsistency which yields several systems called *literal dialogues* (shorter: **L-D**) and takes its permissive non-referential interpretation seriously. I will adapt **L-D** to the purposes of the present paper.

3.3.2 The Dialogical Approach to Paraconsistent Logic and Frege's Nightmare

As already mentioned MacColl's symbolic universe contains non-existent objects and (formally) existent ones. Non-existent objects are in my reconstruction those objects which are named by constants that have been *used* — i.e. which occur in a formula stated in a dialog — without being introduced (in the sense of (DFL3)) before. Now, contradictory objects about objects are in MacColl's view to be included in the sub-universe of non-existent objects, and this is quite in the sense of a permissive interpretation of paraconsistency. Thus, I will provide the system(s) of free logic **DFL** with a rule introducing paraconsistency — I call this rule the *negative literal rule* (DFL7) — but with the following caveat:

(DFL7) *(Negative literal rule)* The Proponent is allowed to attack the negation of an atomic (propositional) statement (the so called *negative literal*) if and only if the Opponent has already attacked the *same* statement before.

(DFL8) *(Permissive caveat)* The negative literal rule applies only for formulae in which constants occur that have not been introduced in the sense of (DFL3).

The structural rule (DFL7) can be considered analogous with the formal rule for positive literals. The idea behind this rule can be connected with MacColl's concept of symbolic existence in the following way: A contradiction between literals, say, a and $\neg a$, expresses that one proposition ascribes a predicator to a given object and the other proposition denies that a predicator applies to this object. Now, if the Opponent is the one who introduces such a contradiction between literals, this contradiction can be seen as having a pure problematic modality, i.e. as being stated symbolically. This means that the Proponent — who has proposed, say, $(a \wedge \neg a) \rightarrow \neg a$ — is also allowed to attack (after the Opponent's concession that $a \wedge \neg a$ and the Opponents attack on $\neg a$) the corresponding negation $\neg a$ (and no other) of the Opponent. Expressed intuitively: "If you (the Opponent) attack my statement that the figure a is not flat conceding that a is flat, so can I (the Proponent)".

When I want to distinguish between the intuitionistic and the classical version I write $\mathbf{L\text{-}D_I}$ (for the intuitionistic version) and $\mathbf{L\text{-}D_C}$ (for the classical version). To be precise we should call these logical systems literal dialogues with classical structural rule and literal dialogues with intuitionistic structural rule respectively. Actually *strictu sensu* they are neither classical nor intuitionistic because neither in **L-D$_I$** nor in **L-D$_C$** are *ex falso sequitur quodlibet*, $(a \to b) \to ((a \to \neg b) \to \neg a)$, or $a \to \neg\neg a$ winnable.

In **L-D** the (from a paraconsistent point of view) dangerous formulae $(a \wedge \neg a) \to b$, $a \to (\neg a \to b)$ and $(a \to b) \to ((a \to \neg b) \to \neg a)$ are not valid. Let us see the corresponding literal dialogues in **L-D$_C$** for the first and the last of the three:

	O	**P**	
		$(a \wedge \neg a) \to b$	(0)
(1)	$?_0\ a \wedge \neg a$		
(3)	$!_2\ a$	$?_{1/\text{left}}$	(2)
(5)	$!_2\ \neg a$	$?_{1/\text{right}}$	(4)

O wins.

The Proponent loses because he is not allowed to attack the move (5) (see negative literal rule). In other words, the Opponent has stated the contradiction $a \wedge \neg a$ about an object but this contradiction, being conceded as part of the symbolic reasoning in the argument, cannot be attacked by the Proponent until the Opponent starts an attack on the negative literal $\neg a$ — an attack which in this case will not take place.

Similar considerations hold for $(a \to b) \to ((a \to \neg b) \to \neg a)$:

	O	**P**	
		$(a \to b) \to ((a \to \neg b) \to \neg a)$	(0)
(1)	$?_0\ a \to b$	$!_1\ (a \to \neg b) \to \neg a$	(2)
(3)	$?_2\ a \to \neg b$	$!_3\ \neg a$	(4)
(5)	$?_4\ a$	$\otimes$	
(7)	$!_6\ b$	$?_1\ a$	(6)
(0)	$!_8\ \neg b$	$?_3\ a$	(8)

O wins.

The Proponent loses here because he cannot attack $\neg b$.

All classically valid formulae without negation are also valid in **L-D$_C$**. All intuitionistically valid formulae without negation are also valid in **L-D$_I$**. As in da Costa's system $\mathbf{C}_1$ neither of the following are valid in $\mathbf{L}\text{-}\mathbf{D}_{\mathbf{C}}$:

$(a \wedge \neg a) \rightarrow b$	$(a \rightarrow (b \vee c)) \rightarrow ((a \wedge \neg b) \rightarrow c)$
$(a \wedge \neg a) \rightarrow \neg b$	$((a \rightarrow \neg a) \wedge (\neg a \rightarrow a)) \rightarrow \neg b$
$\neg(a \wedge \neg a)$	$((a \wedge b) \rightarrow c) \rightarrow ((a \vee \neg c) \rightarrow \neg b)$
$a \rightarrow \neg\neg a$	$(a \rightarrow b) \vee (\neg a \rightarrow b)$
$(a \rightarrow b) \rightarrow ((a \rightarrow \neg b) \rightarrow \neg a)$	$((a \vee b) \wedge \neg a)) \rightarrow b$
$((a \rightarrow b) \wedge (a \rightarrow \neg b)) \rightarrow \neg a$	$(a \vee b) \rightarrow (\neg a \rightarrow b)$
$((\neg a \rightarrow b) \wedge (\neg a \rightarrow \neg b)) \rightarrow a$	$(a \rightarrow b) \rightarrow (\neg b \rightarrow \neg a)$

$\neg a \rightarrow (a \rightarrow b)$	$(\neg a \vee \neg b) \rightarrow \neg(a \wedge b)$
$\neg a \rightarrow (a \rightarrow \neg b)$	$(\neg a \wedge \neg b) \rightarrow \neg(a \vee b)$
$a \rightarrow (\neg a \rightarrow b)$	$(\neg a \vee b) \rightarrow (a \rightarrow b)$
$a(\neg a \rightarrow \neg b)$	$(a \rightarrow b) \rightarrow \neg(a \wedge \neg b)$
$((a \rightarrow \neg a) \wedge (\neg a \rightarrow a)) \rightarrow b$	$\neg a \rightarrow ((a \vee b) \rightarrow b)$

In $\mathbf{L}\text{-}\mathbf{D}_{\mathbf{I}}$ all the intuitionistically non-valid formulae have to be added to the list, for example:

$\neg\neg a \rightarrow a$	$a \vee (a \rightarrow b)$
$a \vee \neg a$	$a \vee ((a \vee b) \rightarrow b)$
$((a \rightarrow b) \rightarrow a) \rightarrow a$	$\neg(a \rightarrow b) \rightarrow a$

The extension of literal dialogues for propositional logic to first-order quantifiers is straightforward. To build *Quantified Literal Dialogues*, we have only to extend the structural negative literal rule to elementary statements of first-order logic. The way to do that is to generalize the rule for elementary statements:

- *((General) negative literal rule)* The Proponent is allowed to attack the negation of an elementary statement (i. e., the *negative literal*) if and only if the Opponent has already attacked the *same* statement before.

Notice that to obtain Frege's Nightmare the above mentioned permissive caveat (DFL8) about the introduction of singular terms should be added to the first order paraconsistent logic.

Let us look at an example:

	O	P	
		$\bigwedge_x((\boldsymbol{A}(x) \wedge \neg \boldsymbol{A}(x)) \rightarrow \boldsymbol{B}(x))$	(0)
(1)	$?_{0/\tau}$	$!_1\ (\boldsymbol{A}(\tau) \wedge \neg \boldsymbol{A}(\tau)) \rightarrow \boldsymbol{B}(\tau)$	(2)
(3)	$?_2\ (\boldsymbol{A}(\tau) \wedge \neg \boldsymbol{A}(\tau))$		
(5)	$!_4\ \boldsymbol{A}(\tau)$	$!_{3/\text{left}}$	(4)
(7)	$!_6\ \neg \boldsymbol{A}(\tau)$	$!_{3/\text{right}}$	(6)

O wins.

The Proponent loses here because (according to the general negative literal rule) he is not allowed to attack move (7) using the Opponent's move (5).

Similarly, the literal rule blocks the validity of $\bigwedge_x(\boldsymbol{A}(x) \rightarrow (\neg \boldsymbol{A}(x) \rightarrow \boldsymbol{B}(x)))$ and the quantified forms of other non-paraconsistent formulae.

Here again it is possible to define quantified literal dialogues for intuitionistic and classical logic. Let us consider an example of a thesis which is not intuitionistically but classically winnable: A quantified literal dialogue in **L-D$_\mathbf{I}$** for $\bigwedge_x \neg\neg \boldsymbol{A}(x) \rightarrow \neg\neg \bigwedge_x \boldsymbol{A}(x)$ runs as follows:

	O	P	
		$\bigwedge_x \neg\neg \boldsymbol{A}(x) \rightarrow \neg\neg \bigwedge_x \boldsymbol{A}(x)$	(0)
(1)	$?_0 \bigwedge_x \neg\neg \boldsymbol{A}(x)$	$!_1 \neg\neg \bigwedge_x \boldsymbol{A}(x)$	(2)
(3)	$?_2 \neg \bigwedge_x \boldsymbol{A}(x)$	$\otimes$	
	$\otimes$	$?_3 \bigwedge_x \boldsymbol{A}(x)$	(4)
(5)	$?_{4/\tau}$		
(7)	$!_6 \neg\neg \boldsymbol{A}(\tau)$	$?_{1/\tau}$	(6)
	$\otimes$	$?_7 \neg \boldsymbol{A}(\tau)$	(8)
(9)	$?_8\ \boldsymbol{A}(\tau)$	$\otimes$	

O wins.

The Proponent loses in **L-D$_\mathbf{I}$** because he is not allowed to defend himself against the attack of the Opponent in move (5) — the last Opponent's attack not already defended by the Proponent was stated in move (9).

The Proponent wins in **L-D$_\mathbf{C}$** because the restriction mentioned above does not hold. Thus the Proponent can answer the attack of move (5) with move

(10) in the following dialogue in (quantified) $\mathbf{L\text{-}D_C}$ and win:

	O	**P**	
		$\bigwedge_x \neg\neg \boldsymbol{A}(x) \rightarrow \neg\neg \bigwedge_x \boldsymbol{A}(x)$	(0)
(1)	$?_0 \bigwedge_x \neg\neg \boldsymbol{A}(x)$	$!_1 \neg\neg \bigwedge_x \boldsymbol{A}(x)$	(2)
(3)	$?_2 \neg \bigwedge_x \boldsymbol{A}(x)$	$\otimes$	
	$\otimes$	$?_3 \bigwedge_x \boldsymbol{A}(x)$	(4)
(5)	$?_{4/\tau}$	$!_5 \boldsymbol{A}(\tau)$	(10)
(7)	$!_6 \neg\neg \boldsymbol{A}(\tau)$	$?_{1/\tau}$	(6)
	$\otimes$	$?_7 \neg \boldsymbol{A}(\tau)$	(8)
(9)	$?_8 \boldsymbol{A}(\tau)$	$\otimes$	

P wins.

It is possible to define tableaux for the winning strategies which correspond to these dialogue systems — see Rahman and Carnielli [22]. To obtain paraconsistent tableaux systems for Frege's Nightmare add the following restriction to the closing rules:

- *(Paraconsistent Restriction)* Check after finishing the tableau and before closing branches that for every elementary **P**-statement (in which no constants labelled with an asterisk occur and) which follows from the application of an **O**-rule to the corresponding negative **O**-literal (i. e. for every attack on a negative **O**-literal) there is an application of a **P**-rule to a negative **P**-literal which yields an **O**-positive literal with the same atomic formula as the above-mentioned attack of the Proponent. Those elementary **P**-attacks on the corresponding negative **O**-literals which do not meet this condition cannot be used for closing branches and can thus be deleted.

The idea of the permissive interpretation is, that paraconsistency does not necessarily leads to accept true contradictions:

> *I suggest to address the inconsistency issue differently. We may well explore the rich representational devices allowed by the use of paraconsistency in inconsistent domains, but withholding any claim to the effect that there are 'inconsistent objects' in reality.* (Da Costa [4], p. 33).
>
> *This allows for the accommodation of inconsistency by acknowledging that it is not a* permanent *feature of* reality *to which theories*

> *must correspond, but is rather a* temporary *aspect of such* theories *[...]. In this view, to accept a theory is to be committed, not to believing it to be true* per se, *but to holding it as* if *it were true, for the purposes of further elaboration, development and investigation.* (da Costa / Bueno / French [6], p. 616–617).

Frege's Nightmare is a logic that takes the non ontological commitment of inconsistencies seriously. That is, the temporary acceptance of inconsistencies will be abandoned as soon as the singular terms occurring in the elementary propositions producing this inconsistencies are ontologically committed. In other words, if the Proponent has accepted the Opponent's inconsistency $\boldsymbol{A}(\tau) \wedge \neg\boldsymbol{A}(\tau)$ he has also accepted that the constant τ carries no ontological commitment. More precisely in Frege's Nightmare the following holds:

$$(\boldsymbol{A}(\tau) \wedge \neg\boldsymbol{A}(\tau)) \rightarrow \neg\bigvee_x((x = \tau) \wedge (\boldsymbol{A}(\tau) \wedge \neg\boldsymbol{A}(\tau)))$$

This approach to paraconsistency blocks triviality for the literal case only, that is, a thesis of the form $((a \wedge b) \wedge \neg(a \wedge b)) \rightarrow c$ is still valid. One way to see the literal rule is to think of it as distinguishing between the internal or copulative negation from the external or sentential negation.[10] That is, in the standard approaches to logic, the elementary proposition $\boldsymbol{A}(n)$ has the internal logical form: $n\varepsilon\boldsymbol{A}$ (where ε stands for the copula: n is $\boldsymbol{A}$) and the negation of it the form: $n\varepsilon'\boldsymbol{A}$ (n is not $\boldsymbol{A}$). Now in this standard interpretation the negative copula is equivalent to the expression $negA$, where A can also be complex. This equivalence ignores the distinction between the internal (copulative) form and the external or sentential form of elementary propositions. The literal approach to paraconsistency takes this distinction seriously with the result that contradictions which cannot be carried on at the literal level should be freed of paraconsistent restrictions. This seems to be the core of the permissive interpretation of paraconsistency: it makes sense to ask for the ontological commitment (or non-commitment) of elementary contradictions, but not of complex ones. The distinction between a copulative and a sentential negation reflects this fact. But this is not the same as to say that the paraconsistency should not be introduced at the level of complex propositions: actually it can be, but with another motivation other than stating propositions with and about contradictory objects.[11]

---

[10] The difference between internal and external negation has been worked out for other purposes by Sinowjew (Sinowjew [27] and Wessels and Sinowjew [28]).

[11] The motivation is that of blocking triviality. This can be achieved by means of restricting the number of attacks. More precisely a dialogical paraconsistent logic results from combining the literal rule with the following structural rule:

3.4 Conclusions

This article is one of a series based on the seminar "Erweiterungen der Dialogischen Logik" ("extensions to dialogical logic") held in Saarbrücken in the summer of 1998 by Shahid Rahman and Helge Rückert. The same seminar has motivated the publication of The Dialogical Approach to Paraconsistency by Rahman and Carnielli [22], On Dialogues and Ontology. *The Dialogical Approach to Free Logic* by Rahman, Rückert and Fischmann [13], *Dialogische Modallogik für T, B, S4 und S5* [18], *Dialogische Logik und Relevanz* [17] and *Die Logik der zusammenhängenden Aussagen: ein dialogischer Ansatz zur konnexen Logik* [19] by Rahman and Rückert. One important aim of these articles (and the present paper) is to show how to build a common semantic language for different non-standard logics in such a way that (1) the semantic intuitions behind these logics can be made transparent, (2) combinations between these logics can be easily achieved, (3) a common basis is proposed for discussion of the philosophical consequences of these logics — the philosophical point here is to undertake the task of discussing the semantics of non-classical logics from a pragmatical point of view which commits itself neither to a correspondence theory of truth nor to a possible-world semantics.

One of the consequences of the dialogical approach is that two of the above mentioned logics can be seen as extending the formal rule for elementary propositions, namely free and paraconsistent logics. This offers a perspective of these logics which seems to be close to Hugh MacColl's reflections on symbolic existence and demands a new concept of logical form. This new concept of logical form should allow valid and invalid forms to be differentiated without going back to a mere syntactic notion — but this is another interesting story.

Acknowledgments. The results of this paper are the achievements of a collaboration project between the Archives — Centre d'Etudes et de Recherches Henri Poincaré (Prof. Gerhard Heinzmann), Université Nancy 2 and FR 5.1 Philosophie (Prof. Kuno Lorenz), Universität des Saarlandes, supported by the Fritz-Thyssen-Stiftung which I wish to thank expressly.

- *(Dual intuitionistic Rule)* In any move, each player may defend himself of every attack or he may attack *the last (complex) defense*.

If the Proponent starts an attack with the atomic formula a introduced before by the Opponent in move n, he can not start another attack based in an application of the formal rule to the same move n.

After an attack by **X** on a negation no other attack by **X** is possible. Thus, as soon as, say **X**, defends himself from an attack of **Y**, **Y** can only attack this defense if complex or the anterior one if this defense is not complex (see Rahman and Roetti [20]).

I also wish to thank Eric Krabbe, Narahari Rao (Saarbrücken), one anonymous referee and Helge Rückert (Saarbrücken) for their critical comments on earlier versions of this paper, Mrs. Cheryl Lobb de Rahman for her careful grammatical revision, and Matthias Fischmann (Saarbrücken) for proof reading and type setting of the final draft.

SHAHID RAHMAN
Philosophie, Université de Lille III
E-mail: Shahid.Rahman@clsh.univ-nancy2.fr and s.rahman@rz-uni.sb.de

Bibliography

[1] M. Astroh. Präsupposition und Implikatur. In [7], p. 1391–1406.

[2] M. Bremer. Wahre Widersprüche: Einführung in die parakonsistente Logik. Sankt Augustin: Academia, 1998.

[3] N. C. A. Da Costa. On the Theory of Inconsistent Formal Systems. *Notre Dame Journal of Formal Logic*, 15:497–510, 1974.

[4] N. C. A. Da Costa. Paraconsistent Logic. In *Stanislaw Jáskowski Memorial Symposium. Paraconsistent Logic, Logical Philosophy, Mathematics & Informatics at Torún*, pages 29–35, 1998.

[5] N. C. A. Da Costa, O. Bueno, and S. French. Is there a Zande Logic? *History and Philosophy of Logic*, XIX(1):41–54, 1998.

[6] N. C. A. Da Costa, O. Bueno, and S. French. The Logic of Pragmatic Truth. *Journal of Philosophical Logic*, XXVII:603–620, 1998.

[7] M. Dascal, D. Gerhardus, K. Lorenz, G. Meggle (Hg.), *Sprachphilosophie/Philosophy of Language/La philosophie de langage.* De Gruyter, Berlin. 1996, vol. 2.

[8] W. Felscher. Dialogues, Strategies and Intuitionistic Provability. *Annals of Pure and Applied Logic*, 28:217–254, 1985.

[9] S. Jaskowski. Rachunek zdańdla systemów dedukcyjnych sprzecznych. *Studia Soc. Scient. Torunensis*, A1(5):55–77, 1948. English translation in [10].

[10] S. Jaskowski. Propositional Calculus for Contradictory Deductive Systems. *Studia Logica*, 24:143–157, 1969. English translation of [9].

[11] P. Lorenzen and K. Lorenz. *Dialogische Logik.* Wissenschaftliche Buchgesellschaft, Darmstadt, 1978.

[12] H. MacColl. Symbolical Reasoning (VI). *Mind*, 14:74–81, 1905.

[13] S. Rahman, H. Rückert, and M. Fischmann. On Dialogues and Ontology. The Dialogical Approach to Free Logic. *Logique et Analyse*, 160:357–375, 1997.

[14] S. Rahman. *Über Dialoge, protologische Kategorien und andere Seltenheiten.* Peter Lang, Frankfurt a. M.; Berlin; New York; Paris; Wien, 1993.

[15] S. Rahman, S. Rueckert, H. and Fischmann, M. On Dialogues and Ontology. The dialogical approach to free logic. *Logique et Analyse*, vol. 160, 327-374, 1997.

[16] S. Rahman and H. Rückert. Die pragmatischen Sinn- und Geltungskriterien der Dialogischen Logik beim Beweis des Adjunktionssatzes. In *Philosophia Scientiae*, (3) 3:145-170, 1998–1999.

[17] S. Rahman and H. Rückert. Dialogische Logik und Relevanz. FR 5.1 Philosophie - Universität des Saarlandes, Memo Nr. 26, July 1998.

[18] S. Rahman and H. Rueckert. Dialogische Modallogik für T, B, S4 und S5. To appear in Logique et Analyse.

[19] S. Rahman and H. Rückert. Die Logik der zusammenhängenden Aussagen: ein dialogischer Ansatz zur konnexen Logik. FR 5.1 Philosophie - Universität des Saarlandes, Memo Nr. 28, December 1998.

[20] S. Rahman and J. A. Roetti. The Dual of Intuitionism and the Non-Committal Formulation of Paraconsistency. (in preparation).

[21] S. Rahman Ways of Understanding Hugh MacColls Concept of Symbolic Existence. *Nordic Journal of Philosophical Logic*, vol. 3 (1-2), 35-58, 1999.

[22] S. Rahman and W. Carnielli. The Dialogical Approach to Paraconsistency. *Synthese*, vol. 125 (1-2), 201-232, 2000.

[23] S. Rahman and H. Rueckert. Dialogical Connexive Logic. *Synthese*, vol. 127, (1-2), 105–139, 2001.

[24] N. Rao. Dialogical Logic and Ontology. In preparation., 1999.

[25] S. Read. *Thinking About Logic.* Oxford University Press, Oxford; New York, 1994.

[26] R. Routley. Exploring Meinong's Jungle and Beyond. Canberra: Canberra Australasian National University., 1979.

[27] A. A. Sinowjew. *Komplexe Logik. Grundlagen einer logischen Theorie des Wissens.* VEB Deutscher Verlag der Wissenschaften / Friedr. Vieweg + Sohn GmbH / Verlag und C. F. Winter'sche Verlagshandlung., Berlin; Braunschweig; Basel, 1970.

[28] A. A. Sinowjew and H. Wessel. *Logische Sprachregeln. Eine Einführung in die Logik.* Wilhelm Fink Verlag., München; Salzburg, 1975.

[29] R. Smullyan. *First-Order Logic.* Springer, Heidelberg, 1968.

[30] M. S. Stepanians. *Frege und Husserl über Urteilen und Denken.* Ferdinand Schöning, Paderborn; München; Wien; Zürich, 1998.

[31] F. Suárez. *Disputationes Methaphysicae — Disputaciones Metafísicas.* Gredos–Biblioteca Hispánica de Filosofía, Madrid, 1960.

Chapter 4

Truthmakers, Entailment and Necessity

Stephen Read

The aim is to show that necessity does not supervene on contingency. Classically, such supervenience is immediate: any necessary truth is entailed by every contingent truth, and so is made true by those contingent truthmakers, whatever they are. In relevance logic, however, there is a class of necessary propositions entailed only by other members of that class. Consequently, they can be made true only by their own class of truthmakers. It follows that the Entailment Thesis is false: this popular thesis says that whatever makes a proposition true makes true whatever that proposition entails. On further examination, however, we find that the truthmaker of a proposition does not itself make true what the proposition entails, but only together with the truthmaker of the entailment in question. Those truthmakers might be the set of all possible worlds—modal Platonism; or linguistic conventions; or proofs. Platonism and conventionalism are rejected in favour of a (moderate) realist account of proofs, abstract structures whose necessary existence entails the necessary truth of necessary propositions.

4.1 Truthmakers

There is a widespread belief that necessary truths do not need anything to make them true. This contrasts with the case of contingent truths. Contingent truths correspond to some event, state of affairs, fact or whatever, whose obtaining is required for their truth. The basic axiom of the Correspondence Theory is qualified by the exclusion of necessary truths: "whatever is (contingently) true, something makes it true." Indeed, in its most resolute version, for example, in Wittgenstein's *Tractatus*, truthmakers were required only for a class of atomic or elementary truths. The truth of all other propositions flowed from them. With increasing doubt as to the existence of such a class of basic truths to which all others could be reduced (the colour exclusion problem played a leading role), truthmakers were expanded once again to cover truths in general. But the belief remained that necessary truths supervened in some sense on contingent truthmaking. The thought seems to have been that the necessary truths will be true regardless of which contingent truths turn out true. Therefore, while something is needed to determine the truth of the contingent truths, namely, the existence of their truthmakers (facts, states of affairs or whatever), nothing is needed to decide that of the necessities, for they are true regardless.

Before we can judge whether the thesis of the supervenience of necessity is correct, we need to spell out in more detail the central notions of truthmaking. Let us write $s \models p$ as shorthand for 's makes p true'. At the heart of the conception lies the Truthmaker Axiom:

Postulate 4.1.1 *(Truthmaker,* **TA***) For all p, if p is true then something makes it true, i.e., $\forall p$, if p is true then $\exists s, s \models p$.*

TA is agnostic on the exact nature of truthmakers. Much ink has been spilt in trying to answer that question. The modern resurgence of interest in the Correspondence Theory of Truth has largely abandoned that quest, trying instead to set out the formal or structural framework for truthmaking, defining truth "from the top down" instead of "bottom-up" from the detailed nature of truthmakers. Accordingly, truthmakers will be whatever satisfy the basic postulates, just as numbers are whatever satisfy Dedekind's or Peano's postulates.[1]

Implicit in what has been said so far is that truthmaking is factive, that is,

[1]One should perhaps be equally agnostic about the truthbearers. I am assuming they are propositions, but nothing hangs on this assumption.

Postulate 4.1.2 *(Factive Condition,* **FC***) If* $\exists s, s \models p$ *then p is true. In other words, if something makes p true then it really is true.*

TA and **FC** can be combined, capturing the "correspondence intuition", that the truth of every true proposition is to be explained by the existence of something whose very existence suffices for the truth of that proposition.

Theorem 4.1.3 *(Correspondence Intuition,* **CI***) For all p, p is true iff* $\exists s, s \models p$.

Proof: immediate from **TA** and **FC**. □

Along with the rejection of a basic or elementary level of propositions and truthmakers goes a theory of the interaction of the truthmakers of negative, conjunctive and disjunctive propositions with those of their parts. First, we adopt a truth-principle for negation (where $\neg p$ stands for the negation of p):

Definition 4.1.4 *(***T**$\neg$*)* $\neg p$ *is true iff p is not.*

Theorem 4.1.5 *(Non-Contradiction,* **NC***)*

$$\exists s, s \models \neg p \text{ iff } \neg\exists t, t \models p.$$

Proof: suppose $s \models \neg p$ and $t \models p$. Then both p and $\neg p$ are true, by **FC**. But that is impossible, by **T**$\neg$. So if $\exists s, s \models \neg p$ then $\neg\exists t, t \models p$. Conversely, suppose $\neg\exists t, t \models p$. Then by **TA**, p is not true, so $\neg p$ is true (by **T**$\neg$), whence $\exists s, s \models \neg p$. So $\exists s, s \models \neg p$ iff $\neg\exists t, t \models p$. □

Theorem 4.1.6 *(Bivalent Truthmaker,* **BTA***) For all p, either* $\exists s, s \models p$ *or* $\exists s, s \models \neg p$.

Proof: Since $p \vee \neg p$ is true (for all p), either p is true or $\neg p$ is true (a disjunction cannot be true unless one part of it is true). So either $\exists s, s \models p$ or $\exists s, s \models \neg p$.

□

Obviously, the proofs of **NC** and **BTA** would be rejected by, for example, a constructivist who did not assent unrestrictedly to the Law of Excluded Middle, or a supervaluationist, for whom truth-value gaps provide no obstacle to the truth of disjunctions neither of whose parts is true.[2]

[2] One possibility, not explored here, would be to develop, in parallel with the theory of

4.2 Entailment

The focus of our discussion will be what is often known as the Entailment Thesis, **ET** (Theorem 4.2.2), that truthmaking is closed under entailment. I will argue that the thesis is mistaken and needs revision (Theorem 4.5.2). But it is important here to distinguish two different thoughts, the Entailment Analysis from the Entailment Thesis. Let $p \Rightarrow q$ mean 'p entails q'.

Definition 4.2.1 *(The Entailment Analysis,* **EA***) True propositions are entailed by the existence of their truthmakers:* $s \models p$ *iff* s *exists and* s *exists* $\Rightarrow p$.[3]

This explicates or defines truth as consisting in the existence of a truthmaker. The existence of the truthmaker of each true proposition entails that proposition (and so entails that it is true). It is supposed to capture the thought that truth supervenes on how things are, so that for p to fail to be true, some truthmaker must fail to exist, i.e., there is no change in truth without a change in the world. I will argue in §4.3 that **EA** does not properly capture the supervenience of truth, and so will reject Definition 4.2.1.

Theorem 4.2.2 *(The Entailment Thesis,* **ET***) Whatever makes a proposition true makes true whatever that proposition entails: if* $s \models p$ *and* $p \Rightarrow q$ *then* $s \models q$.

Proof: The Entailment Thesis follows from the Entailment Analysis, though the former can be retained independently. For if truthmaking is analysed as in **EA**, then clearly if $p \Rightarrow q$ and s exists $\Rightarrow p$ then s exists $\Rightarrow q$ (entailment is transitive), so if $s \models p$ then $s \models q$. □

The supervenience of necessity seems now to be confirmed by the following result, which depends on the spread law, that anything entails a necessary truth:

Theorem 4.2.3 *(Supervenience of Necessity,* **SN***) Given the spread law for entailment, if* p *is necessarily true then* $s \models p$ *for all* s.

truthmakers, a theory of falsity-makers, without any commitment to the question whether any proposition might be made both true and false or neither. **T¬**, however, commits us (via **NC**) to the realist position that each proposition has a falsity-maker just when it lacks a truthmaker.

[3]See, e.g., [11] p. 189 and [4] p. 127.

Proof: Let p be any necessary truth and s any truthmaker. Then, $\exists q, s \models q$. Since p is necessarily true, $q \Rightarrow p$ by the spread law for entailment. So $s \models p$ by **ET**. □

There is some plausibility that what makes necessary truths true is simply contingent matters of fact—but in such a way that they are true regardless of what those facts are. Take $p \vee \neg p$, for example. If p is true, $p \vee \neg p$ is true; equally, if p is false, $\neg p$ is true, so $p \vee \neg p$ is true. So either way, $p \vee \neg p$ is true. By **ET**, what makes it true is whatever makes p true or false. For something must make p true or false (**BTA**); and whichever it is, will make $p \vee \neg p$ true.

But although the truth of p is clearly relevant in this way to that of $p \vee \neg p$, why should the truth of an arbitrary true proposition get involved? To be sure, $p \vee \neg p$ is true come what may, that is, come p or $\neg p$. **SN**, however, says that, if q, whatever it may be, is true, then what makes q true has an equal role in making $p \vee \neg p$ true. That is why **SN** is mistaken. It is mistaken for the same reason that classical and intuitionistic logic are mistaken, in taking q to entail any logical truth. **SN** depends on the classical spread law, that $q \Rightarrow p$ whenever p is necessarily true. There are familiar reasons to reject this principle. I don't intend to go into these here.[4] What I want to explore are the consequences of doing so for the theory of truthmaking.

Suppose we reject the spread law for entailments. The proof of Theorem 4.2.3 (**SN**) consequently fails. Nonetheless, it might still be true that each necessary truth is made true by some contingent truthmaker, even if not by all. A result of Alberto Coffa's [7], however, shows (roughly) that some entailments, by the lights of relevance logic, are entailed only by entailments. So **ET** will not suffice to provide truthmakers for them by transfer from some contingent truth.

Coffa's result needs careful formulation and statement. Suppose p is necessarily true and q is contingent. Then $p \& q$ is contingent. By **TA**, $\exists s, s \models p \& q$. By **ET**, $s \models p$. So it seems that any necessary truth is made true by a contingent truthmaker. But this is sophistical. The necessary truth, p, is entailed by the contingent truth, $p \& q$. Yet the latter provides no support for the necessity of p. Suppose $u \models p$ and $v \models q$. What have u and v to do with the truth of $p \& q$?

To deal with conjunction, we need some way of combining truthmakers. A common way to do so (though one which I will ultimately reject) is to use the fusion operation of mereology, producing the "sum" of two truthmakers, which are then its parts (as are their parts, also):[5]

Definition 4.2.4 *(Mereology) A* **mereology** *is a poset (partially ordered set)*

[4] See, e.g., [27] ch. 2.
[5] See, e.g., [5].

$\langle A, \subseteq \rangle$ *closed under arbitrary suprema, i.e., such that for all non-empty* $B \subseteq A$, *sup* B *exists. If* $B = \{b_1, \ldots, b_n\}$, *we write sup* B *as* $b_1 + \ldots + b_n$. *(We read* $s \subseteq t$ *as 's is part of t', and* $s + t$ *as 'the sum—or fusion—of s and t'.)*[6]

Lemma 4.2.5 *(i)* $s \subseteq t$ *iff* $s + t = t$;

(ii) $s + s = s$;

(iii) $s \subseteq s + t$.

Proof:

(i) $s + t = sup\{s, t\} = t$ iff $s \subseteq t$.

(ii) $s \subseteq s$, so $s + s = s$ by 1.

(iii) $s \subseteq sup\{s, t\} = s + t$. □

Postulate 4.2.6 *(Truthmaker Fusion,* **TF***)*

$$\text{If } s \models p \text{ and } t \models q \text{ then } s + t \models p\&q.$$

Reverting to u and v, the truthmakers of p and q: it follows that $u + v \models p\&q$, so by **ET**, $u+v \models p$. The supposed contingent truthmaker, s, of $p\&q$ (and so of p) is itself no more than a fusion of a contingent truthmaker, v, and whatever does make p (necessarily) true. To ignore the contribution of u to $u + v$ is already to suppose that necessary truths do not have their own truthmakers. All the argument shows is that, given **ET**, the same truthmaker makes both a contingent truth and a necessary truth true. It does not show that necessary truths do not have, or need, truthmakers distinct from the truthmakers of contingencies.

Moreover, consider $p \vee \neg p$, and suppose, w.l.g., that p is contingently true. Then $\exists s, s \models p$, so by **ET**, $s \models p \vee \neg p$. But though s, the contingent truthmaker of p, can explain why $p \vee \neg p$ is true, just as it explains why $p \vee q$ is true for any q, it does not explain why $p \vee \neg p$ has to be true, why $p \vee \neg p$ is necessarily true. We need to distinguish two questions:

- why is a necessary truth true
- why is a necessary truth necessary.

[6]Thus a mereology is a complete upper semi-lattice. See, e.g., [10] p. 36; [31] p. 34.

There may be many explanations of the first of these which provide no answer to the second. But a proper account of the truthmakers of necessary truths will explain both why they are necessary and why they are true. The supervenience of necessity (**SN**), were it correct, could do that. The necessary truths are not only true (since any truthmaker makes them true) but are necessarily true (because every truthmaker makes them true). We could, in the context of classical or intuitionistic logic, define the necessary truths as those made true by every truthmaker.

But **SN** is mistaken, and we are left with the question, what makes necessary truths necessarily true? What Coffa did was screen out cases like $p\&q \Rightarrow p$, where the necessary truth p is entailed by itself in conjunction with some proposition q whose contingency infects $p\&q$; and cases like $p \Rightarrow p \vee \neg p$, whose consequent, though necessary, is a substitution-instance of a proposition $p \vee q$ in general as contingent as p may be. First, we need a definition:

Definition 4.2.7 *A wff p is a* **necessitive** *if $p \Leftrightarrow \Box q$ for some q.*

Take a logic in which the spread law fails, such as E or $\mathsf{R}^{\Box}$,[7] the logics of relevant entailment or of relevance and necessity. The necessitives of E are entailments, $p \Rightarrow q$; the entailments of $\mathsf{R}^{\Box}$ are necessitives, $\Box(p \rightarrow q)$, abbreviated $p \Rightarrow q$. Let N be a class of necessitives of such a logic. Coffa defined a class $S(N)$, relative to N, and showed that if $p \Rightarrow q$ in that logic and $q \in S(N)$, then $p \in S(N)$ too. Thus members of $S(N)$, if true, are not only necessarily true (since E and $\mathsf{R}^{\Box}$ incorporate an $\mathsf{S4}$ notion of necessity), but are entailed only by necessitives. It follows that their truth, let alone their necessity, cannot be inherited from any contingency. If true, they are necessarily true, and as such, demand an explanation of why they are so.

4.3 Necessity

Thus the question, what makes necessary truths true, no longer admits the answer that nothing does, that there are no special truthmakers of necessities in that they are entailed by whatever is contingently true, however it turns out. Necessity cannot supervene on contingency. Members of the class of necessitives, $S(N)$, when true, are shown to be true of necessity, since their own special truthmakers, when they exist, exist of necessity. What shows them to be true also shows them to be necessary.

---

[7] See, e.g., [2] and [27].

But now the Entailment Thesis (**ET**) is revealed to be as sophistical as the argument for supervenience. The latter concluded that contingency sufficed to explain the truth of necessities by ignoring the need for a truthmaker for entailment. But what makes $p \vee \neg p$ true is not just what makes p true (if it is—or what makes $\neg p$ true, if it is not), but what makes p true in combination with what makes it true that p entails $p \vee \neg p$. Call this latter truthmaker, the truthmaker of the entailment, v. Then if $u \models p$ and $v \models p \Rightarrow p \vee \neg p$, then $u + v \models p \vee \neg p$.[8] Similarly, if p is false, $\exists u, u \models \neg p$ and $u + v \models p \vee \neg p$. Hence, either way, $\exists t = u + v, t \models p \vee \neg p$. That is, a truthmaker of $p \vee \neg p$ exists of necessity. So $p \vee \neg p$ is not only true, it is necessarily true. Thus we have an explanation not only of the truth of $p \vee \neg p$ but also of its necessity.

However, the Entailment Thesis infers from the fact that $u \models p$ and $p \Rightarrow p \vee \neg p$ that $u \models p \vee \neg p$, i.e., that u alone makes $p \vee \neg p$ true. This is precisely to ignore the truthmaker of the entailment—it is to assume that nothing is needed to make the entailment true. Indeed, **ET** was central to the proof of **SN** in Theorem 4.2.3. But we have rejected **SN**. So **ET** must be wrong too. It follows that the Entailment Analysis (**EA**) must also be mistaken, since **ET** follows immediately from **EA** (Theorem 4.2.2). What we should have is that, whenever s exists and s exists $\Rightarrow p$, $s + t \models p$, where $t \models s$ exists $\Rightarrow p$. Now suppose $u \models p$. Then u splits into two components, one of which makes it true that the existence of the other entails p, i.e., $\exists s, t, u = s + t, s$ exists and $t \models s$ exists $\Rightarrow p$. But, by the S4-principle that necessary truths (in particular, entailments) are necessarily true, t exists of necessity (if s exists $\Rightarrow p$). So the question is whether the necessary existence of t can be overlooked, so that the existence of s alone suffices for the truth of p. Can necessary truths be suppressed? We say that a type of wff, ϕ, can be suppressed if, whenever $X \Rightarrow p$ and for some q, of type ϕ, $q \in X$, then $X - \{q\} \Rightarrow p$. To say that necessary truths can be suppressed is to claim that they can be omitted *salva veritate* from the antecedent of entailments.

Recall that we have rejected the idea that an arbitrary proposition entails a necessary truth. Clearly, $p \& q \Rightarrow p$, by the meaning of &. (We could write $p, q \Rightarrow p$ if $\Rightarrow$ were multigrade.) Suppose p is a necessary truth. Then, if necessary truths could be suppressed, $q \Rightarrow p$. But that is the classical spread law. So Suppression (of necessary truths) is a fallacy.

We can conclude, then, that **EA** is mistaken and **ET** is false. Necessary truths require their own truthmakers, so that if $s \models p$ and $p \Rightarrow q$ then, although something makes it true that p entails q, it is only that further truthmaker, in

[8] I express it this way for the moment. Of course, a regress is threatening, since the entailment $(p \& (p \Rightarrow q)) \Rightarrow q$ also needs a truthmaker. This anxiety will be dealt with in §4.5.

conjunction with what makes p true, i.e., s, that makes q true, not (necessarily) s alone.

However, **EA** was supposed to capture an important aspect of truth, that truth supervenes on the world. Does the failure of **EA** mean that truth is not supervenient? No. We must instead state **EA** more circumspectly. The exact way in which we do so must wait until §4.5 and Definition 4.5.1.

So what does make necessary truths true? What makes contingent truths true is how things are, the nature of the actual world. The actual world is the mereological sum of all contingent truthmakers. The insight attributed to Leibniz and developed by Kripke and David Lewis,[9] among others, was that necessary truth supervenes on the class of all possible worlds just as contingent truth supervenes on the actual world. There can be no difference, no change, in the set of contingent truths without a change in the facts, in the sum of all contingent facts which constitute the actual world. Similarly, there can be no alteration, no difference, in the class of necessary truths without some alteration in some world somewhere. (Of course, since they are necessarily true, there can be no change in the class of necessary truths. What we mean is that what that class is, is determined by what happens across the entire spread of possible worlds.)

The metaphysics of contingent truthmakers is a credible theory. There is a world, described by our language, which contains facts, states of affairs or whatever whose existence makes contingent truths true. In contrast, Lewis' elaboration of a metaphysics of possible worlds whose existence and reality are supposed to explain the truth of modal propositions was met with an "incredulous stare" ([18] p. 133). And rightly so. It is not credible that what makes it true that I might now be subjected to insufferable torture is that some counterpart of me in another possible world actually does undergo such torture. It's a useful metaphor to speak in these terms, but it is an error to suppose that these other worlds, and their constituents, actually exist. They might have existed—indeed, some of them are us, and we might have turned handstands or whatever. But we didn't. Yet the modal truth-conditions require that for 'I might have suffered awful pain' to be true there be a world in which I (or my counterpart) does so.[10] That's a useful fiction, but it is a profligate and incredible metaphysics which interprets it as requiring that that world and that event really exist to act as a truthmaker of the modal proposition.

Similarly, for propositions to be necessary. Modal Platonism says that what makes a necessary proposition necessarily true is that it is true of all the man-

---

[9]See, e.g., [18].
[10]The objection was put by Adams in [1].

ifold really existing possible worlds. The metaphor is that if the proposition is necessarily true then however the world had turned out it would have been true of it; the rotten metaphysics is to take the metaphor literally and infer that its necessity is constituted by that manifold uniformity.

4.4 Reductionism

One overzealous reaction to metaphysical profligacy of Lewis' sort is eliminativism or reductionism, to reduce all supposed talk of necessity to convention, or language, or meaning. It is to deny that there really are any necessary truths in the intended sense. Instead, necessary truths are construed as analytically true, true by virtue of meaning or by convention. There are two reductionist strategies here, and they need separate treatment. The strong conventionalist strategy is to claim that the conventions of meaning are insufficient to determine the truth of any propositions, in particular of necessary truths, which are true only in virtue of further conventions. The weak conventionalist, in contrast, claims that those meaning-conventions are themselves sufficient to determine the truth of necessary truths. Obviously, everyone (except Fabre d'Olivet[11]) agrees that words have the meaning they do as a matter of convention. What distinguishes the (weak and strong) conventionalists is that they deny that anything non-conventional determines the truth of necessities. The weak conventionalist says that those meaning-conventions suffice;[12] the strong conventionalist, while denying that, invokes no metaphysics but further conventions to assure the truth of necessary truths.[13]

The problem with strong conventionalism is its sheer implausibility. Take a deep and difficult mathematical result, for example, Fermat's Last Theorem or the Four-Colour Theorem. Those results do not appear to be conventions. Their proofs were the result of lengthy investigation, preceded by many false starts and mistaken attempts. The strong conventionalist is suggesting that we could set these proofs aside and go ahead with the rejection of these results, claiming, for example, that there is a solution to Fermat's equation with exponent greater than 2, or that there is a map which cannot be coloured with only four colours. Admittedly, he need not claim that doing so would be easy—we may be psychologically constrained to follow a certain furrow. But to refuse to accept these mathematical proofs, without feeling any obligation to point to

[11] See, e.g., John B. Carroll, "Introduction" to [36] pp. 8-9.

[12] This I take to be the view expressed in, e.g., [3] and [30], and criticised in [22].

[13] This I take to be the view expressed in, e.g., the later Wittgenstein, [24] and [15], and attacked in [21]: see, e.g., p. 164: "The thesis is rather that, even *given* what we mean by 'distance', there is no fact of the matter as to which is the true distance."

mistakes in them— for the strong conventionalist denies that the meanings and rules force any single answer to the truth of these necessary propositions—is absurd. The point of the proofs is to show how those meanings and rules do force a particular answer on us as a matter of necessity.

What, then, of the weak conventionalists' position? Their claim is that all necessity follows from the meanings of the terms involved—that is, they are all analytic. A first doubt about this claim arises from the same sort of example: the four-colour theorem, or any other reasonably deep mathematical claim. Is it plausible to say that they differ from simple equations like $1+1=2$ (whose analyticity is at least more credible) only in their psychological obscurity? It takes us to the heart of the philosophy of mathematics: can one explain the necessity of mathematical truths while showing how they also have application? The temptation in finding an explanation of their necessity is to belittle their substance (and saying they are analytic is the most extreme such position). But to explain their application and usefulness, some sense of their substantive content is needed, to contrast 'Every plane map can be coloured with at most four colours' with 'Vixens are female foxes'.

But is even 'Vixens are female foxes', i.e., 'All vixens are female foxes', true solely in virtue of its meaning? What the meaning of 'vixen' shows is that it reduces to

All female foxes are female foxes

and the meaning of 'female fox' is irrelevant to that. Its form is:

$$\forall x(Fx \to Fx) \qquad (*)$$

All instances of $(*)$ are true in virtue of the meaning of $\forall$ and $\to$. But what that means must wait until §4.5.

The other problem with weak conventionalism is its reference to the truth of necessary propositions "following from" the meanings of their terms. What is meant by "follows from" here is "follows of necessity from"—if further contingencies were involved in the consequence all would be lost. But then the account is circular unless some prior account of "following of necessity" is given.[14]

---

[14]See, e.g., [22] p. 97.

4.5 Proofs

What then does make entailments true? They cannot supervene on contingency, nor can their necessary truth consist in the existence of, on the one hand, the manifold of possible worlds, or on the other, of linguistic conventions. The answer comes from reflecting further on the character of the propositions in $S(N)$. Let p be an arbitrary true member of $S(N)$. Then p is a truth-functional combination of entailments. So ultimately what makes p true is the truth of its constituent entailments. Our question, therefore, reduces to the question what makes an entailment true; and what makes an entailment (necessarily) true is the fact that its consequent follows validly from its antecedent. What sort of fact is that?

Once again, it's not that the former is true in every model of the latter, though that will undoubtedly be the case. Rather, we must recognise that there are further truthmakers over and above the contingent truthmakers. If an entailment holds, there must be some fact about the premises and conclusion which rules out the possibility that the premises are true and the conclusion false.[15]

One thing that is distinctive about necessary truths is that they admit of proof. Proofs are what show that necessary truths are true, and not only true, but necessarily so. If we can prove them, then, apart from any error in our grasp of the proof, they can't fail to hold, and so are necessarily true. Of course, a proof, if valid, is only as good as the premises on which it depends. But the purpose of the theory of those necessary truths—logic, mathematics, perhaps metaphysics, too—is to establish axioms definitive of the subject matter of the theory, whose certainty and self-evidence can then be transmitted to the theorems and establish them as necessarily true.

There are two obvious objections to the suggestion that proofs are truthmakers for necessities. First, the fact that higher-order and arithmetic truth are not recursively enumerable surely shows that proof and truth come apart. The point about proofs is that, though there may be no algorithm for proof search in, say, first-order logic, or even in propositional relevance logic, a proof must be recognisable once found. The proof-predicate must be decidable. Proofs are in principle surveyable. Given this conception of proof, we know from Gödel's incompleteness results that there are truths of arithmetic and of higher-order logic, necessary truths, which have no proof. Hence proofs cannot be what make them true.

Indeed, the second objection elaborates the first. To suppose that proofs make anything true is surely to confuse two different questions:

[15] See, e.g., [25] §4.

- what makes something true
- what shows that it is true

and, intersecting these two questions with our earlier distinction:

- what makes a necessary truth necessarily true
- what shows that a necessary truth is necessarily true.

Proofs are a means of demonstrating that something is necessarily true. But how can they themselves make them true or necessary? That would seem to confuse epistemology with metaphysics.

Constructivists will be unabashed at these objections. They will happily identify proofs with truthmakers.[16] For example, what makes an existential claim, $\exists x\phi(x)$, true is "a pair (a_1, a_2) such that a_1 is a proof of $\phi(\overline{a_2})$,"[17] and what makes an implication $p \rightarrow q$ true is "a construction $[s]$ that converts each proof t of p into a proof $s(t)$ of q."[18] For the constructivist refuses to countenance the idea that proof and truth could separate in this way. Dummett writes: "the truth of [a mathematical statement] can consist only in the existence of ... a proof."[19] Truth for the constructivist is an epistemic notion.

Much of the most exciting work in proof theory in recent decades has been in intuitionistic proof theory. One of the stimulants to these developments was the Curry/Howard isomorphism, whereby formulae are understood as the types of their proofs in an intuitionistic type theory. The formulae-as-types interpretation is the predominant notion in contemporary proof theory. What are constructed in the process are proof-terms, what one might call proof-makers, or "constructive truth"-makers.

From the realist perspective of this paper, however, truth is not an epistemic notion, and realism is marked by its belief that what is known (or knowable) may not exhaust what is true. Theorem 4.1.6 may guarantee that every proposition is true or false, but it cannot guarantee that every proposition can be known to be true or false. That does not mean, however, that a realist account of the truthmakers of necessary truths cannot draw on the insights of constructivist proof theory.

---

[16]See, e.g., [34].
[17][35] p. 231.
[18]*ibid.*
[19][8] p. 6.

Take '&'-introduction, for example. The "proofmaker" for $p\&q$ is given by the Cartesian product of the proofmakers of p and q:

$$\frac{s : p \quad t : q}{(s,t) : p\&q}\ \&\text{-intro.}$$

so that proofs of p and of q can be extracted from a canonical proof of $p\&q$:

$$\frac{s : p\&q}{\mathit{first}(s) : p}\ \&\text{-elim.} \qquad \frac{s : p\&q}{\mathit{second}(s) : q}\ \&\text{-elim.}$$

where *first* and *second* are projection functions yielding the first and second places, respectively, of their arguments. The analogy with the fusion of truth-makers is very close. What makes p true is part of what makes $p\&q$ true, as is what makes q true: $s \in (s,t)$ and $t \in (s,t)$. Moreover, this reinforces our rejection of **ET**, the Entailment Thesis, since, e.g., a proof of $p\&q$ is not itself a proof of p. But it contains all that is needed for a proof of p.

We can now give truthmakers (proofmakers) a far richer structure than mereology can offer. The proofmaker for an entailment $p \Rightarrow q$, for example, is an abstraction:

$$\frac{s : q}{\lambda x.s : p \Rightarrow q}\ \Rightarrow\text{-intro.}$$

(subject to suitable constraints on s and x),[20] and $\Rightarrow$-elimination is then a case of functional application:

$$\frac{s : p \Rightarrow q \quad t : p}{s(t) : q}\ \Rightarrow\text{-elim.}$$

I can now fulfil the outstanding promise to restate **EA**, showing how truth is properly supervenient on the existence of truthmakers:

Definition 4.5.1 *(The Supervenience of Truth,* **ST***)* $s \models p$ *iff* $\exists u, v,\ s = v(u)$, u *exists and* $v \models u$ *exists* $\Rightarrow p$.

Then if p fails to be true, either u does not exist or $v \not\models u$ exists $\Rightarrow p$. But since v is the truthmaker of a (true) entailment, v exists of necessity. So if p fails, u does not exist, and this is how truth supervenes on the world, i.e., on the existence of truthmakers. No change in truth without change in truthmaker.

But note that Definition 4.5.1 does not in fact say that true propositions are entailed by the existence of their truthmakers, but rather, by *part* of their truthmakers. Nonetheless, the claim is still true:

[20]For relevance, we require that x be a variable of type p occurring free in s; for the necessity of the entailment, further restrictions are needed. See, e.g., [14] ch. 3.

Theorem 4.5.2 *(The Revised Entailment Thesis,* **ET′***)*

(i) True propositions are entailed by the existence of their truthmakers, i.e., $\forall s, p$, if $s \models p$ then s exists and s exists $\Rightarrow p$.

(ii) $\forall s, p, q$, if $s \models p$ and $p \Rightarrow q$ then $\exists t$, $t \models p \Rightarrow q$ and $t(s) \models q$.

Proof:

(i) suppose $s \models p$. Then by Definition 4.5.1, $\exists u, v$, $s = v(u)$, u exists and $v \models u$ exists $\Rightarrow p$. Since $s = v(u)$, s exists $\Leftrightarrow u$ exists and v exists. So s exists $\Rightarrow p$ by the transitivity of entailment, and since u and v exist, s exists. So s exists and s exists $\Rightarrow p$.

(ii) suppose $s \models p$ and $p \Rightarrow q$. Then $\exists t$, $t \models p \Rightarrow q$. So $t(s) \models q$. □

For all this to work, however, two realist generalizations of the constructivist notion of proof are needed. First, when the constructivist speaks of, for example, "a construction which selects an object a (of the domain) ..." (cf. [33] p. 154), he means a construction which can be finitely or effectively carried out. Not so the realist. The realist speaks, for example, of Cauchy's or Dedekind's methods of *construction* of the real numbers as limits of sequences of, or cuts of rationals.[21] Such a construction is an infinitary one. The Dedekind construction identifies, e.g., the irrational $\sqrt{2}$ with the set of all rationals whose square is less than 2. Such a set is an infinitary object beyond the constructivist's pale.[22] In the case of proofs, such an infinitary object is indeed what makes its conclusion true, not what shows it to be true. It is true in virtue of there being such a proof. What shows it to be true is our exhibiting the proof. That answers the second of the above objections to proofs as truthmakers.

The second generalization is also infinitary, to allow infinitary modes of proof. Thereby we overcome the first objection. It is indeed true that, as the term 'proof' is normally used—even in realist contexts—a proof is a finitary array of formulae, by definition an array of formulae which can be effectively verified as in accordance with a given set of rules. When we say that a class of formulae,

[21] E.g., [9] p. 37: "If we carry out the Dedekind cut construction once again on $\mathcal{R}$, we obtain nothing new." Again, on p. 40: "Quite apart from its use in the definition of real numbers, the CANTOR construction with fundamental sequences has turned out to be the most fruitful." Cf. [32] p. 173: "we must solve the problem of constructing a complete ordered field $\mathcal{R}$ starting from $\mathcal{N}_I$ ... First the integers $\mathcal{Z}$ are constructed from $\mathcal{N}_I$, and the rationals $\mathcal{Q}$ from $\mathcal{Z}$. To construct $\mathcal{R}$ from $\mathcal{Q}$ is a more taxing operation ...." Finally, note the heading of §2.2 "Dedekind's construction" in [13] p. 8.

[22] I described a similar infinitary "construction" used in the proof of König's Lemma in [28] p. 216.

e.g., the valid wffs of first-order logic, are not themselves decidable, but semi-decidable, we mean that there is a proof system which is complete for these validities, and each such proof must be finitely and effectively checkable as a proof in accord with the system.

Gödel's Theorem assures us that there are classes of necessary truths which are not even semi-decidable. The truths of arithmetic are one such class. The Gödel sentence is true but not provable—not provable in this standard sense. The Gödel sentence appears, therefore, to be a counterexample to the thesis that the truthmakers of necessary truths are proofs, for here is a necessary truth which is not provable.

Gödel's Theorem does not show that no system of proof is adequate for arithmetic—provided "proof" is suitably generalized. The appropriate generalization is to admit a rule of infinitary induction. Applied to the case of arithmetic, we obtain what is often called the ω-rule:

$$\frac{A(0) \quad A(1) \quad A(2) \quad \ldots}{(\forall n)A(n)}\ \omega\text{-rule}$$

The ω-rule has infinitely many premises, one for each natural number. Adding the ω-rule to Peano's first four axioms suffices for a complete system of proof for arithmetic. Call it P_∞. Proofs in this system can, however, be infinitely large, and so cannot be effectively checked for compliance with the rules. It follows that there may be proofs of whose existence we will remain forever ignorant. They establish the truth of the verification-transcendent truths whose possible existence characterizes realism.

Nonetheless, it is quite clear (to a realist) what it is for a proof in this system to be correct. We can effectively specify the nature of proofs in P_∞. P_∞ is a well-defined system; and it is almost trivially complete (since the ω-rule exactly matches the truth-clause for $\forall$).

Recall the example of 'Vixens are female foxes'. We noted that its form was $(*)\ \forall x(Fx \to Fx)$, and that it was true in virtue of the meaning of $\forall$ and $\to$ (and 'vixen'). We now see that what that means is that there is a proof of it using the rules for $\forall$ and $\to$:

$$\cfrac{\cfrac{Fx^1}{Fx \to Fx}\ {\to}\text{I}(1)}{\forall x(Fx \to Fx)}\ \forall\text{I}$$

It is the existence of the proof that is crucial to showing that $(*)$ is necessarily true. In virtue of the meaning of its terms, there is a proof of it. The meaning of '$\to$' is that one can deduce its consequent from its antecedent. So its meaning is given by the rule:

$$\frac{\begin{array}{c}(p)\\ q\end{array}}{p \to q}\ \to\mathrm{I}$$

Similarly, the meaning of '∀' is given by its introduction-rule. We abbreviate the infinitary rule above by letting a single premise go proxy for the infinity of cases. Then the meanings conferred on '→' and '∀' by these being the rules for the assertion of $p \to q$ and $\forall x Fx$ respectively (and no other) justifies the corresponding elimination-rules.[23] The meaning of '→' and '∀' are such that there is a proof of every instance of $\forall x(Fx \to Fx)$. So it is necessarily true. But what makes it true (and necessarily so) is the existence of its proof. Its meaning is as much as and no more part of what makes it true than is the meaning of any contingent proposition. Its meaning is what makes its truthmaker the appropriate truthmaker for it. This is true for both contingent and necessary propositions. The meaning of 'Vixens are female foxes' is what makes the proof of (∗) an appropriate truthmaker for it.

4.6 Conclusion

The identification of the truthmakers of necessary truths in §4.5 with their proofs is clearly programmatic. It leaves many questions open—indeed, it opens as many questions as it closes. But to answer them goes beyond the remit of this paper. What I hope to have shown here is that:

(i) the correspondence intuition (**CI**) is the basis of a promising theory of truth;

(ii) within that theory, at least some necessary truths require their own truthmakers, and cannot supervene on contingent truths or their truthmakers;

(iii) consequently, the entailment thesis (**ET**), and its basis, the entailment analysis (**EA**), are mistaken, in implying such supervenience;

(iv) their motivation is properly expressed in the thesis of the supervenience of truth (**ST**) and the revised entailment thesis (**ET′**); and

(v) it is at least plausible that a notion of proof can be developed which reveals the truthmakers of necessary truths as the existence of corresponding proofs.

---

[23] See, e.g., [26] §§2.4-2.5.

This notion of proof will then yield a moderate realist account of necessary truth preferable to the profligacy of modal Platonism and the defeatism of conventionalism.

STEPHEN READ
Department of Logic and Metaphysics, University of St Andrews
Fife KY16 9AL Scotland, U.K.
E-mail: slr@st-and.ac.uk

Bibliography

[1] R.M. Adams, 'Theories of Actuality', *Nous* 8 (1974) 211-31.

[2] A. Anderson and N.D. Belnap, *Entailment: the logic and relevance and necessity*, vol. I (Princeton: Princeton U.P., 1975).

[3] A.J. Ayer, *Language, Truth and Logic* (Oxford: Oxford U.P., 1936).

[4] J. Bigelow, *The Reality of Numbers* (Oxford: Oxford U.P., 1988).

[5] R. Cartwright, 'Scattered objects', in [17] pp. 153-71.

[6] M. Detlefsen, ed., *Proof, Logic and Formalization* (London: Routledge, 1992).

[7] J.A. Coffa, 'Fallacies of Modality', in [2] §22.1.2 pp. 244-52.

[8] M. Dummett, *Elements of Intuitionism* (Oxford: Oxford U.P., 1977).

[9] H.-D. Ebbinghaus et al., *Numbers* (Berlin: Springer, 1991).

[10] R.A. Eberle, *Nominalistic Systems* (Dordrecht: Reidel, 1970).

[11] J.F. Fox, 'Truthmaker', *Australasian Journal of Philosophy* 65 (1987) pp. 188-207.

[12] D. Gabbay and F. Guenthner ed., *Handbook of Philosophical Logic*, vol. III *Alternatives to Classical Logic* (Dordrecht: Reidel, 1986).

[13] D. Goldrei, *Classic Set Theory* (London: Chapman and Hall, 1996).

[14] G. Helman, *Restricted Lambda Abstraction and the Interpretation of some Non-Classical Logics*, Ph.D. thesis, University of Pittsburgh 1977.

[15] P. Horwich, 'A defence of conventionalism', in [19] pp. 163-87.

[16] D. Isaacson, 'Some considerations on arithmetical truth and the ω-rule', in [6] pp. 94-138.

[17] K. Lehrer ed., *Analysis and Metaphysics* (Dordrecht: Reidel, 1975).

[18] D.K. Lewis, *On the Plurality of Worlds* (Oxford: Blackwell, 1986).

[19] G. Macdonald and C. Wright ed., *Fact, Science and Morality* (Oxford: Blackwell, 1986).

[20] H. Putnam, *Mind, Language and Reality* (Philosophical Papers, vol. 2) (Cambridge: Cambridge U.P., 1975).

[21] H. Putnam, 'The refutation of conventionalism', in [20] pp. 153-91.

[22] W.V. Quine, 'Truth by convention', in [23] pp. 70-99.

[23] W.V. Quine, *Ways of Paradox* (New York: Random House, 1966).

[24] W.V. Quine, *Word and Object* (Cambridge, Mass.: M.I.T. Press, 1960).

[25] S. Read, 'Formal and material consequence', *Journal of Philosophical Logic* 23 (1994) pp. 247-65.

[26] S. Read, 'Harmony and Autonomy in Classical Logic', *Journal of Philosophical Logic* 29 (2000) pp. 123-54.

[27] S. Read, *Relevant Logic* (Oxford: Blackwell, 1988).

[28] S. Read, *Thinking about Logic* (Oxford: Oxford U.P., 1995).

[29] G. Restall, 'Truthmakers, entailment and necessity', *Australasian Journal of Philosophy* 74 (1996) pp. 331-40.

[30] A. Sidelle, *Necessity, Essence and Individuation* (Ithaca: Cornell U.P., 1989).

[31] P. Simons, *Parts* (Oxford: Clarendon, 1987).

[32] I. Stewart and D. Tall, *The Foundations of Mathematics* (Oxford: Oxford U.P., 1977).

[33] G. Sundholm, 'Constructions, proofs and the meaning of the logical constants', *Journal of Philosophical Logic* 12 (1983) 151-72.

[34] G. Sundholm, 'Existence, proof and truth-making', *Topoi* 13 (1994) 117-26.

[35] D. van Dalen, 'Intuitionistic logic', in [12] pp. 225-339.

[36] B.L. Whorf, *Language, Thought and Reality* (Cambridge, Mass.: M.I.T. Press, 1956).

Chapter 5

Global Definability in Basic Modal Logic

MAARTEN DE RIJKE and HOLGER STURM

5.1 Introduction

In modal logic, the fundamental semantic relation is 'truth of a modal formula φ in a pair $(\mathfrak{M}, w)$,' where $\mathfrak{M}$ is a model and w is a world chosen from this model. Such a pair is called a *pointed* model [5, 18] or a model-world pair [1]. We use $(\mathfrak{M}, w) \Vdash \varphi$ to say that φ is true in $(\mathfrak{M}, w)$. Based on this relation, further semantical concepts are defined as usual. That a formula φ follows from a set of formulas Γ holds, for instance, if for every pointed model $(\mathfrak{M}, w)$ in which all $\psi \in \Gamma$ are true, we have $(\mathfrak{M}, w) \Vdash \varphi$. Or, in modal terms: it is not possible that Γ is true in some possible state without φ being true there as well.

Both the satisfaction relation and the consequence relation reflect a *local* perspective on the modal language and its models. Formulas are evaluated inside models, at some particular world w (the 'actual' world). In contrast, we can take a *global* perspective, under which models, and not pointed models, are regarded as the fundamental semantic units. The global counterparts of the satisfaction and the consequence relation are then defined as follows. A formula φ is said to be *true in a model* $\mathfrak{M}$, abbreviated by $\mathfrak{M} \models \varphi$, if φ is true in every pointed model $(\mathfrak{M}, w)$ based on $\mathfrak{M}$; and φ follows globally from Γ, if for all models $\mathfrak{M}$ with $\mathfrak{M} \models \Gamma$ it holds that $\mathfrak{M} \models \varphi$. As several authors have observed [5, 13, 24], a large number of logical properties, like completeness, canonicity, finite model property, and interpolation, come in two flavors: a local one and a global one. For instance, the notions of local and global consequence do not coincide: $\Box\psi$ follows locally from ψ, but not globally, yet the following general fact holds: a formula φ follows locally from a set Γ iff φ follows globally from the set $\{\Box^n\psi \mid \psi \in \Gamma, n \in \omega\}$. So, in a sense, the global approach can be simulated within the local setting; moreover, by adding some non-standard modal connectives to our language, the other direction holds as well; see [24, Appendix B] for details.

On the other hand, the global perspective is worth exploring for its own sake. Why? First, via a straightforward translation modal formulas φ may be regarded as terms t_φ of an algebraic language, so that φ turns out to be true in a model $\mathfrak{M}$ iff the equality $t_\varphi = 1$ holds in the corresponding algebra $\mathfrak{M}^*$ [5]. Hence, from the algebraic point of view the global setting proves the more natural one. Second, principles of supervenience, as they were applied in different areas of philosophy, are usually discussed on the level of models [12]. Third, sometimes we are interested in certain features of the whole model, independent of the fact whether they are enforceable by pointwise reasoning [1]. And fourth, global constraints on models play a key role in the closely related area of terminological reasoning [6].

The latter two points raise an important question: what is the expressive power of the given modal language? In other words: which properties of structures are definable or describable within the language? The view of properties that underlies this account is purely extensional; roughly, a property is identified with the class of structures which have this property. Therefore, a property, that is, a class K of structures, is said to be *definable* if there is a set of formulas Γ such that K equals the class of structures in which Γ holds. We can rephrase our original question as follows: is there a general characterization of the classes of structures that are definable in the above sense? What this questions asks for is a characterization of the elementary classes of the logic under investigation. Answers to such questions are usually given by stating algebraic closure conditions that are necessary and sufficient for a class K to be definable. Clearly, in the case of modal logic the characterization problem has two versions: a global and a local one. Our paper contains solutions for both versions. In Section 5.3 we deal with the local version, whereas Section 5.4 is reserved for the global setting.

Semantics-based translations form a valuable tool for investigating the meta-properties of a logic more deeply, by relating it to other logics. In the case of basic modal logic there exists a natural translation into first-order logic. Using this translation we may view modal logic as a fragment of first-order logic. Moreover, this fragment has a nice semantical characterization in terms of its preservation behavior. A famous result by van Benthem [2] tells us that a first-order formula lies in this fragment if and only if it is preserved under so-called bisimulations (see Section 5.3). The global counterpart of this result is proved in Section 5.4. Then, in Section 5.5 we compare our global definability results to earlier results obtained by Hansoul [11]. We mention a number of definability and preservation results concerning particular classes of models in Section 5.6. We conclude with some suggestions for future research in Section 5.7.

5.2 Basic Concepts

Fix a countable set $\mathcal{P} := \{p_n \mid n \in \omega\}$ of proposition letters. The set $\mathcal{ML}$ of modal formulas (over $\mathcal{P}$) is defined as the least set X such that every proposition letter from $\mathcal{P}$ belongs to X, X contains the logical constant $\bot$ (falsum), and X is closed under the boolean connectives $\neg$, $\vee$, and $\wedge$ as well as under the modal operators $\Box$ and $\Diamond$.

A *model* for $\mathcal{ML}$ is a triple $\mathfrak{M} = (W, R, V)$, where W is a non-empty set, R a binary relation on W, and V a valuation function from $\mathcal{P}$ into the power set of W. As usual, the truth of modal formulas is defined recursively with respect to pairs $(\mathfrak{M}, w)$, consisting of a model $\mathfrak{M}$ and a distinguished element $w \in W$. The atomic and boolean cases of the definition are clear. For the modal operators we put

$$\begin{array}{lll} (\mathfrak{M}, w) \Vdash \Diamond\varphi & \text{iff} & \text{there is a } w' \in W \text{ with } Rww' \text{ and } (\mathfrak{M}, w') \Vdash \varphi, \\ (\mathfrak{M}, w) \Vdash \Box\varphi & \text{iff} & \text{for all } w' \in W \text{ with } Rww' \text{ we have } (\mathfrak{M}, w') \Vdash \varphi. \end{array}$$

If $\mathfrak{M}$ is a model and φ a modal formula, we use $\mathfrak{M} \models \varphi$ to say that for all $w \in W$ it holds that $(\mathfrak{M}, w) \Vdash \varphi$. If Φ is a set of modal formulas, $\mathfrak{M} \models \Phi$ says that $\mathfrak{M} \models \varphi$ for every $\varphi \in \Phi$. $\mathrm{Mod}(\Phi)$ denotes the class of models $\mathfrak{M}$ such that $\mathfrak{M} \models \Phi$. A class K of models is *globally definable* if there is a set Φ with $\mathsf{K} = \mathrm{Mod}(\Phi)$. Analogously, we call a class K of pointed models *locally definable* if $\mathsf{K} = \{(\mathfrak{M}, w) \mid (\mathfrak{M}, w) \Vdash \Phi\}$, for some $\Phi \subseteq \mathcal{ML}$.

A pointed model $(\mathfrak{M}, w)$ may also be viewed as a first-order model suitable for a first-order vocabulary, say τ, consisting of a countable set $\{P_n \mid n \in \omega\}$ of predicate symbols, a binary relation symbol S and an individual constant

c.[1] This, together with the fact that the truth clauses for modal formulas are stated in a first-order metalanguage, suggests a standard translation ST from $\mathcal{ML}$ into the set of first-order sentences over τ:

$$\begin{aligned}
ST(p_n) &= P_n c, \text{for } n \in \omega \\
ST(\bot) &= \bot \\
ST(\neg\varphi) &= \neg ST(\varphi) \\
ST(\varphi \vee \psi) &= ST(\varphi) \vee ST(\psi) \\
ST(\varphi \wedge \psi) &= ST(\varphi) \wedge ST(\psi) \\
ST(\Diamond\varphi) &= \exists x(Scx \wedge ST(\varphi)[x/c])^{2,3} \\
ST(\Box\varphi) &= \forall x(Scx \to ST(\varphi)[x/c])
\end{aligned}$$

The following lemma is then proved by an easy induction. In fact, this is the result which allows us to regard modal logic as a fragment of first-order logic.

Lemma 5.2.1 *For every modal formula φ, every model $\mathfrak{M} = (W, R, V)$ and every $w \in W$: $(\mathfrak{M}, w) \Vdash \varphi$ if and only if $(\mathfrak{M}, w) \Vdash ST(\varphi)$.*

As has been emphasized in the introduction, throughout this paper there are two consequence relations in use, a local one, $\models_l$, and a global one, $\models_g$. The first is defined with respect to pointed models, the second with respect to models. Below, these two relations will also be applied to (sets of) first-order sentences. For instance, let $\Delta \cup \{\alpha\}$ be a set of first-order sentences over τ, then $\Delta \models_l \alpha$ says that for every pointed model $(\mathfrak{M}, w)$, $(\mathfrak{M}, w) \Vdash \Delta$ implies $(\mathfrak{M}, w) \Vdash \alpha$.

5.3 Local Definability

In this section we introduce a well-known type of equivalence relations between models, so-called bisimulations. What makes them important is the fact that modal formulas cannot distinguish between bisimilar models, that is, if there is a bisimulation between two models $\mathfrak{M}$ and $\mathfrak{N}$ which relates worlds w and v, then w and v satisfy exactly the same modal formulas. This result is stated

[1] This is possible because, neglecting some harmless notational differences, $(\mathfrak{M}, w)$ may be seen as a convenient way of denoting the first-order model $(W, R, (V(p_n))_{n \in \omega}, w)$.

[2] Here, and in the following clause, the variable x is assumed to be the first variable chosen from a list of variables that do not occur in $ST(\varphi)$.

[3] In general, for a first-order formula α and individual terms t_1 and t_2, $\alpha[t_1/t_2]$ denotes the formula one gets by replacing every occurrence of t_2 in α by t_1.

in Lemma 5.3.2. Moreover, recent work has shown that bisimulations form an important tool in modal model theory. A central result along this line is Theorem 5.3.3 below, which provides an algebraic characterization of the elementary classes of pointed models, that is, the classes of pointed models that are definable by (sets of) modal formulas. This result was first stated and proved in [18].

Definition 5.3.1 Let $\mathfrak{M} = (W, R, V)$ and $\mathfrak{N} = (W', R', V')$ be models. A non-empty relation $Z \subseteq W \times W'$ is a *bisimulation* between $\mathfrak{M}$ and $\mathfrak{N}$, if Z satisfies the following conditions:

B1 For every $w \in W$ and $v \in W'$, if Zwv then $(\mathfrak{M}, w) \Vdash p_n \Leftrightarrow (\mathfrak{N}, v) \Vdash p_n$, for every $n \in \omega$.

B2 For every $w, w' \in W$ and $v \in W'$, if Zwv and Rww', then there is some $v' \in W'$ such that $R'vv'$ and $Zw'v'$.

B3 For every $w \in W$ and $v, v' \in W'$, if Zwv and $R'vv'$ then there is some $w' \in W$ such that Rww' and $Zw'v'$.

We write $(\mathfrak{M}, w) \sim (\mathfrak{N}, v)$ to say that there is a bisimulation Z from $\mathfrak{M}$ to $\mathfrak{N}$ with Zwv.

If Z is a bisimulation such that for every $v \in W'$ there is some $w \in W$ with Zwv, then Z is called a *surjective* bisimulation from $\mathfrak{M}$ to $\mathfrak{N}$. Z is a *total* bisimulation from $\mathfrak{M}$ to $\mathfrak{N}$, if for every $w \in W$ there is some $v \in W'$ with Zwv.

Lemma 5.3.2 *Let Z be a bisimulation between $\mathfrak{M}$ and $\mathfrak{N}$ such that Zwv. Then for every modal formula φ, $(\mathfrak{M}, w) \Vdash \varphi$ iff $(\mathfrak{N}, v) \Vdash \varphi$.*

Theorem 5.3.3 *For a class K of pointed models the following equivalences hold.*

(i) *K is (locally) definable by a set of modal formulas iff K is closed under bisimulations and ultraproducts, and the complement of K, abbreviated by $\overline{\mathsf{K}}$, is closed under ultrapowers.*

(ii) *K is (locally) definable by a single modal formula iff both K and $\overline{\mathsf{K}}$ are closed under bisimulations and ultraproducts.*

Proof. We only give a sketch. For details the reader is referred to [5].

1. The *only if* direction follows from Lemma 5.3.2 and a well-known result from classical model theory. For the converse suppose that K and $\overline{\mathsf{K}}$ fulfill the closure conditions stated above. Clearly, $\overline{\mathsf{K}}$ is also closed under bisimulations. Define $\Phi := \{\varphi \in \mathcal{ML} \mid \forall(\mathfrak{M}, w) \in \mathsf{K} : (\mathfrak{M}, w) \Vdash \varphi\}$. Obviously, $\mathsf{K} \subseteq \{(\mathfrak{M}, w) \mid (\mathfrak{M}, w) \models \Phi\}$. For the other direction, assume $(\mathfrak{M}, w) \Vdash \Phi$. Put $\Delta := \{ST(\psi) \mid (\mathfrak{M}, w) \Vdash \psi\}$. It is easy to see that Δ is finitely satisfiable in K, that is, for every finite subset δ of Δ there is a pointed model $(\mathfrak{N}_\delta, v_\delta) \in \mathsf{K}$ in which δ holds. By standard first-order reasoning we find an ultraproduct $(\mathfrak{N}, v) := \prod_{\delta \subseteq_\omega \Delta}(\mathfrak{N}_\delta, v_\delta)/\mathcal{U}$ such that $(\mathfrak{N}, v) \Vdash \Delta$, and, since K is closed under ultraproducts, $(\mathfrak{N}, v) \in \mathsf{K}$. Moreover, by the choice of Δ, $(\mathfrak{N}, v) \equiv_{\mathcal{ML}} (\mathfrak{M}, w)$. Now, a modal version of the Keisler-Shelah theorem tells us that there exist ultrapowers $(\mathfrak{N}', v')$, $(\mathfrak{M}', w')$ of $(\mathfrak{N}, v)$, $(\mathfrak{M}, w)$ respectively such that $(\mathfrak{N}', v') \sim (\mathfrak{M}', w')$. Utilizing the closure conditions on K we obtain $(\mathfrak{N}', v') \in \mathsf{K}$ and $(\mathfrak{M}', w') \in \mathsf{K}$ in turns. Finally, that $\overline{\mathsf{K}}$ is closed under ultrapowers, implies $(\mathfrak{M}, w) \in \mathsf{K}$. This completes the first part of the proof.

2. Again, the *only if* direction is straightforward. The other direction follows from the first claim by an easy compactness argument. ⊣

From this theorem we easily obtain van Benthem's bisimulation theorem:

Corollary 5.3.4 *A first-order sentence α (over τ) is equivalent to the translation of a modal formula if and only if α is locally preserved under bisimulations.*[4]

In [20], Sahlqvist described a general method of transforming a pointed model $(\mathfrak{M}, w)$ into a tree-like model, called the unraveling of $(\mathfrak{M}, w)$, which is bisimilar and thus modally equivalent to the original model.

Definition 5.3.5 Let $\mathfrak{M} = (W, R, V)$ be a model and $w \in W$. The unraveling of $(\mathfrak{M}, w)$ is the model $(\mathfrak{M}^u, w^u)$, defined as follows. The domain W^u consists of all finite sequences $(w_0, w_1, \ldots, w_n)$ of elements from W such that $w_0 = w$ and Rw_iw_{i+1}, for every $i < n$. Let $R^u(w_0, \ldots, w_n)(v_0, \ldots, v_m)$ if $m = n + 1$, Rw_nv_m and $w_i = v_i$ for every $i \leq n$. Put $(w_0, \ldots, w_n) \in V^u(p)$ if $w_n \in V(p)$. And, finally, let $w^u := (w)$.

It is easy to see that the canonical mapping $f_{(\mathfrak{M},w)} : (w_0, \ldots, w_n) \mapsto w_n$ defines a bisimulation from $(\mathfrak{M}^u, w^u)$ to $(\mathfrak{M}, w)$. Moreover, if the original model $\mathfrak{M}$ is generated by w, then $f_{(\mathfrak{M},w)}$ is surjective.

[4]Here we say that a first-order sentence α is *locally preserved* under bisimulations if whenever Z is a bisimulation between models $\mathfrak{M}$ and $\mathfrak{N}$ such that Zwv and $(\mathfrak{M}, w) \Vdash \alpha$, then $(\mathfrak{N}, v) \Vdash \alpha$.

5.4 Global Definability

In the previous section we took a *local* perspective on modal logic and its corresponding first-order fragment. Below we adopt what we call a *global* point of view: modal formulas will be considered on the level of *models*. The main result of this section characterizes the classes of models that are (globally) definable by modal formulas. This time, the key notions are ultraproducts and ultrapowers, as before, as well as surjective bisimulations and disjoint unions. The latter are introduced below.

Definition 5.4.1 Let $\{\mathfrak{M}_i \mid i \in I\}$ be a non-empty family of models. The *disjoint union* of this family, abbreviated by $\biguplus_{i\in I} \mathfrak{M}_i$, is the model $\mathfrak{M} = (W, R, V)$, where

- $W := \bigcup_{i\in I}(W_i \times \{i\})$;
- for $(w, i), (v, j) \in W$, we put $R(w, i)(v, j)$, if $i = j$ and $R_i wv$; and
- we set $(w, i) \in V(p_n)$, for $n \in \omega$ and $(w, i) \in W$, if $w \in V_i(p_n)$.

Obviously, by a straightforward adaptation of the standard translation from Section 5.2 we may view $\mathcal{ML}$ as a fragment of first-order logic on the (global) level of models as well: we just have to correlate a modal formula φ with the universal closure of its standard translation, that is, with the formula $\forall x(ST(\varphi)[x/c])$. By making use of Lemma 5.2.1 it is then easy to see that for every model $\mathfrak{M}$, $\mathfrak{M} \models \varphi$ iff $\mathfrak{M} \Vdash \forall x(ST(\varphi)[x/c])$.

As in the local case, the modal fragment of first-order logic has a semantic characterization in terms of its preservation behavior. This time we can prove that a first-order sentence lies in this fragment iff it is preserved under surjective bisimulations and disjoint unions, where a formula φ is said to be *preserved under disjoint unions* if for every non-empty family $\{\mathfrak{M}_i \mid i \in I\}$ of models such that for every $i \in I$, $\mathfrak{M}_i \models \varphi$, we have $\biguplus_{i\in I} \mathfrak{M}_i \models \varphi$.

Lemma 5.4.2 *For a set Δ of first-order sentences over $\tau \setminus \{c\}$ the following are equivalent:*

(i) There is a set $\Phi \subseteq \mathcal{ML}$ with $\mathrm{Mod}(\Phi) = \mathrm{Mod}(\Delta)$.

(ii) $\mathrm{Mod}(\Delta)$ *is closed under disjoint unions and surjective bisimulations.*

Proof. For the implication from 1 to 2 it is sufficient to prove that modal formulas are preserved under disjoint unions and surjective bisimulations. Here, we only deal with disjoint unions; the case for surjective bisimulations can be proved similarly. Let $\varphi \in \mathcal{ML}$ and let $\mathfrak{M} := (W, R, V)$ be the disjoint union of a family $\{\mathfrak{M}_i \mid i \in I\}$ of models, where $\mathfrak{M}_i \models \varphi$ holds for each $i \in I$. Choose $(w, i) \in W$. By definition, $w \in W_i$. Then, our assumption yields $\mathfrak{M}_i \models \varphi$, hence $(\mathfrak{M}_i, w) \Vdash \varphi$. Now it is easy to see that the following clause defines a bisimulation Z between $\mathfrak{M}_i$ and $\mathfrak{M}$: for every $w', w'' \in W_i$ put $Zw'(w'', i)$, if $w' = w''$. Thus we obtain $(\mathfrak{M}, w) \Vdash \varphi$ by Lemma 5.3.2. Since w was chosen arbitrary, this yields $\mathfrak{M} \models \varphi$.

For the other implication, suppose that Δ is a set of first-order sentences such that $\mathrm{Mod}(\Delta)$ is closed under disjoint unions and surjective bisimulations. Define $\Phi := \{\varphi \in \mathcal{ML} \mid \Delta \models_g \forall x(ST(\varphi)[x/c])\}$. By an application of Lemma 5.2.1 we obtain $\mathrm{Mod}(\Delta) \subseteq \mathrm{Mod}(\Phi)$. To prove the converse inclusion, let $\mathfrak{M}$ be a model with $\mathfrak{M} \models \Phi$. Choose an ω-saturated elementary extension $\mathfrak{M}' = (W', R', V')$ of $\mathfrak{M}$. Clearly, $\mathfrak{M}' \models \Phi$.

Next we prove the following claim

($\star$) for each $w \in W'$ there is a pointed model $(\mathfrak{N}_w, v_w)$ and a relation Z_w such that $Z_w : (\mathfrak{N}_w, v_w) \sim (\mathfrak{M}', w)$ and $\mathfrak{N}_w \models \Delta$.

Assuming for a moment that ($\star$) has already been proved, we can proceed as follows. First, let $\mathfrak{N} := \biguplus_{w \in W'} \mathfrak{N}_w$. Since Δ is preserved under disjoint unions and $\mathfrak{N}_w \models \Delta$ holds for each $w \in W'$, we infer $\mathfrak{N} \models \Delta$. Second, define a relation Z as follows: for every (v, w) from $\mathfrak{N}$ and every $w' \in W'$ put $Z(v, w)w'$ if $v = w'$. Moreover, by a routine argument, it is easy to prove that Z forms a surjective bisimulation from $\mathfrak{N}$ to $\mathfrak{M}'$. Thus, as Δ is preserved under surjective bisimulations, $\mathfrak{M}' \models \Delta$. As $\mathfrak{M}'$ is an elementary extension of $\mathfrak{M}$, we get $\mathfrak{M} \models \Delta$. This establishes $\mathrm{Mod}(\Phi) \subseteq \mathrm{Mod}(\Delta)$, as desired.

Therefore, to conclude the proof it remains to establish ($\star$). So, let $w \in W'$. Define $\Gamma := \Delta \cup \{ST(\psi) \mid \psi \in \mathcal{ML}, (\mathfrak{M}', w) \Vdash \psi\}$. Γ is finitely satisfiable. For suppose not. Then there is a modal formula ψ such that $(\mathfrak{M}', w) \Vdash \psi$ and $\Delta \models_l \neg ST(\psi)$, hence $\Delta \models_l ST(\neg\psi)$. Since the constant c does not occur in Δ, we obtain $\Delta \models_g \forall x(ST(\neg\psi)[x/c])$. Thus, by definition, $\varphi \in \Phi$. But this contradicts the assumption $\mathfrak{M}' \models \Phi$. Thus Γ is finitely satisfiable, and so, by compactness, satisfiable. Hence, there is a pointed model $(\mathfrak{N}_w, v_w)$ with $(\mathfrak{N}_w, v_w) \models \Gamma$. Without any restrictions we may assume that $(\mathfrak{N}_w, v_w)$ is ω-saturated. From $(\mathfrak{N}_w, v_w) \models \Gamma$ we easily obtain $\mathfrak{N}_w \models \Delta$ and $(\mathfrak{N}_w, v_w) \equiv_{\mathcal{ML}} (\mathfrak{M}', w)$. Now, from modal logic we know that if two ω-saturated models are modally equivalent, then they are bisimilar. Hence there exists a bisimulation

Z_w between $(\mathfrak{N}_w, v_w)$ and $(\mathfrak{M}', w)$. This establishes $(\star)$ and concludes the proof of the lemma. $\dashv$

Theorem 5.4.3 *For a class* K *of models the following equivalences hold.*

(i) K *is (globally) definable by a set of modal formulas iff* K *is closed under surjective bisimulations, disjoint unions and ultraproducts, and* $\overline{\mathsf{K}}$ *is closed under ultrapowers.*

(ii) K *is (globally) definable by means of a single modal formula iff* K *is closed under surjective bisimulations and disjoint unions, and both* K *and* $\overline{\mathsf{K}}$ *are closed under ultraproducts.*

Proof. 1. Suppose K is globally definable by a set Φ of modal formulas, that is $\mathsf{K} = \mathrm{Mod}(\Phi)$. Obviously, K is also definable by a set of first-order sentences, namely by $\Delta := \{\forall x(ST(\varphi)[x/c]) \mid \varphi \in \Phi\}$. So, a well-known result from model theory tells us that K is closed under ultraproducts, and $\overline{\mathsf{K}}$ under ultrapowers. That K is closed under disjoint unions and surjective bisimulations is an immediate consequence of Lemma 5.4.2.

For the other direction assume that K fulfills the closure conditions stated in 1. It follows that K and $\overline{\mathsf{K}}$ are closed under isomorphisms. For note that if a function f is an isomorphism from a model $\mathfrak{M}$ onto a model $\mathfrak{N}$, then f is a surjective bisimulation from $\mathfrak{M}$ to $\mathfrak{N}$, and the inverse of f is a surjective bisimulation from $\mathfrak{N}$ onto $\mathfrak{M}$. From general first-order model theory we infer that K is first-order definable, that is: there is a set Δ of first-order sentences such that $\mathsf{K} = \mathrm{Mod}(\Delta)$. By assumption, $\mathrm{Mod}(\Delta)$ is closed under disjoint unions and surjective bisimulations. An application of Lemma 5.4.2 concludes the first part of the proof.

2. For the *only if* direction suppose that K is definable by a modal formula φ. Hence, by the first claim, K is closed under surjective bisimulations, disjoint unions and ultraproducts. Further, it is easy to see that $\overline{\mathsf{K}}$ is first-order definable by the single sentence $\neg\forall x(ST(\varphi)[x/c])$. Hence $\overline{\mathsf{K}}$ is closed under ultraproducts. This concludes the *only if* direction.

For the other direction, suppose that K and its complement satisfy the closure conditions stated above. By the first claim there is a set Φ of modal formulas such that $\mathsf{K} = \mathrm{Mod}(\Phi)$. Moreover, as in the proof of the first claim we infer that K and $\overline{\mathsf{K}}$ are closed under isomorphisms. Therefore, $\overline{\mathsf{K}}$ is definable by means of a single first-order sentence α, that is $\overline{\mathsf{K}} = \mathrm{Mod}(\alpha)$. Obviously, the set $\{\alpha\} \cup \{\forall x(ST(\varphi)[x/c]) \mid \varphi \in \Phi\}$ is not satisfiable. Hence, by compactness, there are modal formulas $\varphi_1, \ldots, \varphi_n \in \Phi$ such that $\{\alpha\} \cup$

$\{\forall x(ST(\varphi_1)[x/c]), \ldots, \forall x(ST(\varphi_n)[x/c])\}$ is not satisfiable. It is easy to see that the conjunction $\varphi := (\varphi_1 \wedge \cdots \wedge \varphi_n)$ defines K. $\dashv$

Corollary 5.4.4 *For a first-order sentence α over $\tau \setminus \{c\}$ the following are equivalent:*

(i) There is a modal formula φ such that $\models \alpha \leftrightarrow \forall x(ST(\varphi)[x/c])$.

(ii) α is preserved under disjoint unions and surjective bisimulations.

Proof. The claim follows from Lemma 5.4.2 by compactness. $\dashv$

Our next aim is to relativize Corollary 5.4.4 to the setting of finite models, which brings us into the area of finite model theory. Though it has its origins in classical model theory and complexity theory, finite model theory has developed into an independent research area with its own methods and a whole stock of fascinating results (see [7] for an excellent overview). The investigation of finite models owes its importance to the deep connections between complexity classes and the expressive power on finite models of particular logics. In addition, the study of finite models forms a natural task in computational linguistics as well as in database theory. In the context of modal logic the viewpoint of finite model theory has first been taken in a paper by Rosen [19]. The main result of this paper shows that van Benthem's bisimulation result remains true over the class of finite models. Below we will adopt this result to the global setting.

We need some new notions and notation. We write $\mathfrak{M} \equiv_n^{fo} \mathfrak{N}$ to denote that $\mathfrak{M}$ and $\mathfrak{N}$ agree on all first-order sentences of quantifier rank at most n. Moreover, we need so-called *n-approximations* $\sim_n$ to bisimulations; we say that $(\mathfrak{M}, w) \sim_n (\mathfrak{N}, v)$ if there exists a sequence of relations $Z_0, \ldots, Z_n$, each on the domains of $\mathfrak{M}$ and $\mathfrak{N}$, such that

(i) Z_0wv.

(ii) For all $m < n$, if $Z_mw'v'$, and $Rw'w''$, then there is some v'' in $\mathfrak{N}$ such that $Rv'v''$ and $Z_{m+1}w''v''$ (and vice-versa).

(iii) For all $m \leq n$, if $Z_mw'v'$, then $(\mathfrak{M}, w') \Vdash p_n$ iff $(\mathfrak{N}, v') \Vdash p_n$, for every $n \in \omega$.

Next, we need a technical lemma that combines a number of results due to Rosen [19] into a single statement.

Lemma 5.4.5 *There is a unary function f with the following property. Let $r \in \omega$, and assume that $(\mathfrak{M}, w) \sim_{f(r)} (\mathfrak{N}, v)$. Then there exist models $(\mathfrak{M}^*, w^*) \sim (\mathfrak{M}, w)$ and $(\mathfrak{N}^*, v^*) \sim (\mathfrak{M}, w)$ with $(\mathfrak{M}^*, w^*) \equiv_r^{fo} (\mathfrak{N}^*, v^*)$ as displayed in the following diagram:*

$$\begin{array}{ccc}
(\mathfrak{M}, w) & \overset{\sim_{f(r)}}{\longrightarrow\!\!\!\!\!-\!\!\!-} & (\mathfrak{N}, v) \\
\sim \Big| & & \Big| \sim \\
(\mathfrak{M}^*, w^*) & \overset{\equiv_r^{fo}}{\longrightarrow\!\!\!\!\!-\!\!\!-} & (\mathfrak{N}^*, v^*)
\end{array}$$

Moreover, it may be assumed that there is a surjective bisimulation linking $(\mathfrak{M}^*, w^*)$ to $(\mathfrak{M}, w)$, and a surjective bisimulation linking $(\mathfrak{N}, v)$ to $(\mathfrak{N}^*, v^*)$.

Proof. The proof is a combination of Lemmas 2, 3, and 4 in Rosen [19] plus the well-known observation that every model is a p-morphic image of the disjoint union of its point-generated submodels. $\dashv$

Theorem 5.4.6 *For a first-order sentence α the following are equivalent:*

(i) There is a modal formula φ such that $\forall x(ST(\varphi)[x/c])$ and α are equivalent.

(ii) α is preserved under surjective bisimulations (between finite models) and finite disjoint unions.

Proof. The direction from 1 to 2 follows from Theorem 5.4.3. For the other direction suppose α is a first-order sentence that satisfies the closure conditions stated in 2. Let τ be the smallest (finite) vocabulary in which α lives. For every $n \in \omega$, define

$$\Delta_n := \{\forall x(ST(\varphi)[x/c]) \mid \varphi \in \tau, dg(\varphi) \leq n, \alpha \models \forall x(ST(\varphi)[x/c])\}.$$

Observe that we may assume each Δ_n to be finite.

It suffices to show that, for some $n \in \omega$, $\Delta_n \models \alpha$, for then α will be equivalent to a finite conjunction of formulas of the required universal form (which is itself equivalent to a formula of the required form). To arrive at a contradiction, let us assume that

$$(\dagger) \qquad \Delta_n \not\models \alpha, \text{ for each } n \in \omega.$$

Then, for every $n \in \omega$, there is a model $\mathfrak{M}_n$ such that $\mathfrak{M}_n \models \Delta_n$ and $\mathfrak{M}_n \not\models \alpha$. The following observations will prove to be useful below:

(i) Δ_n is true in every point-generated submodel of $\mathfrak{M}_n$.

(ii) There is a point-generated submodel of $\mathfrak{M}_n$ which falsifies α.

The last observation follows from $\mathfrak{M}_n \not\models \alpha$, by the closure conditions on α. As a consequence, we may assume that $\mathfrak{M}_n$ itself is point-generated, say by w_n. By a well-known result from modal logic, there is a modal formula θ of degree n such that for every pointed model $(\mathfrak{N}, v)$, $(\mathfrak{N}, v) \models \theta$ if and only if there is an n-bisimulation from $(\mathfrak{N}, v)$ to $(\mathfrak{M}_n, w_n)$, in symbols $(\mathfrak{N}, v) \sim_n (\mathfrak{M}_n, w_n)$. It is easy to see that the formula $(\alpha \wedge ST(\theta))$ is satisfiable. Otherwise we would obtain $\alpha \models \forall x(ST(\neg\theta)[x/c])$, hence $\forall x(ST(\neg\theta)[x/c]) \in \Delta_n$, which contradicts $\mathfrak{M}_n \models \Delta_n$. So there is a pointed model $(\mathfrak{N}_n, v_n)$ with $(\mathfrak{N}_n, v_n) \models \theta$, thus $(\mathfrak{N}_n, v_n) \sim_n (\mathfrak{M}_n, w_n)$, and $\mathfrak{N} \models \alpha$. Again, we can assume that $\mathfrak{N}_n$ is point-generated, namely by v_n.

Thus, we have shown the following:

($\star$) for each $n \in \omega$ there are point-generated models $(\mathfrak{N}_n, v_n)$, $(\mathfrak{M}_n, w_n)$ such that $(\mathfrak{N}_n, v_n) \sim_n (\mathfrak{M}_n, w_n)$, $\mathfrak{N}_n \models \alpha$ and $\mathfrak{M}_n \not\models \alpha$.

Now, to arrive at a contradiction, we reason as follows. Let r be the quantifier rank of α. Use ($\star$) with $n = f(r)$, where f is the function mentioned in Lemma 5.4.5. Then we find models $(\mathfrak{M}_{f(r)}, w_{f(r)}) \not\models \alpha$ and $(\mathfrak{N}_{f(r)}, v_{f(r)}) \models \alpha$ with

$$(\mathfrak{M}_{f(r)}, w_{f(r)}) \sim_{f(r)} (\mathfrak{N}_{f(r)}, v_{f(r)}).$$

By the conclusion of Lemma 5.4.5, we obtain models $(\mathfrak{M}^*, w^*)$ and $(\mathfrak{N}^*, v^*)$ with

$$(\mathfrak{M}_{f(r)}, w_{f(r)}) \sim (\mathfrak{M}^*, w^*) \equiv_r^{fo} (\mathfrak{N}^*, v^*) \sim (\mathfrak{N}_{f(r)}, v_{f(r)}).$$

As $\mathfrak{M}_{f(r)} \not\models \alpha$ and as there is a surjective bisimulation linking $(\mathfrak{M}^*, w^*)$ to $(\mathfrak{N}_{f(r)}, v_{f(r)})$, we can conclude that $\mathfrak{M}^* \not\models \alpha$. Similarly, we find that $\mathfrak{N}^* \models \alpha$ — but this contradicts $(\mathfrak{M}^*, w^*) \equiv_r^{fo} (\mathfrak{N}^*, v^*)$. Hence, we conclude that our original assumption (†) was mistaken. That is: there exists n with $\Delta_n \models \alpha$, as required. ⊣

5.5 Hansoul's Theorem

In the previous section we presented an algebraic characterization of the elementary classes of $\mathcal{ML}$. This result is not the first global definability result with respect to classes of models. In [11], Hansoul gave an alternative characterization.[5] The purpose of this section is to relate Hansoul's definability result to ours. In Theorem 5.5.6 we compare the conditions that were imposed by Hansoul on a class K to be definable by a set of modal formulas with the conditions that were used in our Theorem 5.4.3. We will show that both sets of conditions are equivalent in the sense that a class K satisfies Hansoul's conditions if and only if it satisfies ours.

Before we state Hansoul's result, it will be helpful to recall some modal notions. Let $\mathfrak{M} := (W, R, V)$ be a model. For each $\varphi \in \mathcal{ML}$ we define $V(\varphi)$ as the set $\{w \in W \mid (\mathfrak{M}, w) \Vdash \varphi\}$. By a well-known construction we can associate an algebra $\mathfrak{A}_{\mathfrak{M}} := (A_{\mathfrak{M}}, \cap, \cdot^c, W, l_R)$ with the model $\mathfrak{M}$. This algebra consists of the following ingredients: $A_{\mathfrak{M}}$ is the set of all truth-sets of the form $V(\varphi)$, with $\varphi \in \mathcal{ML}$, $\cap$ and $\cdot^c$ are the set-theoretic operations of intersection and complement, respectively, and l_R is the algebraic counterpart of the necessity operator, defined as follows, for $X \in \mathfrak{A}_{\mathfrak{M}}$:

$$l_R(X) := \{w \in W \mid \forall v \in W(Rwv \to v \in X)\}.$$

It is easy to verify that $\mathfrak{A}_{\mathfrak{M}}$ is a *modal* algebra. Then, the canonical structure of $\mathfrak{A}_{\mathfrak{M}}$, $\mathcal{C}(\mathfrak{M})$ in symbols, is the following model $(W_{\mathfrak{M}}, R_{\mathfrak{M}}, V_{\mathfrak{M}})$:

- for $W_{\mathfrak{M}}$, we take the set of ultrafilters over $\mathfrak{A}_{\mathfrak{M}}$;
- for $w, v \in W_{\mathfrak{M}}$, we put $R_{\mathfrak{M}}wv$ if $\forall X \in A_{\mathfrak{M}}(l_R(X) \in u \Rightarrow X \in v)$;
- finally, for $u \in W_{\mathfrak{M}}$, we put $u \in V_{\mathfrak{M}}(p)$ if $V(p) \in u$.

An important feature of $\mathcal{C}(\mathfrak{M})$ is stated in Lemma 5.5.1. The proof is fairly standard, and we skip it here (for details, see [5]).

Lemma 5.5.1 *Let $\mathfrak{M}$ be a model. For every modal formula φ and every ultrafilter $u \in W_{\mathfrak{M}}$, $(\mathcal{C}(\mathfrak{M}), u) \Vdash \varphi$ if and only if $V(\varphi) \in u$.*

We are now ready to state Hansoul's result in our own words, avoiding the topological notions used by Hansoul.

Theorem 5.5.2 (Hansoul's Theorem) *A class K of models is globally definable if and only if K is closed under isomorphisms, generated submodels and disjoint unions, and for each model $\mathfrak{M}$, $\mathfrak{M} \in \mathsf{K}$ iff $\mathcal{C}(\mathfrak{M}) \in \mathsf{K}$.*[6]

[5] In [1] another definability result was proved with respect to infinitary modal languages.

[6] The experienced reader may realize that Hansoul's result shows great similarity to a famous result by Goldblatt [9], which characterizes modally definable classes of generalized frames.

Throughout this section we make use of a special class of models, so-called *modally saturated* models. By a modally saturated model we mean a model $\mathfrak{M} := (W, R, V)$ that satisfies the following condition: for every $w \in W$ and $\Phi \subseteq \mathcal{ML}$, if for each finite subset $\Phi' \subseteq \Phi$ there is some $v \in W$ with Rwv and $(\mathfrak{M}, v) \Vdash \Phi'$, then there is some $v \in W$ with Rwv and $(\mathfrak{M}, v) \Vdash \Phi$.

For things to come the reader should have the following two facts concerning modally saturated models in mind:

(i) Modal saturation is a weaker notion than ω-saturation; that means that every ω-saturated model is modally saturated, but the converse fails.

(ii) The class of modally saturated models forms a so-called Hennessy-Milner class, that is a class of models in which the relation of modal equivalence between pointed models from this class is a bisimulation.

Both results are well-known; for proofs the reader may consult [5].

The main result of this section, Theorem 5.5.6, will, essentially, be proved by combining the following three lemmas.

Lemma 5.5.3 *Let $\mathfrak{M} := (W, R, V)$ be a model and let $\mathfrak{N} := (W', R', V')$ be an ω-saturated elementary extension of $\mathfrak{M}$. Then there exists a total and surjective bisimulation from $\mathfrak{N}$ to $\mathcal{C}(\mathfrak{M})$.*

Proof. Suppose $\mathfrak{N}$ is an ω-saturated elementary extension of a model $\mathfrak{M}$. By (i), $\mathfrak{N}$ is modally saturated. Further, by a routine argument, it is easy to check that $\mathcal{C}(\mathfrak{M})$ is modally saturated as well. Next, define Z as follows: for $w \in W'$ and $v \in W_{\mathfrak{M}}$, put Zwv if $(\mathfrak{N}, w) \equiv_{\mathcal{ML}} (\mathcal{C}(\mathfrak{M}), v)$. According to (ii), Z is a bisimulation from $\mathfrak{N}$ to $\mathcal{C}(\mathfrak{M})$. It remains to show that Z is total and surjective.

For totality, choose $w \in W'$. Define $\Delta_w := \{\varphi \in \mathcal{ML} \mid (\mathfrak{N}, w) \Vdash \varphi\}$. Let $\varphi \in \Delta_w$. Then $(\mathfrak{N}, w) \Vdash \varphi$. Hence $(\mathfrak{N}, w) \Vdash ST(\varphi)$, by Lemma 5.2.1. Thus $\mathfrak{N} \Vdash \exists x(ST(\varphi)[x/c])$. Since $\mathfrak{N}$ is an elementary extension of $\mathfrak{M}$, we infer $\mathfrak{M} \Vdash \exists x(ST(\varphi)[x/c])$. So there is some $v \in W$ such that $(\mathfrak{M}, v) \Vdash \varphi$. Since Δ_w is closed under conjunction, it follows that Δ_w is finitely satisfiable in $\mathfrak{M}$. From this we easily obtain that $X := \{V(\varphi) \mid \varphi \in \Delta_w\}$ has the finite intersection property. Moreover, $X \subseteq A_{\mathfrak{M}}$. Hence, there is some ultrafilter $u \in W_{\mathfrak{M}}$ with $X \subseteq u$. Thus, we get $V(\varphi) \in u$, for every $\varphi \in \Delta_w$. By an application of Lemma 5.5.1 we then obtain $(\mathcal{C}(\mathfrak{M}), u) \Vdash \varphi$, for every $\varphi \in \Delta_w$. This establishes $(\mathfrak{N}, w) \equiv_{\mathcal{ML}} (\mathcal{C}(\mathfrak{M}), u)$, which yields, by definition, Zwu. So we have shown that Z is total.

To prove that Z is surjective, let $u \in W_{\mathfrak{M}}$. Put $\Gamma_u := \{\varphi \in \mathcal{ML} \mid (\mathcal{C}(\mathfrak{M}), u) \Vdash \varphi\}$. Choose $\varphi \in \Gamma_u$. By Lemma 5.5.1, $V(\varphi) \in u$. Thus $V(\varphi) \neq \emptyset$. Hence, there is some $w \in W$ such that $(\mathfrak{M}, w) \Vdash \varphi$. From this we deduce that Γ_u is finitely satisfiable in $\mathfrak{M}$; for note that Γ_u is closed under conjunctions. Clearly, then, Γ_u is finitely satisfiable in $\mathfrak{N}$ as well. Since $\mathfrak{N}$ is ω-saturated, Γ_u is satisfiable in $\mathfrak{N}$. Hence there is some $v \in W'$ with $(\mathfrak{N}, v) \Vdash \Gamma_u$, and therefore, Zvu. So Z is surjective. This completes the proof of the lemma. ⊣

Lemma 5.5.4 *Let $\mathfrak{M} := (W, R, V)$ and $\mathfrak{M}' := (W', R', V')$ be models, and let Z be a total and surjective bisimulation from $\mathfrak{M}$ to $\mathfrak{M}'$. Then $\mathcal{C}(\mathfrak{M})$ and $\mathcal{C}(\mathfrak{M}')$ are isomorphic.*

Proof. Suppose $\mathfrak{M}$, $\mathfrak{M}'$ and Z satisfy the conditions stated above. It suffices to show that the associated algebras $\mathfrak{A}_{\mathfrak{M}}$ and $\mathfrak{A}_{\mathfrak{M}'}$ are isomorphic. To prove this, we only need to verify that the mapping $f : V(\varphi) \mapsto V'(\varphi)$ is an isomorphism between $\mathfrak{A}_{\mathfrak{M}}$ and $\mathfrak{A}_{\mathfrak{M}'}$. Obviously, the domain of f is $A_{\mathfrak{M}}$.

To see that f is a function, suppose that $V(\varphi) = V(\psi)$. Choose $v \in V'(\varphi)$. As Z is surjective, there is some $w \in W$ with Zwv. Hence $w \in V(\varphi)$. Thus $w \in V(\psi)$, by assumption. From this we obtain $v \in V'(\psi)$. Therefore, $V'(\varphi) \subseteq V'(\psi)$. A similar argument yields the other direction. So $V'(\varphi) = V'(\psi)$. Hence f is a function.

The injectivity of f can be proved in a similar way. This time one makes use of the fact that Z is total. It remains to show that f is a homomorphism in the sense that it commutes with the algebraic operations $\cap$, $\cdot^c$ and l_R. But this is an easy task which we leave to the reader. ⊣

Lemma 5.5.5 *Let K be a class of models that is closed under isomorphisms, generated submodels, disjoint unions and ultrapowers. Then K is closed under ultraproducts.*

Proof. The claim of this lemma is a version of a well-known result from the theory of frames due to Goldblatt [9]. We only need to replace the family M by a family of frames, and we immediately get Goldblatt's Theorem 1.16.4. Since Goldblatt's proof can easily be adjusted to the context of models, we dispense with a proof. However, we will give a hint that should help the reader to find the proof: Suppose $\mathsf{M} := \{\mathfrak{M}_i \mid i \in I\}$ is a non-empty family of models and suppose $\mathfrak{N}$ is an ultraproduct of this family. Then one has to show that $\mathfrak{N}$ is isomorphic to a generated submodel of some ultrapower for the disjoint union of M. When this has been done, the claim of the lemma follows as an easy corollary. ⊣

Before we get to the main result of this section, a short remark is in order. In Theorem 5.4.3 we required that a class K of models be closed under ultraproducts for it to be modally definable. A careful examination of the proof of this theorem shows that we can do with a slightly weaker condition. It suffices to call for closure under ultraproducts modulo ultrafilters of a special sort, namely countably incomplete ultrafilters. The reason why this suffices is rather obvious: countably incomplete ultrafilters provide ω-saturated ultraproducts, and the latter are the kind of ultraproducts we are in need of.

Theorem 5.5.6 *For a class K of models the following conditions are equivalent:*

(i) K *is closed under surjective bisimulations, disjoint unions and ultraproducts modulo countably incomplete ultrafilters, and* $\overline{\mathsf{K}}$ *is closed under ultrapowers modulo countably incomplete ultrafilters.*

(ii) K *is closed under generated submodels, isomorphisms and disjoint unions, and for each model* $\mathfrak{M}$, $\mathfrak{M} \in \mathsf{K}$ *iff* $\mathcal{C}(\mathfrak{M}) \in \mathsf{K}$.

Proof. For the *only if* direction assume that K satisfies the closure conditions stated in 1. Clearly, K is closed under generated submodels and isomorphisms. Next, suppose $\mathfrak{M} \in K$. Choose a countably incomplete ultrafilter $\mathcal{U}$ over ω and let $\mathfrak{M}' := (W', R', V')$ be the ultrapower of $\mathfrak{M}$ modulo $\mathcal{U}$. By the closure conditions on K, $\mathfrak{M}' \in \mathsf{K}$. Further, from general first-order model theory we know that $\mathfrak{M}'$ is ω-saturated. Hence, by Lemma 5.5.3, there is a total surjective bisimulation Z from $\mathfrak{M}'$ to $\mathcal{C}(\mathfrak{M})$. As K is closed under surjective bisimulations, we obtain $\mathcal{C}(\mathfrak{M}) \in \mathsf{K}$. For the other direction suppose $\mathcal{C}(\mathfrak{M}) \in \mathsf{K}$. Let $\mathfrak{M}'$ and Z be as above. It is easy to see that Z^{-1} is a surjective bisimulation from $\mathcal{C}(\mathfrak{M})$ to $\mathfrak{M}'$. Thus, $\mathfrak{M}' \in \mathsf{K}$. Since $\overline{\mathsf{K}}$ is closed under ultrapowers, we obtain $\mathfrak{M} \in \mathsf{K}$. This concludes the proof of the *only if* direction.

For the converse, assume that K satisfies the closure conditions stated in 2. To show that K is closed under surjective bisimulations, let $\mathfrak{M}$ and $\mathfrak{M}'$ be models such that $\mathfrak{M} \in \mathsf{K}$, and suppose that Z is a surjective bisimulation from $\mathfrak{M}$ to $\mathfrak{M}'$. Let $\mathfrak{N} := (W'', R'', V'')$ be the submodel of $\mathfrak{M}$ generated by the domain of Z. As K is closed under generated submodels, $\mathfrak{N} \in \mathsf{K}$. Moreover, it is obvious that $Z \cap (W'' \times W')$ is a bisimulation from $\mathfrak{N}$ to $\mathfrak{M}'$ which is total and surjective. Hence, by Lemma 5.5.4, $\mathcal{C}(\mathfrak{N}) \cong \mathcal{C}(\mathfrak{M}')$. By the closure under $\mathcal{C}$, $\mathcal{C}(\mathfrak{N}) \in \mathsf{K}$. As K is closed under isomorphisms, $\mathcal{C}(\mathfrak{M}') \in \mathsf{K}$, which yields $\mathfrak{M}' \in \mathsf{K}$. This shows that K is closed under surjective bisimulations.

Let $\mathfrak{M} \in \mathsf{K}$, and let $\mathfrak{N}$ be an ultrapower modulo a countably incomplete ultrafilter of $\mathfrak{M}$. By the closure conditions on K, $\mathcal{C}(\mathfrak{M}) \in \mathsf{K}$. From Lemma 5.5.3

we infer that $\mathfrak{N} \in \mathsf{K}$ if and only if $\mathcal{C}(\mathfrak{M}) \in \mathsf{K}$. Hence $\mathfrak{N} \in \mathsf{K}$. Thus K is closed under the right kind of ultrapowers. By a similar argument we can show that $\overline{\mathsf{K}}$ is closed under suitable ultrapowers. An application of Lemma 5.5.5 concludes the proof. $\dashv$

As a corollary to Theorem 5.5.6 we find that Hansoul's characterization of the globally definable classes of models (Theorem 5.5.2) is equivalent with ours (Theorem 5.4.3).

5.6 Universal Classes

Applying arguments and tools similar to the ones in the previous section, we can also obtain global definability and preservation results for modal formulas satisfying various syntactic constraints. Below, we restrict our attention to universal formulas. By a *universal* formula we mean a modal formula that has been built up from atomic formulas and negated atomic formulas, using $\wedge$, $\vee$ and $\Box$ only. We use Π to denote the set of universal formulas. Analogously, the set Σ of existential formulas is defined as the smallest subset of $\mathcal{ML}$ that contains all atomic formulas and their negations, and is closed under $\wedge$, $\vee$ and $\Diamond$.

When we drop clause B3 in Definition 5.3.1, we arrive at the notion of simulation. We write $(\mathfrak{M}, w) \rightsquigarrow (\mathfrak{N}, v)$ to denote that there is a simulation Z from $\mathfrak{M}$ to $\mathfrak{N}$ with Zwv. It is easy to prove that universal formulas are anti-preserved under simulations, that is, if $(\mathfrak{M}, w) \rightsquigarrow (\mathfrak{N}, v)$ then for every universal formula φ, if $(\mathfrak{N}, v) \Vdash \varphi$ then $(\mathfrak{M}, w) \Vdash \varphi$.

The main result of this section, Theorem 5.6.3, provides a precise characterization of the conditions under which classes of models are globally definable by sets of *universal* formulas. From this we easily get a preservation result for universal formulas, stated as Corollary 5.6.4. In the proof of Lemma 5.6.2, which forms the key to the proof of Theorem 5.6.3, we make use of the following lemma. (For a proof the reader is referred to [22]; this work also contains local counterparts of the results of this section.)

Lemma 5.6.1 *Let $(\mathfrak{M}, w)$, $(\mathfrak{N}, v)$ be unraveled pointed models with $(\mathfrak{M}, w) \rightsquigarrow (\mathfrak{N}, v)$. Then there is an unraveled model $(\mathfrak{N}', v)$ such that $(\mathfrak{M}, w) \subseteq (\mathfrak{N}', v)$ and a surjective bisimulation from $(\mathfrak{N}, v)$ to $(\mathfrak{N}', v)$.*

Lemma 5.6.2 *For a set Φ of modal formulas the following are equivalent:*

(i) There is a set Ψ *of universal formulas such that* $\mathrm{Mod}(\Phi) = \mathrm{Mod}(\Psi)$.

(ii) $\mathrm{Mod}(\Phi)$ *is closed under submodels.*

Proof. For the implication from 1 to 2 we need to show that universal formulas are preserved under submodels, which can be proved by an easy induction. For the other direction, suppose Φ is a set of modal formulas such that $\mathrm{Mod}(\Phi)$ is closed under submodels. Define $\Psi := \{\psi \in \Pi \mid \Phi \models_g \psi\}$. We must show that $\Psi \models_g \Phi$. So suppose $\mathfrak{M} := (W, R, V)$ is a model with $\mathfrak{M} \models \Psi$. It suffices to prove that Φ holds in each point-generated submodel of $\mathfrak{M}$.

To see why this is enough, let $\mathfrak{M}'$ be the disjoint union of the set of all point-generated submodels of $\mathfrak{M}$. Now, suppose we have shown that Φ holds in each point-generated submodel of $\mathfrak{M}$. Since $\mathrm{Mod}(\Phi)$ is closed under disjoint unions, this yields $\mathfrak{M}' \models \Phi$. Moreover, it is easy to see that there exists a surjective bisimulation from $\mathfrak{M}'$ to $\mathfrak{M}$. By closure under surjective bisimulations we obtain the desired result.

So, let $w \in W$, and let $\mathfrak{M}_w$ be the submodel of $\mathfrak{M}$ which is generated by w. Clearly, $\mathfrak{M}_w \models \Psi$. Our next aim is to show that there is a model $\mathfrak{N}_w$, generated by a point v, such that $\mathfrak{N}_w \models \Phi$ and each existential formula true in $(\mathfrak{M}_w, w)$ also holds in $(\mathfrak{N}_w, v)$. To do this, it is enough to show that the following two sets Γ_1 and Γ_2 are simultaneously satisfiable:

$$\begin{aligned} \Gamma_1 &:= \{\forall x(ST(\varphi)[x/c]) \mid \varphi \in \Phi\} \\ \Gamma_2 &:= \{ST(\psi) \mid \psi \in \Sigma, (\mathfrak{M}_w, w) \Vdash \psi\}. \end{aligned}$$

Suppose not. Then there are $\psi_1, \ldots, \psi_n \in \Sigma$ with $(\mathfrak{M}_w, w) \Vdash \psi_i$, for $i \leq n$, such that $\Gamma_1 \models_l \neg(ST(\psi_1) \wedge \cdots \wedge ST(\psi_n))$. Hence $\Gamma_1 \models_l \neg ST(\psi_1 \wedge \cdots \wedge \psi_n)$. Let $\psi := (\psi_1 \wedge \cdots \wedge \psi_n)$. Since Σ is closed under conjunctions, $\psi \in \Sigma$. Hence $ST(\psi) \in \Gamma_2$. Now, note that c does not occur in Γ_1. So we obtain $\Gamma_1 \models_g \forall x(\neg ST(\psi)[x/c])$, hence $\Gamma_1 \models_g \forall x(ST(\neg\psi)[x/c])$. The latter implies $\Phi \models_g \psi^*$, where ψ^* is the negation normal form of ψ. Obviously, $\psi^* \in \Pi$, hence $\psi^* \in \Psi$, which contradicts $\mathfrak{M}_w \models \Psi$. From this we can conclude that $\Gamma_1 \cup \Gamma_2$ is satisfiable.

So there is a pointed model $(\mathfrak{N}_w, v)$ with $\mathfrak{N}_w \models \Phi$ and such that for each existential formula ψ, if $(\mathfrak{M}_w, w) \Vdash \psi$ then $(\mathfrak{N}_w, v) \Vdash \psi$. Choose ω-saturated elementary extensions $(\mathfrak{M}'_w, w)$, $(\mathfrak{N}'_w, v)$ of $(\mathfrak{M}_w, w)$, $(\mathfrak{N}_w, v)$ respectively. By a standard argument we obtain $(\mathfrak{M}'_w, w) \rightsquigarrow (\mathfrak{N}'_w, v)$. Further, let $(\mathfrak{M}^u_w, w)$, $(\mathfrak{N}^u_w, v)$ be the unraveling of $(\mathfrak{M}'_w, w)$, $(\mathfrak{N}'_w, v)$ respectively. It is easy to see that $(\mathfrak{M}^u_w, w) \rightsquigarrow (\mathfrak{N}^u_w, v)$ holds. By an application of Lemma 5.6.1 we obtain a pointed model $(\mathfrak{N}, v_w)$ with $(\mathfrak{M}^u_w, w) \subseteq (\mathfrak{N}, v)$ and a surjective bisimulation from $(\mathfrak{N}^u_w, v)$ to $(\mathfrak{N}, v)$. See Figure 5.1.

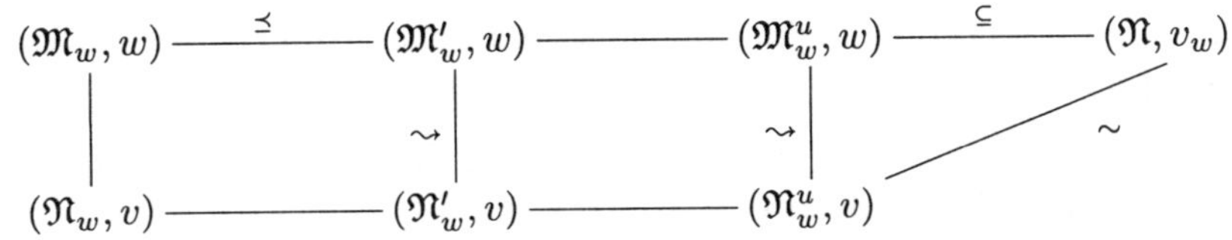

Figure 5.1: A chain of models

To conclude the proof, we argue as follows. By construction it holds that $\mathfrak{N}_w \models \Phi$, hence, by elementary extension, $\mathfrak{N}'_w \models \Phi$. Consider the submodel $\mathfrak{N}''$ of $\mathfrak{N}'$ that is point-generated by v_w. Observe that the converse relation of $f_{(\mathfrak{N}'', v_w)}$ forms a surjective bisimulation from $\mathfrak{N}'$ to $\mathfrak{N}^u$. This, together with Theorem 5.4.2, implies $\mathfrak{N}^u_w \models \Phi$ and, hence, $\mathfrak{N} \models \Phi$. That Φ is preserved under submodels implies $\mathfrak{M}^u_w \models \Phi$. Again, by making use of the fact that modal formulas are preserved under surjective bisimulations and elementary extensions, we finally obtain $\mathfrak{M}_w \models \Phi$. This concludes the proof. $\dashv$

Theorem 5.6.3 *A class* K *of models is definable by a set of universal formulas iff* K *is closed under surjective bisimulations, disjoint unions, submodels and ultraproducts.*

Proof. Suppose K is globally definable by a set of universal formulas. Then K satisfies the above closure conditions by Theorem 5.4.3 and Lemma 5.6.2. For the other direction we reason as follows. Suppose K is closed under surjective bisimulations, disjoint unions and ultraproducts. Since every model is (isomorphic to) a submodel of its ultrapowers, $\overline{\mathsf{K}}$ is closed under ultrapowers as well. Thus by Theorem 5.4.3 there is a set Ψ of modal formulas such that $\mathrm{Mod}(\Psi) = \mathsf{K}$. Using the closure of K under submodels, an application of Lemma 5.6.2 concludes the proof. $\dashv$

Corollary 5.6.4 *A modal formula* φ *is globally preserved under submodels iff there is a universal formula* ψ *such that* φ *and* ψ *are true on exactly the same models.*

Proof. The claim of the corollary follows from Lemma 5.6.2 by compactness. Recall that the set of universal formulas is closed under conjunction. $\dashv$

We hasten to add that similar results also exist for positive, that is negation-free formulas: formulas built up from proposition letters using only $\wedge$, $\vee$, $\Diamond$ and

□. In particular, in Theorem 5.6.5 we give necessary and sufficient conditions for a class of models K to be globally definable by a set of positive formulas.

In the following, a model $\mathfrak{N} = (W', R', V')$ is said to be a *weak extension* of a model $\mathfrak{M} = (W, R, V)$, if $W = W'$, $R = R'$, and $V(p_n) \subseteq V'(p_n)$, for every $n \in \omega$.

Theorem 5.6.5 *A class K of models is definable by a set of positive formulas iff K is closed under surjective bisimulations, disjoint unions, weak extensions and ultraproducts, and $\overline{\mathsf{K}}$ is closed under ultrapowers.*

Proof. The proof closely resembles the proof of Theorem 5.6.3; hence, we only give a brief sketch. For a start, one has to find a kind of bisimulations suitable for positive formulas. These are positive bisimulations, where a relation Z is said to be a *positive* bisimulation, if Z satisfies B2 and B3 from Definition 5.3.1 together with the following weakening of clause B1: for $w \in W$, $v \in W'$, if Zwv then $(\mathfrak{M}, w) \Vdash p_n$ implies $(\mathfrak{N}, v) \Vdash p_n$, for every $n \in \omega$. Then, one has to prove the following statement (see [21, 22]):

> Suppose $(\mathfrak{M}, w)$, $(\mathfrak{N}, v)$ are unraveled pointed models and Z is a positive bisimulation from $(\mathfrak{M}, w)$ to $(\mathfrak{N}, v)$. Then there exist unraveled models $(\mathfrak{M}', w)$, $(\mathfrak{N}', v)$ such that $(\mathfrak{N}', v)$ is a weak extension of $(\mathfrak{M}', w)$, and there are surjective bisimulations from $(\mathfrak{M}, w)$, $(\mathfrak{N}, v)$ to $(\mathfrak{M}', w)$, $(\mathfrak{N}', v)$ respectively.

Next, using this result, one can show that a set of modal formulas Φ is preserved under weak extensions if and only if there is a set of positive formulas Ψ with $\mathrm{Mod}(\Psi) = \mathrm{Mod}(\Phi)$. The characterization for positive classes then follows by an easy argument, similar to the argument in the proof of Theorem 5.6.3. ⊣

From this theorem we easily infer a preservation result for positive formulas:

Corollary 5.6.6 *A modal formula φ is globally preserved under weak extensions iff there is a positive formula ψ such that φ and ψ are true on exactly the same models.*

5.7 Concluding Remarks

In this paper we have presented a number of definability and preservation results for (basic) modal logic. Contrary to common practice, we have emphasized the global perspective. Of course, the above results can only be considered as a modest beginning; a lot of work remains to be done. Our future research should concentrate on the following aspects and questions.

First, what other local results (and tools) can be adapted to the global setting? For example, consider existential formulas and try to prove results in the spirit of Section 5.6. Note that, on the global level, a modal existential formula like $\Diamond p$ does not translate into an existential first-order sentence, but into a sentence with the prefix $\forall\exists$. Another interesting task is to analyze modal Horn formulas along the same line; for local results see [23].

Second, in recent years logicians have introduced bisimulations for a great number of modal and modal-like languages and proved (local) definability results with respect to them. Examples are temporal languages with Since and Until [15], description logics [17] and negation-free languages [16]. Many of the results proved in these papers can be globalized along the lines followed in Section 5.4. How far does this method go? In particular, does it also apply to modal languages that live outside first-order logic, like PDL or infinitary languages?

Third, to go one step further, it would be worthwhile to look for a uniform way of connecting the local and the global setting. Indeed, we have a general result with respect to preservation, but it is not completely satisfactory. First, it looks slightly proof-generated and, second, it makes use of the notion of ω-saturated models which restricts its applicability to modal languages that lie inside first-order logic. However, the result may serve as a good starting point for further work.

In this context, Kracht and Wolter's work on transfer results [13, 14] deserves attention. They investigate the metalogical properties of modal logics, thereby considering both levels, the local and the global one. Though they take a different perspective on modal logic — their aim is to explore the lattice of normal modal logic — there are interesting connections between their research and ours. This holds, in particular, when we no longer analyze definability with respect to the class of all models only, but consider definability within certain subclasses (induced by special frame properties) as well.

Fourth, we may also change tack, and try to match up the semantic operations that were used in this paper with syntactic characterizations in the following sense. Find syntactic characterizations for the classes of models closed under surjective bisimulations, and establish a preservation result for surjective bisimulations. Tackle analogous questions for disjoint unions as well.

The case of surjective bisimulations is fairly easy. By a standard argument we are able to prove that a class K is $\bigvee$-definable iff K is closed under surjective bisimulations and ultraproducts, and $\overline{\mathsf{K}}$ is closed under ultrapowers. Here, by $\bigvee$-definable we mean definable in the set $\Theta := \{\forall x(ST(\varphi_1)[x/c]) \vee \cdots \vee \forall x(ST(\varphi_n)[x/c]) \mid \varphi_i \in \mathcal{ML}\}$. The corresponding preservation result may again be obtained as an immediate consequence. It tells us that a first-order sentence (over $\tau \setminus \{c\}$) is equivalent to some $\varphi \in \Theta$ if and only if it is preserved under surjective bisimulations.

The case of disjoint unions turns out to be much harder. Van Benthem [3] gave a characterization of the first-order sentences that are invariant under disjoint unions. This result only considers the frame language, that is the first-order vocabulary consisting of the relation symbol S and the identity symbol. It is easy to turn van Benthem's result into a result that characterizes the sentences in the modal language, that is $\tau \setminus \{c\}$, that are preserved under disjoint unions. Moreover, by using techniques developed in the present paper, we are able to give a similar characterization for the language we obtain by dropping the identity symbol. Although this is a nice result, it strikes us as not completely satisfactory. What we are after is a characterization of those first-order sentences that are *preserved* — and not invariant — under disjoint unions. The solution to this problem must be left to future research.

As a final point, we mention the connections that exist between the results in this paper and work on the universal modality [8, 10]. These links are interesting for a number of reasons. First, the global translations of $\mathcal{ML}$-formulas are expressible in the language with the universal modality. In general, the universal modality makes it possible to talk about global properties from the local point of view. Second, in [4] van Benthem formulated a preservation theorem that says that a first-order sentence is equivalent to a modal formula from the universal language if and only if it is preserved under total bisimulations. And third, the algebraic criteria that were given in [10] for a class of generalized frames to be definable in the language with universal modality may be adopted to the level of models. This should lead to a characterization result in the style of Hansoul's theorem. Moreover, the latter result and van Benthem's theorem might be linked up in the spirit of our Theorem 5.5.6.

Acknowledgments. Maarten de Rijke was supported by the Spinoza project 'Logic in Action' at ILLC, the University of Amsterdam.

MAARTEN DE RIJKE
ILLC, University of Amsterdam
1018 TV Amsterdam, The Netherlands
E-mail: mdr@science.uva.nl

HOLGER STURM
Fachbereich Philosophie, Universität Konstanz
78457 Konstanz, Germany
E-mail: Holger.Sturm@uni-konstanz.de

Bibliography

[1] J. Barwise and L.S. Moss. Modal correspondence for models. *Journal of Philosophical Logic*, 27:275–294, 1998.

[2] J.F.A.K. van Benthem. *Modal Correspondence Theory*. PhD thesis, University of Amsterdam, 1976.

[3] J.F.A.K. van Benthem. *Modal Logic and Classical Logic*. Bibliopolis, Napoli, 1985.

[4] J.F.A.K. van Benthem. The range of modal logic. Technical Report, ILLC, University of Amsterdam, 1997.

[5] P. Blackburn, M. de Rijke, and Y. Venema. *Modal Logic*, Manuscript, ILLC, University of Amsterdam, 1998. Available at `http://www.illc.-uva.nl/~mdr/Publications/modal-logic.html`.

[6] F.M. Donini, M. Lenzerini, D. Nardi, and A. Schaerf. Reasoning in description logics. In G. Brewka, editor, *Principles of Knowledge Representation*, Studies in Logic, Language and Information, pages 191–236. CSLI Publications, 1996.

[7] H.-D. Ebbinghaus and J. Flum. *Finite Model Theory*. Springer, Berlin 1995.

[8] G. Gargov and V. Goranko. Modal logic with names. *Journal of Philosophical Logic*, 22:607–636, 1993.

[9] R. Goldblatt. Metamathematics of modal logic I. *Reports on Mathematical Logic*, 6:41–78, 1976.

[10] V. Goranko and S. Passy. Using the universal modality. *Journal of Logic and Computation*, 1:5–31, 1992.

[11] G. Hansoul. Modal-axiomatic closure of Kripke models. In: H. Andréka, D. Monk, and I. Németi, editors, *Algebraic Logic*. North-Holland, 257–264, 1991.

[12] J. Kim. *Supervenience and Mind.* Cambridge University Press, Cambridge 1993.

[13] M. Kracht. *Tools and Techniques in Modal Logic.* Habilitationsschrift, Berlin 1996.

[14] M. Kracht and F. Wolter. Simulation and transfer results in modal logic – a survey. *Studia Logica*, 59:149–177, 1997.

[15] N. Kurtonina and M. de Rijke. Bisimulations for temporal logic. *Journal of Logic, Language and Information*, 6:403–425, 1997.

[16] N. Kurtonina and M. de Rijke. Simulating without negation. *Journal of Logic and Computation*, 7:501–522, 1997.

[17] N. Kurtonina and M. de Rijke. Expressiveness of concept expressions in first-order description logics. *Artificial Intelligence*, 107:303-333, 1999.

[18] M. de Rijke. *Extending Modal Logic.* PhD thesis, ILLC, University of Amsterdam, 1993.

[19] E. Rosen. Modal logic over finite structures. *Journal of Logic, Language and Information*, 6:427–439, 1997.

[20] H. Sahlqvist. Completeness and correspondence in the first and second order semantics for modal logic. In: S. Kanger, editor, *Proc. 3rd. Scand. Logic Symp.* North-Holland, 110–143, 1975.

[21] H. Sturm. *Modale Fragmente von* $\mathcal{L}_{\omega\omega}$ *und* $\mathcal{L}_{\omega_1\omega}$. PhD thesis, CIS, University of Munich, 1997.

[22] H. Sturm. Elementary classes in basic modal logic. *Studia Logica*, 64:193–213, 2000.

[23] H. Sturm. Modal horn classes. *Studia Logica*, 64:301–313, 2000.

[24] Y. Venema. *Many-Dimensional Modal Logic.* PhD thesis, University of Amsterdam, 1991.

Chapter 6

Ackermann's Implication for Typefree Logic

KLAUS ROBERING

We study the positive fragment of a system of partial logic which has been developed by Ackermann in the course of his typefree foundation of mathematics. One of the prominent features of this system is its implication, which has been supplied with a deductive interpretation according to which $A \to B$ expresses that B is derivable from A. The first section provides Ackermann's original Hilbert-style formulation of the positive part of his logic and a new formulation using natural deduction. Elaborating Ackermann's idea concerning the interpretation of $\to$, another new characterization of his positive logic is given in terms of a sequence of consecutive deductive systems. The last section contains a brief account of the algebraic semantics of Ackermann's system, which has not been considered in the literature up to now.

6.1 Ackermann's Typefree Logic

6.1.1 Deductive and Combinatorial Completeness

In a series of papers starting with [1], Wilhelm Ackermann constructed several systems of logic which lack any type restrictions and dispose of a full form of comprehension; cp. [2], [4], [5], [6], [7]. A class term $\{x \mid A\}$ may be formed in these systems for each formula A where the term and the formula are connected by the following principles of conversion:

$$t \in \{x \mid A\} \rightarrow [t/x]A, \qquad (\text{abs}_1)$$
$$[t/x]A \rightarrow t \in \{x \mid A\}. \qquad (\text{abs}_2)$$

Following the terminology of combinatory logic, Ackermann [5, p. 3] calls a system of set theory in which these two principles are valid "combinatorially complete".

Partial predicates which lead up to formulas lacking a truth value are admitted by Ackermann in order to avoid antinomies like Russell's[1]. Thus the principle of *tertium non datur* does not hold in Ackermann's systems. As is well known, however, giving up this principle does not suffice to avoid antinomies since Curry's antinomy is derivable even in the implicational fragment of positive logic. Let $c = \{x \mid x \in x \rightarrow \curlywedge\}$ be the class of those classes for which self-membership implies the *falsum* $\curlywedge$. Assuming (abs_1) and (abs_2), it becomes possible to derive the *falsum* using only *modus ponens* (mp) and the deduction theorem (dt); cp. the following derivation:

(1)	$c \in c \dot{\rightarrow} c \in c \rightarrow \curlywedge$	abs_1
(2)	$c \in c$	assumption
(3)	$c \in c \rightarrow \curlywedge$	(2), (1), (mp)
(4)	$\curlywedge$	(2), (3), (mp)
(5)	$c \in c \rightarrow \curlywedge$	(2), (4), (dt)
(6)	$c \in c \rightarrow \curlywedge \dot{\rightarrow} c \in c$	abs_2
(7)	$c \in c$	(5), (6), (mp)
(8)	$\curlywedge$	(7), (1), (mp) twice

[1] Ackermann's procedure here is comparable to that of many-valued logic. In systems of many-valued logic we may admit besides "true" and "false" a third truth-value "indetermined". Russell's antinomy disappears, for instance, in Łukasiewicz's three-valued logic Ł3 since $r \in r \leftrightarrow r \notin r$ is no contradiction in Ł3; see Malinowski [14, p. 19 and sec. 11.2] and compare also the work of Bochvar [9], which is summed up by Malinowski [14, sec. 7.2]. The enrichment of Ł3 with an unrestricted comprehension axiom leads up, however, to other antinomies; cp. Skolem [22, p. 1]. Ł3 differs from Ackermann's logic A in several respects: It has, for instance, the dilution principle $A \dot{\rightarrow} B \rightarrow A$, which is lacking from A, and disposes of an unrestricted deduction theorem (cp. [14, p. 63f]), the absence of which is one of the most characteristic features of A.

In order to block this derivation one has to give up either full comprehension as embodied in the two conversion principles (abs_1) and (abs_2) or either (mp) or (dt)[2]. The unrestricted rule (mp) is given up by Fitch [12]; cp. Ackermann's [3] review of Fitch's book. Ackermann himself dispenses with (dt) instead. He calls a logical system in which (dt) makes it possible to represent the derivability of B from A by the theorem $A \rightarrow B$ "deductively complete"; and he interprets Curry's antinomy as showing that a logical system cannot be both combinatorial and deductively complete; cp. Ackermann [5, p. 58].

6.1.2 A Deductive Interpretation of Implication

Thus besides the giving up of the *tertium non datur* there is a second revision of classical logic in Ackermann's systems. This second revision is motivated by Ackermann's special interpretation of the implication as expressing a deductive link between its antecedent and its consequent. The formula $A \rightarrow B$ expresses that B is "derivable" from A; cp. Ackermann [2, p. 34]. At a first glance, this seems to conflict with Ackermann's abolition of (dt) since the very idea of this principle is that an implication $A \rightarrow B$ is proved by giving a derivation of B from A. But note that Ackermann's deductive interpretation of $\rightarrow$ does not imply that any proof of B from A will suffice to establish $A \rightarrow B$ as a theorem. There might well be special properties to be required of a proof in order to justify the truth of an implication. Ackermann [2], however, is not very specific on this matter and only in [7, § 2] he specifies a system Σ_2 and describes a property of proofs in Σ_2 such that $A \rightarrow B$ is a theorem of Σ_2 if there is a derivation of B from A which possesses this property.

Although Ackermann [2, p. 34] considers the deductive conception of implication as the sole reasonable interpretation ("einzige vernüftige Interpretation") within the framework of typefree logic, he envisages the following obstacle against an explicit characterization of implication in terms of derivability. Suppose S were the system of propositional logic such that $A \rightarrow B$ is a theorem of S iff $A \vdash_S B$. The definition of the derivability relation $\vdash_S$ will depend on the rules of inferences of S. Since $\rightarrow$ belongs to the language of S, there will be inference rules for this connective such as, e. g., (mp). But then the characterization of $\rightarrow$ by means of $\vdash_S$ turns out to be circular. Ackermann [2, p. 34] concludes that providing an axiomatic system is the only way to characterize the deductively interpreted connective $\rightarrow$.

[2]There is another, more subtle strategy to get rid of Curry's paradox. Note that in the last step of its derivation (mp) was used twice. If we spell out the structure of the derivation in terms of sequents, this double application of (mp) corresponds to an application of the structural rule of contraction. Thus giving up contraction - as, e. g., in BCK-logic - is another possibility here; cp. Grishin [13].

In order to motivate his axioms for propositional logic, Ackermann starts with the observation that the formula $A \to B$ asserting - as explained - the existence of a deductive link between A and B thereby differs from its components in having a metatheoretic character. This renders some of the valid formulas of positive logic such as, e. g., the principles (vq) of *verum ex quodlibet* and (sd) of self-distribution invalid:

$$A \dot{\to} B \to A, \qquad \text{(vq)}$$
$$A \dot{\to} B \to C \ddot{\to} A \to B \dot{\to} A \to C. \qquad \text{(sd)}$$

As concerns (vq), Ackermann [2, p. 34f] argues as follows: The formula $B \to A$ concerns the metatheoretic notion of derivability and thus itself cannot be inferred from the formula A but only from the metatheoretic statement that this formula is derivable. Thus (vq) is to be given up, and, since similar considerations apply to (sd), the latter principle is to be abandoned, too. Note that the proof of the deduction theorem for positive (minimal, intuitionistic and classical) logic turns on these two principles, which we have just recognized as invalid in Ackermann's logic.

According to Ackermann, statements are stratified into successive levels. There are the objectual statements at the base level. Deductive relationships between these statements are formulated by means of implication as metatheoretic statements at the second level; deductive relationships between these metatheoretic statements are again formulated by means of implication at the third level, etc. Instances of (vq) and (sd) do not fit into this system of levels and are therefore not to be accepted as logically valid.

6.1.3 The Positive Fragments of Ackermann's Systems

In the following we are only concerned with the positive (negationless) propositional part of Ackermann's logic. This is formulated within the language $\mathcal{L}^+$ with the syntactic operations Υ (0-ary), $\wedge$, $\vee$ and $\to$ (binary). The formulas of $\mathcal{L}^+$ are generated by iterated application of these operations to the elements of the denumerable set $\mathrm{S} = \{p, q, r, ...\}$ of sentence letters. $\mathrm{Form}_{\mathcal{L}^+}$ is the set of formulas thus generated. Of course, $\wedge$, $\vee$ and $\to$ assign to pairs of elements $A, B \in \mathrm{Form}_{\mathcal{L}^+}$ their conjunction $(A \wedge B)$, disjunction $(A \vee B)$ and their implication $(A \to B)$, respectively. The *verum* Υ is to be interpreted as a proposition which is true for logical reasons. We conceive of $\mathcal{L}^+$ as the algebra $\mathcal{L}^+ = (\mathrm{Form}_{\mathcal{L}^+}, \Upsilon, \wedge, \vee, \to)$.

We employ the usual rules for the omission of brackets and furthermore use dots above the implication sign for a further economization of bracket use. A substitution s is a homomorphism from $\mathcal{L}^+$ to itself, i. e. $s \in \mathrm{HOM}(\mathcal{L}^+, \mathcal{L}^+)$. We write "$sA$" for the result of applying s to formula A, and for $M \subseteq \mathrm{Form}_{\mathcal{L}^+}$ sM is the set $\{sA \mid A \in M\}$. If for $s \in \mathrm{HOM}(\mathcal{L}^+, \mathcal{L}^+)$ and $p_i \in \mathrm{S}$ $(1 \leq i \leq m)$ we have $sp_i = B_i$ and $sq = q$ for all $q \in \mathrm{S}$ distinct from every p_i, then we write "$[B_1/p_1, ..., B_m/p_m]A$" instead of "sA". The notation "$\Upsilon^m A$" $(m \in \mathbb{N})$ is defined inductively as follows: $\Upsilon^0 A$ is just the formula A itself; $\Upsilon^{m+1} A$ is the implication $\Upsilon \to A$.

We now give two systems A^+ and Σ^+ for the positive fragment of Ackermann's logic. The Hilbert-type system A^+ is simply the positive subcalculus of the system given in [4]. Σ^+ is a natural deduction calculus. This calculus originates from the system Σ_2 in [7] but it generalizes the treatment of implication given there. Furthermore, there is a difference in the treatment of conjunction and disjunction: Whereas this is in the spirit of Kleene's weak partial logic in Σ_2, in Σ^+ as well as in Ackermann's earlier papers it is more akin to Kleene's strong partial logic.

The Hilbert-type System A^+

These are the axiom schemes of A^+:

A1	$A \to A$,		
A2	$\Upsilon \to A \dot{\to} B \to A \wedge B$,		
A3a	$A \wedge B \to A$,	A3b	$A \wedge B \to B$,
A4a	$A \to A \vee B$,	A4b	$B \to A \vee B$,
A5	$A \wedge (B \vee C) \to B \vee (A \wedge C)$,		
A6	$(A \to B) \wedge (A \to C) \dot{\to} A \to B \wedge C$,		
A7	$(A \to C) \wedge (B \to C) \dot{\to} A \vee B \to C$,		
A8	$(A \to B) \wedge (B \to C) \dot{\to} A \to C$,		
A9	$\Upsilon \to A \dot{\to} B \to A$,		
A10	$\Upsilon \to A \vee B \dot{\to} (\Upsilon \to A) \vee (\Upsilon \to B)$,		
A11	$\Upsilon \to A \dot{\to} A$.		

The description of A^+ is completed by the specification of its two rules:

$$\frac{A \quad A \to B}{B}\ (\mathrm{mp}) \quad \text{and} \quad \frac{A}{\Upsilon \to A}\ (\mathrm{up}) \ .$$

Let $M \subseteq \mathrm{Form}_{\mathcal{L}^+}$ and $A \in \mathrm{Form}_{\mathcal{L}^+}$; then we write "$M \Vdash_{A^+} A$" if A is derivable in A^+ from M[3] where this notion is defined in the standard manner. The following lemma lists some simple facts about the relation $\Vdash_{A^+}$.

Lemma 6.1.1

(i) $\Vdash_{A^+} \curlyvee$;

(ii) $A, B \Vdash_{A^+} A \wedge B$;

(iii) $A \Vdash_{A^+} B \to A$;

(iv) $\Vdash_{A^+} A \to \curlyvee$;

(v) $A \to B, B \to C \Vdash_{A^+} A \to C$;

(vi) $C \to A, C \to B \Vdash_{A^+} C \to A \wedge B$;

(vii) $A \to C, B \to C \Vdash_{A^+} A \vee B \to C$.

PROOF: (i) By A1, A11 and (mp). - The proof of the other parts of the lemma are immediate; cp. Ackermann [2, p. 43]. □

Lemma 6.1.2 Let "$A \leftrightarrow B$" abbreviate "$(A \to B) \wedge (B \to A)$". Then: $A_1 \leftrightarrow A_2, B_1 \leftrightarrow B_2 \Vdash_{A^+} A_1 \oplus B_1 \leftrightarrow A_2 \oplus B_2$ for $\oplus \in \{\wedge, \vee, \to\}$.

PROOF: We consider only the case that $\oplus$ is $\wedge$; the other cases are treated similarly. Using A3a, we may infer $A_1 \to A_2$ from $A_1 \leftrightarrow A_2$. This formula together with $A_1 \wedge B_1 \to A_1$ (A3a) yields (by Lemma 6.1.1-(v)) (1): $A_1 \wedge B_1 \to A_2$. Starting from $B_1 \leftrightarrow B_2$, we may simlarly infer that (2): $A_1 \wedge B_1 \to B_2$. (1) and (2), by Lemma 6.1.1-(vi), yields $A_1 \wedge B_1 \to A_2 \wedge B_2$. The converse of this may be derived in a completely analogous manner. □

Using an induction on the complexity of formulas, we may prove the following replacement theorem from Lemma 6.1.2.

Corollary 6.1.3 Let p be any sentence letter from S. Then: $A \leftrightarrow B \Vdash_{A^+} [A/p]C \to [B/p]C$.

A pair consisting of a formal language and a consequence relation $\vdash$ for this language is called an "implicative logic" if there is a connective $\Rightarrow$ in the

[3] The reason for chosing $\Vdash$ instead of the common $\vdash$ will become apparent in section 1.3.3.

language such that the following five conditions are fulfilled: (a) $\vdash A \Rightarrow A$, (b) $A, A \Rightarrow B \vdash B$, (c) $A \vdash B \Rightarrow A$, (d) $A \Rightarrow B, B \Rightarrow C \vdash A \Rightarrow C$, (e) $A \Rightarrow B$, $B \Rightarrow A \vdash [p/A]C \Rightarrow [p/B]C$; cp. Wójcicki [24, p. 228]. The connective $\Rightarrow$ is, of course, called the implication of the logic. We may collect the stated results into the following theorem.

Theorem 6.1.4 $(\mathcal{L}^+, \Vdash_{A+})$ is an implicative logic with $\rightarrow$ as its implication connective.

The following theorem describes the specific form in which the deduction theorem is valid for A^+.

Theorem 6.1.5 If $A_1, ..., A_m \Vdash_{A+} A_0$, then there is an (effectively determinable) number i such that $\Vdash_{A+} \Upsilon^i A_1 \wedge ... \wedge \Upsilon^i A_m \rightarrow A_0$.

PROOF: The proof for this theorem may be derived from the special case dealt with by Ackermann [4, p. 45]. □

The Natural Deduction System Σ^+

The following rules for Σ^+ employ the usual conventions for natural deduction rules; cp. Prawitz [17, p. 22-24].

$$\frac{}{\Upsilon}\ (\Upsilon\text{int})$$

$$\frac{A \quad B}{A \wedge B}\ (\wedge\text{int}) \qquad \frac{A \wedge B}{A}\ (\wedge\text{el}_r) \qquad \frac{A \wedge B}{B}\ (\wedge\text{el}_l)$$

$$\frac{C \rightarrow A \quad C \rightarrow B}{C \rightarrow A \wedge B}\ (\rightarrow\wedge\text{int})$$

$$\frac{A}{A \vee B}\ (\vee\text{int}_r) \qquad \frac{A}{B \vee A}\ (\vee\text{int}_l) \qquad \frac{A \vee B \quad \begin{matrix} A^{(i)} \\ \vdots \\ C \end{matrix} \quad \begin{matrix} B^{(i)} \\ \vdots \\ C \end{matrix}}{C}\ (i)\ (\vee\text{el})$$

$$\frac{A \to B \quad A \to C}{A \vee B \to C} \; (\vee{\to}\text{int})$$

$$\frac{\begin{matrix} A^{(i)} \\ \vdots \\ B \end{matrix}}{A \to B} \; (i)\ ({\to}\text{int}) \qquad \frac{A}{\Upsilon \to A} \; (\text{up}) \qquad \frac{\Upsilon \to A}{A} \; (\text{down})$$

$$\frac{A \to B \quad B \to C}{A \to C} \; (\text{trans})$$

$$\frac{\Upsilon \to A \vee B}{(\Upsilon \to A) \vee (\Upsilon \to B)} \; ({\to}\vee\text{dist})$$

The rules ($\vee$el) and ($\to$ int) are improper, the other rules - except (up), the status of which is discussed in the following subsection - are proper inference rules of Σ^+; cp. Prawitz [17, p. 23]. Assumptions of improper inference rules which are to be bound in the course of an derivation are marked with a numerical superscript which is repeated at the rule application where the binding takes place.

The rules ($\vee$el) and ($\to$ int) are subject to the restriction that all unbound assumptions in the premiss proofs (of C and B, respectively) are just occurrences of the formulas indicated in the schemes (namely, A and B in the case of $\vee$el and A in the case of ($\to$ int)) and that there are no applications of (up) in these premiss proofs to formulas depending on the assumptions. Since B in ($\to$ int) may thus not be another assumption besides A, the usual proof of $A \to B \to A$ is blocked. A derivation $\mathcal{D}$ of A from M in Σ^+ is a formula tree in which the binding of assumptions has been made explicit by co-indexing. Furthermore, A is attached at the root of $\mathcal{D}$, all unbound assumptions are elements of M, and $\mathcal{D}$ obeys the restrictions on ($\to$ int) and ($\vee$el).

6.1.4 The Two Deducibility Relation of Σ^+

In the introduction we stated that Ackermann gives up (dt) in order to avoid Curry's paradox and that another alternative to do this would be to abandon (mp). Inspection of the system Σ^+ reveals that we might also say that (mp) is given up since it is not a primitive rule of that system. Since Σ^+ is offered as an alternative formulation of A^+ and since the latter system has *modus ponens*, we might suspect, however, that in some sense (mp) is present in Σ^+, too.

Let us consider the question whether we should define the relation of derivability for Σ^+ in such a way that (mp) becomes a derived rule. Given assumptions A and $A \to B$, we could apply (up) to A in order to derive $\Upsilon \to A$ and combine this with $A \to B$ by (trans) which procedure would yield the formula $\Upsilon \to B$. A final application of (down), then, results in B. This argument, however, depends on the use of the rule (up), which in view of ($\vee$el) and ($\to$ int) has a rather special character.

According to Ackermann, the formula $\Upsilon \to A$ expresses that A is derivable (since it is derivable from the derivable Υ). But, clearly, an assumption may not be derivable (although it could be, of course), and thus (up) should not be applied to formulas depending on assumptions. This explains the corresponding restriction on the rule ($\to$ int). The above argument in case of (mp) is acceptable only if A is a theorem of Σ^+. This reminds us of the fact that there are several principles of deduction that might be called "*modus ponens*". Scott [20, p. 148] gives a table of four such principles. The two items of this table which are at issue here are:

$$A, A \to B \vdash_S B; \qquad \text{(dmp)}$$
$$\text{if } \vdash_S A \text{ and } \vdash_S A \to B, \text{ then } \vdash_S B. \qquad \text{(amp)}$$

Assuming that *modus ponens* is not among the primitive rules of S and adopting the accepted terminology for "short cut rules", we may say that according to (dmp) *modus ponens* is a derived rule of S but according to (amp) it is only an admissible one. Each derived rule is also admissible, but the converse of this is not true.

Taking the difference between (dmp) and (amp) into account, we define two derivability relation for Σ^+: $\Vdash_{\Sigma^+}$ and $\vdash_{\Sigma^+}$. *Modus ponens*, then, is derivable according to $\Vdash_{\Sigma^+}$ but admissible according to $\vdash_{\Sigma^+}$. Viewed from our natural deduction framework, the difference between $\Vdash_{\Sigma^+}$ and $\vdash_{\Sigma^+}$ consists in the different treatment of (up): Treating this rule as a proper inference rule results in the derivability relation $\Vdash_{\Sigma^+}$ whereas a treatment as an improper rule requiring that A should not depend on any assumption results in $\vdash_{\Sigma^+}$.

Definition 6.1.6 Let $M \subseteq \mathrm{Form}_{\mathcal{L}^+}$ and $A \in \mathrm{Form}_{\mathcal{L}^+}$. Then:

(i) $M \Vdash_{\Sigma^+} A$ iff there is derivation $\mathcal{D}$ of A from M in Σ^+.

(ii) $M \vdash_{\Sigma^+} A$ iff there is a derivation $\mathcal{D}$ of A from M in Σ^+ such that every unbound assumption of $\mathcal{D}$ is an occurrence of a formula in M and each assumption of $\mathcal{D}$ at the beginning of a branch which passes through an application of (up) becomes bound before or at the highest application of this rule in that branch.

The following theorem describes the relationship between A^+ and Σ^+; cp. Ackermann [7, p. 10].

Theorem 6.1.7

(i) If $\Vdash_{\mathrm{A}^+} A$, then $\Vdash_{\Sigma^+} A$.

(ii) (a) If $\Vdash_{\Sigma^+} A$, then $\Vdash_{\mathrm{A}^+} A$.

(b) If there is a derivation $\mathcal{D}$ for A in Σ^+ without any applications of the rule (up) in which every unbound assumption of $\mathcal{D}$ is an occurrence of B, then $\Vdash_{\mathrm{A}^+} B \to A$.

(iii) $M \Vdash_{\mathrm{A}^+} A$ iff $M \Vdash_{\Sigma^+} A$.

PROOF: (i) This is proved by an induction on the length l of the derivation for A in A^+. If $l = 1$, then A is an instance of one of the schemes A1-A11. All these instances, however, are easily derived in Σ^+. For the sake of illustration, we only deal with A9 and A2. Instances of these schemes may be derived in the following way:

$$\dfrac{\dfrac{\dfrac{\dfrac{A^{(1)}}{\Upsilon}\;\Upsilon\text{int}}{A \to \Upsilon}\;(1)\to\text{int} \qquad \Upsilon \to B^{(2)}}{A \to B}\;\text{trans}}{\Upsilon \to B \;\dot{\to}\; A \to B}\;(2)\to\text{int}$$

$$\dfrac{\dfrac{\dfrac{\dfrac{\dfrac{B^{(1)}}{\Upsilon}\;\Upsilon\text{int}}{B \to \Upsilon}\;(1)\to\text{int} \qquad \Upsilon \to A^{(2)}}{B \to A}\;\to\text{trans} \qquad \dfrac{B^{(2)}}{B \to B}\;(2)\to\text{int}}{B \to A \wedge B}\;\to\wedge\text{int}}{\Upsilon \to A \;\dot{\to}\; B \to A \wedge B}\;(2)\to\text{int}$$

Now assume that $l = m + 1$ and the last step of the derivation of A is an application of (mp) to the formulas $B \to A$ and B. Then, by the induction hypothesis, these formulas are theorems of Σ^+ and we may apply the reasoning sketched before our distinction between (dmp) and (amp) to derive also A in this system. Finally, let A result in A^+ from an application of (up). Then, since (up) is also a rule of Σ^+, we may simply employ the induction hypothesis.

(ii) The two parts of (ii) are proved by simultaneous induction on the height h (i. e., the length of the longest branch) of the derivation $\mathcal{D}$ of this formula in Σ^+. Let $h = 1$: (a) Then A can only be the *verum* $\curlyvee$, which is a theorem of A^+; c.f. Lemma 6.1.1-(iv). (b) In this case A is either $\curlyvee$ again or identical to B. In the first case the assumption holds because of Lemma 6.1.1-(iv) and in the second case because of A1. Now assume that $h = m + 1$. (a) We illustrate the reasoning necessary here only by two examples. Assume that the last step of $\mathcal{D}$ is an application of ($\wedge$int). Using the induction hypothesis and Lemma 6.1.1-(ii)., we may infer that $\Vdash_{\mathrm{A}^+} A$. - If the last step of $\mathcal{D}$ is an application of ($\vee$el), we apply the induction hypothesis with respect to part (b). Because of the restrictions of this rule, we may infer that both $A \to C$ and $B \to C$ are theorems of A^+. Lemma 6.1.1-(vii) then yields $\Vdash_{\mathrm{A}^+} A \vee B \to C$. Since $A \vee B$ is a theorem of A^+ according to the induction hypothesis, the same is true for C. - (b) Now we turn to part (b) of the assertion. We give again only two examples: If $\mathcal{D}$ ends with an application of ($\wedge$int) to formulas A_1 and A_2, then A is the conjunction $A_1 \wedge A_2$. Then we have $\Vdash_{\mathrm{A}^+} B \to A_1$ and $\Vdash_{\mathrm{A}^+} B \to A_2$ by the induction hypothesis. This, according to Lemma 6.1.1-(vi)., yields $\Vdash_{\mathrm{A}^+} B \to A_1 \wedge A_2$. - If the last step of $\mathcal{D}$ consists in an application of ($\to$ int), then A is an implication $C \to D$ and, according to the restriction of ($\to$ int), the formula D immediately preceding A in $\mathcal{D}$ does not depend on any assumptions except C. Just applying the induction hypothesis to C and this formula yields $\Vdash_{\mathrm{A}^+} C \to D$ - i. e., $\Vdash_{\mathrm{A}^+} A$. Using Lemma 6.1.1-(iii). from this we get $\Vdash_{\mathrm{A}^+} B \to A$.

3. This part of the theorem may now be proved again by two inductive arguments. These will make use of (i) and (ii) □

Some properties of $\vdash_{\Sigma^+}$ are provided by the following theorem.

Theorem 6.1.8

(i) $\vdash_{\Sigma^+} \subseteq \Vdash_{\Sigma^+}$.

(ii) If $M \vdash_{\Sigma^+} A$, then $\vdash_{\Sigma^+} \bigwedge N \to A$ for some finite subset $N \subseteq M$. (Here $\bigwedge N$ is the conjunction of the elements of N taken in some arbitrary order.)

(iii) The rule (mp) is admissible with respect to $\vdash_{\Sigma^+}$ - i. e., if both $\vdash_{\Sigma^+} A$ and $\vdash_{\Sigma^+} A \to B$, then $\vdash_{\Sigma^+} B$.

PROOF: (i) is immediate from the definition of the two derivability relations.

(ii) If $M \vdash_{\Sigma^+} A$, then there is a derivation $\mathcal{D}$ of A of the kind required in Definition 6.1.6-(ii) such that every unbound assumption B of $\mathcal{D}$ is an element of M. Obviously, the set N of these assumptions is a finite subset of M. Furthermore, each $B \in N$ may be derived from $\bigwedge N$ by successive applications of ($\wedge$el$_r$) and ($\wedge$el$_l$) in a derivation $\mathcal{D}_B$. If for each $B \in N$ we glue $\mathcal{D}_B$ to each occurrence of B as an unbound assumption in $\mathcal{D}$ we receive a derivation $\mathcal{D}'$ of A from $\bigwedge N$. Furthermore, since no occurrence of a $B \in N$ starts a branch of $\mathcal{D}$ through an application of (up), the same is true for $\mathcal{D}'$ with respect to the new occurrences of $\bigwedge N$. Thus we may apply ($\to$ int) in order to get the theorem $\bigwedge N \to A$.

(iii) We may apply here the argument from the second paragraph of this section. This argument is valid here because A is a theorem according to the assumption of (iii). □

We no define the relation $\equiv$ of deductive equivalence in terms of $\vdash_{\Sigma^+}$; we shall come back to it in section 3.2 below.

Definition 6.1.9 $A \equiv B$ iff $A \vdash_{\Sigma^+} B$ and $B \vdash_{\Sigma^+} A$.

For $\equiv$ we have:

Lemma 6.1.10

(i) The relation $\equiv$ is an equivalence relation on $\text{Form}_{\mathcal{L}^+}$.

(ii) If $A_1 \equiv A_2$ and $B_1 \equiv B_2$, then $A_1 \oplus B_1 \equiv A_2 \oplus B_2$ for $\oplus \in \{\wedge, \vee, \to\}$.

PROOF: (i) This follows directly from the definition of $\equiv$ together with the basic facts about the derivability relation $\vdash_{\Sigma^+}$.

(ii) Given the rules of Σ^+, this is immediate. We only consider the cases for $\vee$ and $\to$. From $A_1 \equiv A_2$ we have: $A_1 \vdash_{\Sigma^+} A_2$, and from this with the help of

($\vee$int$_r$): $A_1 \vdash_{\Sigma^+} A_2 \vee B_2$. Analogously, we get $B_1 \vdash_{\Sigma^+} A_2 \vee B_2$. Because of the restriction in Definition 6.1.6-(ii). we may apply ($\vee$el) in order to get the desired $A_1 \vee B_1 \vdash_{\Sigma^+} A_2 \vee B_2$. The converse of this is proved in the same way. - Now consider the case of implication. From $A_1 \equiv A_2$ we have: $A_2 \vdash_{\Sigma^+} A_1$ and, applying Theorem 6.1.8-(ii) to this: $\vdash_{\Sigma^+} A_2 \rightarrow A_1$. Using this and (trans) we get: $A_1 \rightarrow B_1 \vdash_{\Sigma^+} A_2 \rightarrow B_1$ (1). Now, from $B_1 \equiv B_2$ we have: $B_1 \vdash_{\Sigma^+} B_2$ and, again with Theorem 6.1.8-(ii), $\vdash_{\Sigma^+} B_1 \rightarrow B_2$. Combining this with (1) according to (trans) we receive the desired $A_1 \rightarrow B_1 \vdash_{\Sigma^+} A_2 \rightarrow A_1$. The converse of this is proved analogously. □

6.2 A Hierarchy of Deductive Systems

The system Σ^+ provides us with a better understanding of Ackermann's deductive interpretation of implication; cp. 6.1.2 above. A closer look at the rules of Σ^+ reveals that inferences which involve only the *verum*, conjunction and disjunction are to be considered unproblematic. The rules which involve implication serve to represent derivations with the unproblematic rules by means of formulas. Especially the rule ($\rightarrow$ int) directly embodies the strategy to represent derivations (with a single unbound assumption) by implications.

Putting this together with Ackermann's remarks on the hierarchy of implicational formulas (cp. 6.1.2 above), we reach at the following stepwise interpretation of the sign $\rightarrow$[4]: Consider first implications in which the sign $\rightarrow$ occurs only once. These formulas are to interpreted as stating deductive relationships with respect to a calculus K_0 which does not dispose of any rules about implication. The rule ($\rightarrow$ int) may be conceived as a principle for turning derivations of K_0 into such first level implications. These first level implications may then be added as axioms to K_0 and again be processed according to the rules of this calculus. Let us call the enriched calculus $K_1{}'$. Due to the presence of the new axioms, there will be new deductive relationships in $K_1{}'$ which may again be turned into implications by the use of the principle ($\rightarrow$ int), thus giving rise to second level implications which are processed in the extended calculus $K_2{}'$, etc.

This procedure, though basically correct, overlooks one subtle point. At each stage $n+1$ we add implications $A \rightarrow B$ to the new calculus K'_{n+1} which correspond to the derivability of B from A in K'_n. By this, though we take care of all the instances of $\vdash_{K'_n}$, we neglect the laws governing this relationship.

[4]A similar procedure has been proposed in the framework of Fitch's system in [12] by Myhill [15]. Myhill, however, enriches Fitch's system with a whole sequence $\rightarrow_0$, $\rightarrow_1$, ... of implications instead of one single connective.

As an example, consider that the base calculus K_0 contains a rule which allows to infer $A \wedge B$ from the premisses A and B. Suppose, furthermore, that we have $(A \wedge B) \vee (A \wedge B) \vdash_{\mathrm{K}_0} A$ as well as $(A \wedge B) \vee (A \wedge B) \vdash_{\mathrm{K}_0} B$. Correspondingly, we have both $\vdash_{\mathrm{K}_1'} (A \wedge B) \vee (A \wedge B) \rightarrow A$ and $\vdash_{\mathrm{K}_1'} (A \wedge B) \vee (A \wedge B) \rightarrow B$. But there might be no possibility in $\mathrm{K}_1{}'$ itself to combine these two theorems to $\vdash_{\mathrm{K}_1'} (A \wedge B) \vee (A \wedge B) \rightarrow A \wedge B$ although we have $(A \wedge B) \vee (A \wedge B) \vdash_{\mathrm{K}_0} A \wedge B$. In this case we would not be entitled to add $((A \wedge B) \vee (A \wedge B) \rightarrow A) \wedge ((A \wedge B) \vee (A \wedge B) \rightarrow B) \rightarrow A \wedge B$ as an axiom to $\mathrm{K}_2{}'$.

The example might suggest the following solution. Though it might not be a derivable rule of K_1' to infer $C \rightarrow A \wedge B$ from $C \rightarrow A$ and $C \rightarrow B$, this is surely an admissible one since according to our example we always have $C \vdash_{\mathrm{K}_0} A \wedge B$ if $C \vdash_{\mathrm{K}_0} A$ and $C \vdash_{\mathrm{K}_0} B$. Define for each calculus K $M \vdash_K^\circ A$ by: "if $\vdash_K B$ for all $B \in M$, then $\vdash_K A$" and then - in the same manner as above - represent the $\vdash^\circ$-relations instead of the $\vdash$-relations by $\rightarrow$. This would be a solution to our present problem but at the same time would also give rise to a new one. Suppose our base calculus K_0 is consistent in the sense that $\not\vdash_{\mathrm{K}_0} p$ for each sentence letter p. Then, trivially, we have $p \vdash_{\mathrm{K}_0}^\circ A$. But, surely, we would not like to have every formula $p \rightarrow A$ as a new axiom of $\mathrm{K}_1{}'$.

Thus the $\vdash^\circ$-relations are not very suitable as a means for interpreting $\rightarrow$. Perhaps the relations $\vdash_K^{\circ\circ}$ defined in the following way are better candidates for doing this: $M \vdash_K^{\circ\circ} A$ iff for all substitutions s if $sM \Vdash_K sA$. This might be a possible solution to our problem, but the $\vdash^{\circ\circ}$-relations are rather complicated and not easy to handle.[5] So we chose as a simpler solution to retain the $\vdash$-relations but to add at each stage of our construction not only instances of the derivability relation of the former calculus but also the "implicational translations" of the principles governing this relationship. By the implicational translation of a rule R I mean a rule R' which relates to R as $(\rightarrow \wedge\mathrm{int})$ relates to $(\wedge\mathrm{int})$ and $(\vee \rightarrow \mathrm{int})$ to $(\vee\mathrm{el})$. The whole construction is carried out in the next subsections[6].

---

[5]Viewed from this perspective, our problem of setting up a satisfactory system of implicational logic resembles the problem of constructing structurally complete calculi. A calculus is structurally complete iff each of its admissable rule which is structural is also a derivable rule, cp. [16] and [18].

[6]Similar constructions have been proposed in a more general setting by Schroeder-Heister [19] within a natural deduction framework and by Došen [11] and Kutschera [23] by using systems of higher-order sequents. Schroeder-Heister's approach has been reformulated within a higher-order sequent system by Avron [8].

6.2.1 The Base Calculus K_0

We chose as our base calculus K_0 a system with language $\mathcal{L}^+$ the rules of which only govern the *verum*, conjunction and disjunction. In order to avoid rules like ($\vee$el) and ($\rightarrow$ int) using derivations as their premisses, we chose to allow rules with multiple conclusions; cp. Shoesmith/Smiley [21]. The rules of K_0, then, are: ($\curlyvee$int), ($\wedge$int), ($\wedge$el$_r$), ($\wedge$el$_l$), ($\vee$int$_r$), ($\vee$int$_l$) as well as the multiple conclusion rule ($\vee$mel):

$$\frac{A \vee B}{A \quad B} \ (\vee\text{mel})$$

Taking account of multiple conclusion rules, we conceive of derivations as downward branching trees. In order to give an exact definition, we have to explain two auxiliary concepts: A "file" is an initial segment of a branch of a tree (including the empty segment) and the "rank" of a file is the set of all the nodes which are preceded exactly by the nodes of the file. Note that the unit set containing only the root of a tree $\mathcal{T}$ is the rank of the empty file of $\mathcal{T}$. Following Shoesmith/Smiley [21, p. 44] we define the notion of a derivation as follows:

Definition 6.2.1 Let K be a calculus, L(K) the language in which it is formulated and R(K)[7] the set of its rules; furthermore, let M and N be sets of formulas of L(K). Then a tree $\mathcal{T}$ of formulas of L(K) is a derivation in K from M to N iff for every file f of $\mathcal{T}$ one of the following conditions is fulfilled:

(i) f is a complete branch ending in a node to which an element from N is attached; or

(ii) the rank of f consists only in a single node to which an element of M is attached; or

(iii) $A_1, ..., A_m$ are the formulas attached to the nodes of the rank of f and there are formulas $B_1, ...B_n$ attached to nodes of f and a rule in R(K) which allows to infer $A_1, ..., A_m$ from $B_1, ...B_n$.

We say that N is derivable in K from M - formally, $M \vdash_K N$ - iff there are subsets $M' \subseteq M$ and $N' \subseteq N$ such that there is a derivation of N' from M' in K.

[7]Formally, we may define a possible rule of K as a binary relation on the set of finite sets of formulas of L(K).

The following example of a derivation shows that $A \wedge (B \vee C) \vdash_{K_0} B \vee (A \wedge C)$.

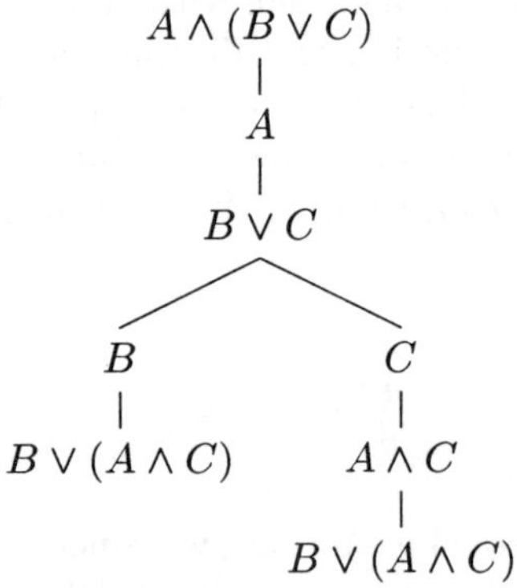

As in the case of natural deduction derivations, we call the length of the longest branch in a derivation with multiple conclusion rules the "height" of the derivation. - The calculus K_0 has the disjunction property; this is stated in the part 2. of the following theorem.

Theorem 6.2.2 The following holds for K_0:

(i) If $\mathcal{T}$ is a derivation of $A \wedge B$ in K_0 with height m, then there are derivations $\mathcal{T}_1$ of A and $\mathcal{T}_2$ of B with lesser heigths $m_1, m_2 < m$.

(ii) If $\mathcal{T}$ is a derivation of $A \vee B$ in K_0, then there is a derivation $\mathcal{T}'$ of K_0 of either A or B with a lesser height $m' < m$.

PROOF: The two parts of the theorem are shown by a simultaneous induction on the number b of branching nodes of $\mathcal{T}$. Let $b = 0$, so that $\mathcal{T}$ is a linear derivation. We employ an induction on the number n of nodes of $\mathcal{T}$. The case $n = 1$ is trivial since the only theorem derivable in a single step is $\curlyvee$, which is neither a conjunction nor a disjunction. Now assume that $n = m + 1$. We consider (i) first. Since $b = 0$, the last step in the derivation $\mathcal{T}$ is either an application of ($\wedge$int) or of one of the elimination rules ($\wedge$el$_r$) or ($\wedge$el$_l$). In the first case there are obviously subderivations of the required kind, and in the second case we simply apply the induction hypothesis twice. Turning to the case of disjunction, we recognize that because of $b = 0$ the last step of $\mathcal{T}$ can only consist of an application of an elimination rule for $\wedge$ or an introduction rule for $\vee$. In the latter case the assertion is evident. In the former case, there are, according to the induction hypothesis, subderivations of both conjuncts of the premiss of the applied rule. One of these conjunct, however, is the disjunction in question. Applying again the induction hypothesis to the derivation of this disjunction yields a subderivation for one of the disjuncts. Now let $b = k + 1$ and assume that the assertion has already been proved for all derivations with at most k branching nodes. Let E be the formula derived in $\mathcal{T}$; thus, E is attached to every maximal node (every leaf) of $\mathcal{T}$. E is either a conjunction (part (i)) or a disjunction (part (ii)); we deal with both parts simultaneously. Take the highest branching node k in the derivation $\mathcal{T}$. The node k is the last node in a linear derivation $\mathcal{T}'$ of a disjunctive formula $C \vee D$. According to the induction hypothesis $\mathcal{T}'$ contains a subderivation $\mathcal{D}''$ either of C or of D. Furthermore, k is immediately succeeded by two nodes k_l and k_r to which the formulas C and D are attached respectively. Depending on whether $\mathcal{T}''$ is a derivation of C or of D, we may simply cut off that part of $\mathcal{T}$ which starts with either k_l (if $\mathcal{T}''$ is a proof of C) or with k_r (if $\mathcal{T}''$ is a proof of D). The application of ($\vee$mel) is replaced by a reference to the disjunct which has already been proved. Thus the new tree is a derivation of E with fewer branching points and thus we may apply the induction hypothesis to it. □

6.2.2 The Calculus K_1

Applying the strategy discussed above, we extend now the base calculus K_0 to K_1 by adding implicational axioms corresponding to instances of derivability relationships in K_0 as well as implicational translations of the rules of K_0 to this calculus:

$$\frac{}{A \to B}\,(\mathrm{mdt}_0) \quad \text{if } A \vdash_{\mathrm{K}_0} B$$

$$\frac{C \to A \quad C \to B}{C \to A \wedge B}\,(\to\wedge\mathrm{int}) \qquad \frac{C \to A \wedge B}{C \to A}\,(\to\wedge\mathrm{el_r}) \qquad \frac{C \to A \wedge B}{C \to B}\,(\to\wedge\mathrm{el_l})$$

$$\frac{C \to A}{C \to A \vee B}\,(\to\vee\mathrm{int_r}) \qquad \frac{C \to B}{C \to A \vee B}\,(\to\vee\mathrm{int_l}) \qquad \frac{\Upsilon \to A \vee B}{\Upsilon \to A \quad \Upsilon \to B}\,(\to\vee\mathrm{el})$$

$$\frac{A \to C \quad B \to C}{A \vee B \to C}\,(\vee\!\to\!\mathrm{int})$$

$$\frac{\Upsilon \to A}{A}\,(\mathrm{down}) \qquad \frac{A \to B \quad B \to C}{A \to C}\,(\mathrm{trans})$$

The modified deduction theorem (mdt_0) is a direct manifestation of the deductive interpretation of implication. The rule (trans) reflects the fact that according to Definition 6.2.1 simpler derivations may be concatenated to more complex ones. Each other of the new rules of K_1 corresponds to one of the rules of K_0 and thus to a subcase of clause (iii) in Definition 6.2.1. Disjunction has a special status in that ($\vee$el) gives rise to two rules: ($\vee$el) is a reflection of Theorem 6.2.2-(ii) and ($\vee \rightarrow$ int) is motivated by the fact that in K_1 derivations of C from A and from B may be combined using ($\vee$el) into a derivation of C from $A \vee B$.

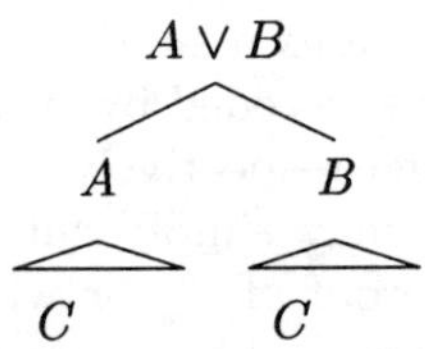

The following lemma provides some simple facts about $\vdash_{K_1}$:

Lemma 6.2.3

(i) $\vdash_{K_1} A \rightarrow A$;

(ii) $\Upsilon \rightarrow A \vdash_{K_1} B \rightarrow A \wedge B$;

(iii) $(A \rightarrow B) \wedge (A \rightarrow C) \vdash_{K_1} (A \rightarrow B \wedge C)$;

(iv) $(A \rightarrow C) \wedge (B \rightarrow C) \vdash_{K_1} (A \vee B \rightarrow C)$;

(v) $\Upsilon \rightarrow A \vdash_{K_1} B \rightarrow A$;

(vi) $\Upsilon \rightarrow A \vee B \vdash_{K_1} (\Upsilon \rightarrow A) \vee (\Upsilon \rightarrow B)$;

(vii) $\Upsilon \rightarrow A \vdash_{K_1} A$.

PROOF: (i) is an instance of (mdt$_0$), (iii) results from ($\rightarrow \wedge$int), (iv) from ($\vee \rightarrow$ int), (vi) from (trans) and (vii) from (down). - For (v) we reason as follows: By (mdt$_0$) we have $\vdash_{K_1} B \rightarrow \Upsilon$ which together with (trans) yields (v). - Consider now part (ii). From $\Upsilon \rightarrow A$ we may infer $B \rightarrow A$ by (v). Combining this with $\vdash_{K_1} B \rightarrow B$ according to ($\rightarrow \wedge$int) yields 2. □

6.2.3 The Full Hierarchy

Now we repeat the step leading from K_0 to K_1. But, as is readily seen, it would be redundant to add implicational translations of the new rules of K_1 to K_2, the addition of an analogue (mdt_1) of (mdt_0) suffices. The iteration of this procedure provides us with a whole sequence $(K_m)_{0 \leq m}$ of calculi.

Definition 6.2.4 For $m \geq 1$ K_{m+1} is the calculus resulting from K_m by adding the rule

$$\frac{}{A \to B}\,{}^{\mathrm{mdt}_m} \quad \text{if } A \vdash_{K_m} B$$

to K_m.

The calculus K_{m+1} has the disjunction property. Furthermore, deductive relationships between pairs of formulas in K_m are completely represented by implicational theorems of K_{m+1}. That each such relationship is represented by an implication is guaranteed by the rule (mdt_m). That, conversely, each derivable implication expresses the derivability of its consequent from its antecedent in K_m is proved by the following theorem.

Theorem 6.2.5 For $n \geq 1$: If $\mathcal{T}$ is a derivation in K_n

(i) of $A \wedge B$, then there are also derivations $\mathcal{T}_1$ of A and $\mathcal{T}_2$ of B in K_n.

(ii) of $A \vee B$, then there is also a derivation $\mathcal{T}'$ in K_n of A or of B.

(iii) of $A \to B$, then $A \vdash_{K_n} B$.

PROOF: The proof is by a simultaneous induction on n. Let $n = 1$. As in Theorem 6.2.2, we first demonstrate the theorem for linear derivations and then apply the cut-and-glue-technique applied in the proof of that theorem.

Let thus $\mathcal{T}$ be a linear derivation of height $h = 1$. Then (i) and (ii) are trivially true since there is no rule starting a derivation with a conjunction or disjunction. Thus $\mathcal{T}$ simply consists of a single formula $A \to B$ which has been derived by means of (mdt_0). Then $A \vdash_{K_0} B$ by the presupposition of this rule. Now assume that $\mathcal{T}$ be a linear derivation of height $h = m+1$ and the theorem has already been proved for all linear proofs of lesser height. In the case of (i) the last rule applied in $\mathcal{T}$ can only be ($\wedge$int) (case (a)), ($\wedge el_r$) or ($\wedge el_l$) (case (b)) or (down) (case (c)). Cases (a) and (b) are treated as in Theorem 6.2.2.

In case (c) we have $\Upsilon \vdash_{K_0} A \wedge B$ by the induction hypothesis relating to (iii). But then also: $\vdash_{K_0} A \wedge B$, and the assertion follows from Theorem 6.2.2-(i). In the case of (ii) the last rule applied in $\mathcal{T}$ can only be ($\vee$int) (case (a)), ($\wedge$el$_r$) or ($\wedge$el$_l$) (case (b)) or again (down) (case (c)). The first two cases are again treated as in Theorem 6.2.2. Case (c) is covered by Theorem 6.2.2-(ii). In the case of (iii) the last step in $\mathcal{T}$ may be an application of ($\wedge$el$_r$) or ($\wedge$el$_l$) (case (a)) or of one of the new rules of K_1 (case (b)). Case (a) is treated by applying the induction hypothesis relating to (i) and (iii). We illustrate the treatment of the subcases of case (b) (except (down)) by the example of ($\rightarrow \wedge$int). Assume the last step of $\mathcal{T}$ is an application of this rule and thus $A \rightarrow B$ is the formula $A \rightarrow B_1 \wedge B_2$. This formula results from premisses $A \rightarrow B_1$ and $A \rightarrow B_2$. Applying the induction hypothesis relating to (iii) to these two formulas we have both $A \vdash_{K_0} B_1$ and $A \vdash_{K_0} B_2$. In view of rule ($\wedge$int) of K_0 this yields the desired $A \vdash_{K_0} B_1 \wedge B_2$. Finally, assume the last step of $\mathcal{T}$ were an application of (down). Then $A \rightarrow B$ would have been derived from $\Upsilon \dot{\rightarrow} A \rightarrow B$. But this is impossible since applying the induction hypothesis to the latter formula would result in $\Upsilon \vdash_{K_0} A \rightarrow B$. There is, however, no rule in K_0 which enables one to derive an implication. This completes the proof of the theorem for the case that $m = 1$ and that $\mathcal{T}$ is a linear proof.

Now assume that $\mathcal{T}$ is a derivation of K_1 with $b = j + 1$ branching points and that the theorem has been proved already for all derivation of K_1 with fewer branching points. We consider the topmost branching point of $\mathcal{T}$. This corresponds either to an application of ($\vee$el) or of ($\rightarrow \vee$int). The procedure in the first case is just the same as in the proof of Theorem 6.2.2. In the second case a formula $\Upsilon \rightarrow C_1 \vee C_2$ is attached to the topmost branching point. Since this formula is the last in a linear proof, we conclude that $\Upsilon \vdash_{K_0} C_1 \vee C_2$. Thus, according to Theorem 6.2.2-(ii), we have: $\Upsilon \vdash_{K_0} C_1$ or $\Upsilon \vdash_{K_0} C_2$. Let C_x ($x \in \{1, 2\}$) be that one of the two formulas C_1 and C_2 which is derivable (from Υ) in K_0, then $\Upsilon \rightarrow C_x$ is derivable in K_1 by (int$_0$). That part of $\mathcal{T}$ which follows the occurrence of $\Upsilon \rightarrow C_x$ immediately under the topmost branching point is also a derivation of the formula derived in $\mathcal{T}$ itself. Since this proof has fewer branching points than $\mathcal{T}$, our theorem holds for it and thus for $\mathcal{T}$, too. This completes the proof of the theorem for the base case $m = 1$.

The case that $m = k+1$ is treated in the same way as the base case. There are only two exceptions. We use the induction hypothesis where in the base case we use Theorem 6.2.2. The second exception pertains to the case of a linear proof for a formula $A \rightarrow B$ (third part of the theorem). In the base case an application of (down) as a last step in such a proof turned out to be impossible; this is no longer true if $m = k+1$. Assume then that $A \rightarrow B$ has been inferred from $\Upsilon \dot{\rightarrow} A \rightarrow B$. Then we must have $\Upsilon \vdash_{K_k} A \rightarrow B$. By the induction hypothesis relating to part (iii) of the theorem this yields $A \vdash_{K_{k-1}} B$. Now K_{k-1} is a subcalculus of K_k, thus also: $A \vdash_{K_k} B$. This completes the proof of the entire theorem. □

The "limit system" K_∞ is the system with the rules: ($\curlyvee$int), ($\wedge$int), ($\wedge$el$_r$), ($\wedge$el$_l$), ($\vee$int$_r$), ($\vee$int$_l$), ($\vee$mel) (these are the rules of K_0), ($\to \wedge$int), ($\to \wedge$el$_r$), ($\to \wedge$el$_l$), ($\to \vee$int$_r$), ($\to \vee$int$_l$), ($\to \vee$el), ($\vee \to$ int), (down), (trans) and (mdt$_m$) for all $m \geq 0$. Thus K_∞ has infinitely many rules. *Modus ponens* and the rule (up) are admissible rules of K_∞. Obviously, if $\vdash_{K_\infty} A$ there is a number m such that already $\vdash_{K_m} A$. This number m is simply determined by the highest index of an (mdt$_n$)-rule applied in the derivation of A in K_∞.

Lemma 6.2.6

(i) All instances of the axiom schemata of A^+ are theorems of K_∞.

(ii) If $\vdash_{K_\infty} A$ and $\vdash_{K_\infty} A \to B$, then $\vdash_{K_\infty} B$.

(iii) If $\vdash_{K_\infty} A$, then $\vdash_{K_\infty} \curlyvee \to A$.

PROOF: (i) As regards A3a, A3b, A4a and A4b, (i) follows from the presence of ($\wedge$el$_r$), ($\wedge$el$_l$), ($\vee$int$_r$) and ($\vee$int$_l$) in K_0. The other cases are covered by Lemma 6.2.3 and, for A5, by the example of a tree proof given in section 2.1 above.

(ii) Since $\vdash_{K_\infty} A$ and $\vdash_{K_\infty} A \to B$, there are $m, n \in \mathbb{N}$ such that $\vdash_{K_m} A$ and $\vdash_{K_n} A \to B$ (see above). The latter yields $A \vdash_{K_{n-1}} B$ by Theorem 6.2.5-(iii). Now let $j = \max(m, n-1)$, then we have $\vdash_{K_j} A$ and $A \vdash_{K_j} B$ because of the cumulativity of the sequence $(K_m)_{0 \leq m}$ and thus $\curlyvee \vdash_{K_j} B$, too. The rule (mdt$_j$) then leads up to the theorem $\curlyvee \to B$ of K_∞ which gives rise to $\vdash_{K_\infty} B$ by an application of (down).

(iii) Since we have $\vdash_{K_\infty} A$, there is a number m such that $\vdash_{K_m} A$. Thus we have $\curlyvee \vdash_{K_m} A$ and by an application of (mdt$_m$) $\vdash_{K_\infty} \curlyvee \to A$. □

The construction of this section was motivated by Ackermann's explanation that the implication $A \to B$ expresses a deductive link between its antecedent A and its consequent B. This explanation may also be spelled out within the framework of a system of higher-order sequents; cp. the references given in fn. 6 above. In the framework of such a system we may just adopt the two higher-order sequents $A \Rightarrow B \Rightarrow A \to B$ and $A \to B \Rightarrow A \Rightarrow B$. Clearly, the logic of the thus characterized implication will depend on the principles governing the sequent-arrow $\Rightarrow$. The frameworks developed by Kutschera [23] and Avron [8] will lead up to an implication for which the full deduction theorem holds and are thus clearly not adequate for Ackermann's logic. We may, however, easily construct a higher-order sequent system for Ackermann's logic by applying the techniques provided by Došen [11] if we - unlike Došen himself - also allow for the horizontalization of "non-level-preserving rules"; cp. [11, p. 151].

6.3 Algebraic Semantics

6.3.1 Ackermann Structures

The intuition backing up Ackermann's (positive) systems may also be described in the following way: The items denoted by formulas are proposition. Let P be the collection of all propositions. Corresponding to the syntactic operations $\curlyvee$, $\wedge$, $\vee$, $\rightarrow$ there are the operations $\top$, $\sqcap$, $\sqcup$ and $\multimap$ on P. A proposition may be true or false.

The propositions are partially ordered by the relation $\sqsubseteq$ of logical consequence. Of course, logical consequence is normally conceived of as a relation between sets $X \subseteq P$ of propositions - the premisses - and single propositions $x \in P$ - the corresponding consequents. But at least in case of a finite set X of premisses we may deal with the proposition $\bigsqcap X$ instead of the set X itself. The operations $\sqcap$ of conjunction and $\sqcup$ of disjunction fulfill the usual conditions with respect to logical consequence. This means that they are respectively the infimum and supremum operation of the lattice of propositions and that $\sqsubseteq$ is the correspondig ordering relation of this lattice; (This means that we identify proposition which entail each other.)

The operation $\multimap$ of implication mirrows the relation of logical consequence. If y is a consequence of x, then $x \multimap y$ is a true proposition. But since logical consequence is a relation which either holds or fails for logical reasons, $x \multimap y$ is not only true but even logically true. Thus we infer that $\top$ implies $x \multimap y$ if y follows from x. Since $\multimap$ mirrors the relation $\sqsubseteq$, the behavior of $\multimap$ resembles in several respects that of the former relation. The consequence relation $\sqsubseteq$ is, for instance, transitive; consequently, $\multimap$ is "transitive" in the following sense: The conjunctive proposition $(x \multimap y) \sqcap (y \multimap z)$ implies the proposition $x \multimap z$.

We sum up our observations about the notions of truth, logical truth and consequence in the following definition.

Definition 6.3.1 **P** is a positive Ackermann lattice [8] ("pal", for short) iff there are P, $\top$, $\sqcap$, $\sqcup$ and $\multimap$ such that $\mathbf{P} = (P, \top, \sqcap, \sqcup, \multimap)$ and the following conditions are fulfilled:

(i) $\top \in P$;

(ii) $\sqcap$ and $\sqcup$ are binary operations on P such that $(P, \sqcap, \sqcup)$ is a distributive lattice with top element $\top$; in the following let $\sqsubseteq$ be the ordering relation of this lattice

(iii) $\multimap$ also is a binary operation on P which fulfills the following conditions:

(a) if $x \sqsubseteq y$, then $\top \sqsubseteq (x \multimap y)$ (and thus, consequently, $(x \multimap y) = \top$),

(b) furthermore:

i. $(\top \multimap x) \sqsubseteq x$,

ii. $(x \multimap y) \sqcap (y \multimap z) \sqsubseteq (x \multimap z)$,

iii. $(x \multimap y) \sqcap (x \multimap z) \sqsubseteq x \multimap (y \sqcap z)$,

iv. $(x \multimap z) \sqcap (y \multimap z) \sqsubseteq (x \sqcup y) \multimap z$,

v. $\top \multimap (x \sqcup y) \sqsubseteq (\top \multimap x) \sqcup (\top \multimap y)$.

Making use of the notion of a pal, we define now two consequence relations.

Definition 6.3.2 Let $\mathfrak{K}$ be a class of pals, $M \subseteq \mathrm{Form}_{\mathcal{L}^+}$ and $A \in \mathrm{Form}_{\mathcal{L}^+}$. Then:

(i) $M \models_{\mathfrak{K}} A$ iff there is a finite subset $N \subseteq M$ such that for every $\mathbf{P} = (P, \top, \sqcap, \sqcup, \multimap) \in \mathfrak{K}$ with ordering relation $\sqsubseteq$ and for all $V \in \mathrm{HOM}(\mathcal{L}^+, \mathbf{P})$: $\bigsqcap V(N) \sqsubseteq V(A)$ (where, of course, $V(N) = \{V(x) \mid x \in N\}$)[9].

(ii) $M \Vdash\!\models_{\mathfrak{K}} A$ iff for all $\mathbf{P} = (P, \top, \sqcap, \sqcup, \multimap) \in \mathfrak{K}$ and for all $V \in \mathrm{HOM}(\mathcal{L}^+, \mathbf{P})$: if $V(B) = \top$ for all $B \in M$, then $V(A) = \top$, too.

Theorem 6.3.3 Let $\mathfrak{K}$ be a class of pals. Then:

---

[8] A lattice with an additional operation $\multimap$ - the "ply operation" - is called an "implicative lattice" in Curry [10, p. 140f] iff the ply operation satisfies two conditions: $x \sqcap (x \multimap y) \sqsubseteq y$ (P_1) and $x \sqsubseteq (x \multimap y)$ if $x \sqcap y \sqsubseteq z$ (P_2). Obviously, these are algebraic counterparts of (mp) and (dt). Together they suffice to derive the conditions listed in (iii)-(b) of the definition of a pal.

[9] A pal was not required to be a complete lattice. So we cannot just postulate $\bigsqcap V(M) \sqsubseteq V(A)$ here.

(i) If $M \vdash_{\Sigma^+} A$, then $M \models_{\mathfrak{K}} A$.

(ii) If $M \Vdash_{\Sigma^+} A$, then $M \Vvdash_{\mathfrak{K}} A$

PROOF: (i) If $M \vdash_{\Sigma^+} A$, then there is a derivation $\mathcal{D}$ of A such that the set N of unbound assumptions in $\mathcal{D}$ is a subset of M. Now let $\mathbf{P} \in \mathfrak{K}$ and $\sqsubseteq$ be the ordering relation of $\mathbf{P}$. It can be shown by an easy induction on the height h of $\mathcal{D}$ that for every valuation $V \in \mathrm{HOM}(\mathcal{L}^+, \mathbf{P})$ $\bigsqcap V(N) \subseteq V(A)$ and thus that $M \models_{\Sigma^+} A$.

(ii) Using (i), we proof part (ii) again by an induction on the heigth h of the derivation $\mathcal{D}$ of Σ^+ leading from M to A. Let again $\mathbf{P} \in \mathfrak{K}$ and $\sqsubseteq$ be the ordering relation of $\mathbf{P}$. For the sake of illustration, we only treat the case that in the last step in $\mathcal{D}$ A is proved by an application of ($\vee$el) to the formula $B \vee C$ and two premiss proofs of A from B and C, respectively. Because of the restriction of this rule and by part (i) of the present theorem we have for each valuation V: $V(B) \sqsubseteq V(A)$ and $V(C) \sqsubseteq V(A)$, and thus (a) $V(B) \sqcup V(C) \sqsubseteq V(A)$. Furthermore, we have by the induction hypothesis that for all valuations V it holds that (b) $V(A) \sqcup V(B) = \top$ if $V(D) = \top$ for every $D \in M$. Obviously, by these two facts (a) and (b): If $V(D) = \top$ for every $D \in M$, then $V(A) = \top$, too. □

6.3.2 The Canonical Ackermann Lattice

Finally, we have a look at the pal which results from factoring our language $\mathcal{L}^+$ by the relation $\equiv$ of Definition 6.1.9. Firstly, we observe:

Lemma 6.3.4 The relation $\equiv$ is a congruence on $\mathcal{L}^+$.

PROOF: This is immediate from the two parts of Lemma 6.1.10. □

The equivalence class of a formula A *modulo* $\equiv$ is denoted by "[A]" and the factor algebra of $\mathcal{L}^+$ is called "$\mathcal{P}$" by us: $\mathcal{P} = (\mathrm{Form}_{\mathcal{L}^+}/_{\equiv}, [\Upsilon], \sqcap_{\mathcal{P}}, \sqcup_{\mathcal{P}}, \multimap_{\mathcal{P}})$. Lemma 6.3.4 allows us to define the operations of $\mathcal{P}$ as follows: $[A] \sqcap [B] =_{\mathrm{def}} [A \wedge B]$, $[A] \sqcup [B] =_{\mathrm{def}} [A \vee B]$, and $[A] \multimap [B] =_{\mathrm{def}} [A \rightarrow B]$. The ordering relation $\sqsubseteq_{\mathcal{P}}$ of the lattice $\mathcal{P}$ (defined in the usual way by: $x \sqsubseteq_{\mathcal{P}} y \Leftrightarrow_{\mathrm{def}} [C] \sqcap_{\mathcal{P}} [D] = [C]$ for some formula $C \in x$ and some formula $D \in y$) is determined by the derivability relation $\vdash_{\Sigma^+}$.

Lemma 6.3.5 $[A] \sqsubseteq_{\mathcal{P}} [B]$ iff $A \vdash_{\Sigma^+} B$.

PROOF: $[A] \sqcap_{\mathcal{P}} [B] = [A]$ iff both $A \wedge B \vdash_{\Sigma+} A$ and $A \vdash_{\Sigma+} A \wedge B$. Given ($\wedge$el$_\text{l}$), from the latter it follows that $A \vdash_{\Sigma+} B$. - Now, assume that $A \vdash_{\Sigma+} B$. Then we also have $A \vdash_{\Sigma+} A \wedge B$ because of $A \vdash_{\Sigma+} A$ and ($\wedge$int). Furthermore, the converse $A \wedge B \vdash_{\Sigma+} A$ is true by ($\wedge$el$_\text{l}$). □

With the help of this Lemma we easily see that $\mathcal{P}$ itself is a pal; we call it "the canonical pal".

Theorem 6.3.6 The factor algebra $\mathcal{P}$ is a pal.

PROOF: We have to show that the conditions of Definition 6.3.1 are fulfilled by $\mathcal{P} = (\text{Form}_{\mathcal{L}^+}/_{\equiv}, [\curlyvee], \sqcap_{\mathcal{P}}, \sqcup_{\mathcal{P}}, \multimap_{\mathcal{P}})$.

(i) Clearly, $[\curlyvee] \in \text{Form}_{\mathcal{L}^+}/_{\equiv}$.

(ii) It is readily seen that the lattice laws and the distributive laws are fulfilled. Furthermore, $A \vdash_{\Sigma+} \curlyvee$; thus $[A] \sqsubseteq_{\mathcal{P}} [\curlyvee]$. So $[\curlyvee]$ is the top element of this lattice.

(iii) (a) Assume that $[A] \sqsubseteq_{\mathcal{P}} [B]$; by Lemma 6.3.5 we have $A \vdash_{\Sigma+} B$, thus by Theorem 6.1.8-(ii) also $\curlyvee \vdash_{\Sigma+} A \to B$ and thus $\top \sqsubseteq_{\mathcal{P}} [A] \multimap [B]$. - (b) The conditions i.-v. follow easily with the help of A11, A8, A6, A7 and A10, Theorem 6.1.7-(i) and Lemma 6.3.5. □

Now we have:

Theorem 6.3.7

(i) If $M \models_{\{\mathcal{P}\}} A$, then $M \vdash_{\Sigma+} A$.

(ii) If $M \Vdash_{\{\mathcal{P}\}} A$, then the following holds true: if $\vdash_{\Sigma+} B$ for all $B \in M$, then $\vdash_{\Sigma+} A$.

PROOF: (i) Suppose that $M \models_{\{\mathcal{P}\}} A$. Then there is a set $\{B_1, ..., B_m\} \subseteq M$ such that for all $V \in \text{HOM}(\mathcal{L}^+, \mathcal{P})$ we have: $V(B_1) \sqcap ... \sqcap V(B_m) \sqsubseteq_{\mathcal{P}} V(A)$. Taking V as the natural homomorphism which maps each formula to its congruence class we get: if $[B_1] \sqcap ... \sqcap [B_m] \sqsubseteq_{\mathcal{P}} [A]$. This gives $B_1, \wedge ... \wedge B_m \vdash_{\Sigma+} A$ according to Lemma 6.3.5. By the elimination rules for $\wedge$ this yields $B_1, ..., B_m \vdash_{\Sigma+} A$ and thus $M \vdash_{\Sigma+} A$.

(ii) Assume $M \models_{\{\mathcal{P}\}} A$ and let $\mathrm{N} \in \mathrm{HOM}(\mathcal{L}^+, \mathcal{P})$ again be the natural homomorphism. Then we have: if $\mathrm{N}(B) = [B] = [\Upsilon]$ for all $B \in M$, then $\mathrm{N}(A) = [A] = [\Upsilon]$, too. Since for all formulas C $[C] = [\Upsilon]$ iff $\vdash_{\Sigma^+} C$, this means: if $\vdash_{\Sigma^+} B$ for all $B \in M$, then $\vdash_{\Sigma^+} A$, too. Thus $M \Vdash_{\Sigma^+} A$. □

KLAUS ROBERING
FB Informatik, Technische Universität Berlin
10587 Berlin, Germany
E-mail: krob@cs.tu-berlin.de

A virtually identical version of this paper has appeared in volume 11 (2001) of the **Journal of Logic and Computation**.

Bibliography

[1] Wilhelm Ackermann. *Ein System der typenfreien Logik*. Forschungen zur Logik und zur Grundlegung der exakten Wissenschaften. NF. Heft 7. Hirzel, Leipzig 1941. Reprinted (together with the other numbers of the series): Gerstenberg, Hildesheim, 1970.

[2] Wilhelm Ackermann. Widerspruchsfreier Aufbau der Logik I.Typenfreies System ohne *tertium non datur*. *The journal of symbolic logic*, 15 (1950), 33-57.

[3] Wilhelm Ackermann. Review of [12]. *The journal of symbolic logic*, 17 (1952), 266-268.

[4] Wilhelm Ackermann. Widerspruchsfreier Aufbau einer typenfreien Logik. (Erweitertes System). *Mathematische Zeitschrift*, 55 (1952), 364-384.

[5] Wilhelm Ackermann. Ein typenfreies System der Logik mit ausreichender mathematischer Anwendungsfähigkeit. *Archiv für mathematische Logik und Grundlagenforschung*, 4 (1958), 3-26.

[6] Wilhelm Ackermann. Grundgedanken einer typenfreien Logik. In: Y. Bar-Hillel, E. I. J. Poznanski, M. O. Rabin, and A. Robinson [eds.], *Essays on the foundations of mathematics. Dedicated to A. A. Fraenkel on his 70th anniversary*, Jerusalem, Magnes Press, 1961,143-155.

[7] Wilhelm Ackermann. Der Aufbau einer höheren Logik. *Archiv für mathematische Logik und Grundlagenforschung*, 7 (1965), 5-22.

[8] Arnon Avron. Gentzenizing Schroeder-Heister's natural extension of natural deduction. *Notre Dame journal of formal logic*, 31 (1990), 127-135.

[9] D. A. Bochvar. On a three-valued logical calculus and its application to the analysis of the paradoxes of the classical extended functional calculus. *Matématičéskij Sbornik* [in Russian], 4 (1938), 287-308. Engl. translation in: *History and philosophy of logic*, 2 (1981), 87-112.

[10] H. B. Curry. *Foundations of mathematical logic*, McGraw-Hill, Toronto, 1963.

[11] Kosta Došen. Sequent-systems for modal logic. *The journal of symbolic logic*, 50 (1985), 149-168.

[12] Frederic B. Fitch. *Symbolic logic. An Introduction.* The Ronald Press, New York, 1952.

[13] Viacheslav N. Grishin. A non-standard logic and its application to set theory. *Studies in Formalized Languages and Nonclassical logics* [in Russian]. Nauka, Moscow, 1974, 135-171.

[14] Grzegorz Malinowski. *Many-valued logics.* Oxford University Press, Oxford, 1993.

[15] John Myhill. Levels of implication. In: A. R. Anderson, R. Barcan Marcus, and R. M. Martin [eds.], *The logical enterprise*, Yale University Press, New Haven and London, 1975, 179-185.

[16] Witold A. Pogorzelski and Piotr Wojtylak. *Elements of the theory of completeness in propositional logic.* Silesian University, Katowice, 1982. [= Prace naukowe Uniwersytetu Slaskiego w Katowicach, 512.]

[17] Dag Prawitz. *Natural Deduction.* Almqvist and Wiksell, Uppsala, 1965.

[18] Vladimir V. Rybakov. *Admissibility of logical inference rules.* North-Holland Pub. Co., Amsterdam, 1997

[19] Peter Schroeder-Heister. A natural extension of natural deduction. *The journal of symbolic logic* 49 (1984), 1284-1300.

[20] Dana Scott. Rules and derived rules. In: S. Stenlund [ed.], *Logical theory and semantic analysis. Essays dedicated to Stig Kanger on his 50th birthday*, Reidel, Dordrecht, 1974, 147-161.

[21] D. J. Shoesmith and T. J. Smiley. *Multiple-conclusion logic.* Cambridge University Press, Cambridge, 1978.

[22] Thoralf Skolem. Bemerkungen zum Komprehensionsaxiom. *Zeitschrift für mathematische Logik und Grundlagen der Mathematik*, 3 (1957), 1-17.

[23] Franz von Kutschera. *Der Satz vom ausgeschlossenen Dritten. Untersuchungen über die Grundlagen der Logik.* Walter de Gruyter, Berlin, 1985.

[24] Ryszard Wójcicki. *Theory of logical calculi. Basic theory of consequence relations.* Kluwer, Dordrecht, 1988.

Chapter 7

Why Dialogical Logic?

HELGE RÜCKERT

The aim of this paper is to present the dialogical approach to logic as an interesting alternative to the model-theoretic approach. In the introduction I plead for pluralism concerning logical systems and logical methodology before giving a short outline of Dialogical Logic. Then, I discuss and reject several prejudices against Dialogical Logic. I present three conceptual distinctions that are characteristic of the dialogical approach to logic (namely, formal vs. general truth, level of games vs. level of strategies and particle rules vs. structural rules) and their fruitfulness for logical research is demonstrated at the hand of some examples.

7.1 Introduction

The title of this volume is *Essays on Non-Classical Logic.* Any logical system that differs from classical two-valued propositional and first order logic can be called non-classical, for example intuitionistic logic, modal logics, relevance logics and such-like. Non-classical logics in this sense are not the main issue of this paper, even though they play an important part in the argumentation.

Instead I consider different approaches to logic or logical methodology. The goal is to defend the dialogical approach, that – at present – seems to be of secondary interest in logical research.[1] I will try to show in what aspects the dialogical approach differs from other logical methods and what its advantages are.

A first dichotomy subdivides logical methodology into syntactic and semantic approaches. Prominent examples of the first are axiomatic systems and systems of natural deduction, while the model-theoretic or referential approach predominates the second category. In this dichotomy Dialogical Logic belongs – together with Hintikka's better known Game Theoretical Semantics[2] – to the semantic side as a version of game-theoretical logical methodology.

The goal of this paper is not to press the superiority of the dialogical approach to all other semantic methodologies, not even to claim that it alone should be used in future logical research. I will not only plead for pluralism concerning the different logical systems, but also for pluralism concerning the different logical methodologies. This means that it is appropriate to use different logical methods to pursue different aims. In my opinion, for many aims Dialogical Logic is a fruitful alternative to the common model-theoretic approach and it deserves more attention than it gets at present.

In the sequel I defend logical pluralism, and I give a short introduction to the dialogical approach. Furthermore some prejudices that are – among other things – responsible for the fact that Dialogical Logic often is completely unknown or considered exotic are corrected. Finally, some peculiarities and some resulting advantages of Dialogical Logic are discussed. I would be happy if this paper could contribute a little bit to change the uncaring attitude towards Dialogical Logic.

7.1.1 Pluralism Concerning Logics and Logical Methodology

I plead for logical pluralism, i.e. I think that among the different logical systems developed so far (and still to be developed), including classical logic, as well as the so-called non-classical logics, there is no system that represents the only correct logic. Thus I do not plead for a certain logic as intuitionistic logic, or a version of relevance logic, but for working with a multitude of formal instruments. Which logical system is the most adequate always depends on the context of application and on the purposes for which one wants to use

[1] There are some signs that the situation is changing and that there is a new start of research in Dialogical Logic (see Rahman/Rückert [30]).

[2] Hintikka's [12] treatment of branching quantifiers in his IF-Logic (independence friendly logic) receives considerable attention from logicians. It would be interesting to examine whether Hintikka's ideas can be reconstructed in dialogical terms.

the formal tools. Thus, different logical systems are formal instruments for different purposes.

The task of the logician should be – among other things – to develop many different interesting logical systems, in which the motivations and underlying ideas are formally worked out. Especially for these purposes I consider the dialogical approach to logic as very suitable, because it often provides the possibility to formally treat interesting ideas in a very simple way. Another advantage is that such formally treated ideas can often be easily combined.

But I do not want to voice the opinion that the dialogical approach provides the best of all available logical methodologies. Even on the methodological level the choice of tools depends on the purposes. Thus – in many contexts – it could be the best choice to use the model-theoretic approach, a Gentzen calculus or another logical method. However, I do think that Dialogical Logic is a fruitful alternative for logical research, especially for developing and combining new logics, and I think that it could be used fruitfully more often than is presently the case.

7.1.2 Dialogical Logic: A Short Outline

Dialogical Logic was suggested at the end of the 1950s by Paul Lorenzen and then worked out by Kuno Lorenz.[3] In a dialogue two parties argue about a thesis respecting certain fixed rules. The defender of the thesis is called Proponent (**P**), his rival, who attacks the thesis is called Opponent (**O**). Each dialogue ends after a finite number of moves with one player winning, while the other loses. The rules are divided into structural rules and particle rules. The structural rules determine the general course of a dialogue game, whereas the particle rules show which moves are allowed to attack the moves of the other player or to defend one's own moves.

a) Structural Rules

(SR 0) (starting rule):
The initial formula is uttered by **P**. It provides the topic of the argumentation. Moves are alternately uttered by **P** and **O**. Each move that follows the initial formula is either an attack or a defence.

(SR 1) (no delaying tactics rule):

[3]Some of the most important early texts about Dialogical Logic are collected in Lorenzen/Lorenz [17].

Both **P** and **O** may only make moves that change the situation.[4]

(SR 2) (formal rule):
P may not introduce atomic formulas, any atomic formula must be stated by **O** first.

(SR 3) (winning rule):
X wins iff it is **Y**'s turn but he cannot move (either attack or defend).

(SR 4i) (intuitionistic rule):
In any move, each player may attack a (complex) formula asserted by his partner or he may defend himself against the last attack that has not yet been answered.

or

(SR 4c) (classical rule):
In any move, each player may attack a (complex) formula asserted by his partner or he may defend himself against any attack (including those that have already been defended).[5]

b) Particle Rules

$\neg, \wedge, \vee, \rightarrow, \forall, \exists$	Attack	Defence
$\neg A$	A	$\otimes$ (No defence, only counterattack, possible.)
$A \wedge B$	?L(eft)	A
	?R(ight) (The attacker chooses.)	B

[4]This rule replaces Lorenz' *Angriffsschranken.* It still needs to be made clear on a formal basis.

[5]Both in SR 4i and SR 4c we have stated the so-called symmetric versions of these rules. It is possible to diminish the rights of **O** without any changes on the level of strategies in the following way: for **P** the rules remain unchanged, but **O** is only allowed either to defend himself against the last move of **P** or to attack this move. These versions of the rules SR 4i and SR 4c are called asymmetric, because now **P** has more rights than **O**.

$\neg, \wedge, \vee, \rightarrow, \forall, \exists$	Attack	Defence
$A \vee B$	?	A / B (The defender chooses.)
$A \rightarrow B$	A	B
$\forall_x A$	$?_n$ (The attacker chooses.)	$A[n/x]$
$\exists_x A$	?	$A[n/x]$ (The defender chooses.)

The given structural and particle rules define the intuitionistic (with SR 4i) and the classical (with SR 4c) dialogue games. Validity is defined as follows:

Validity (definition):
A formula is valid in a certain dialogical system iff **P** has a formal winning strategy for this formula. (To have a formal winning strategy means, that for any choice of moves by your opponent you have at least one possible move at your disposition, so that you finally win.)

It can be shown that with these rules and this definition of logical validity the same valid formulas are obtained as in the common approaches to logic. (To get intuitionistic logic use the intuitionistic rule, and to get classical logic use the classical rule.)[6]

[6]Such proofs can be found for example in Barth/Krabbe [1], in Krabbe [14], and in Rahman [22].

Example 1 (with either SR 4i or SR 4c):

	O			**P**	
				$((a \to b) \wedge a) \to b$	(0)
(1)	$(a \to b) \wedge a$	0		b	(8)
(3)	$a \to b$		1	$?L$	(2)
(5)	a		1	$?R$	(4)
(7)	b		3	a	(6)

P wins.

Example 2 (with SR 4c):

	O		**P**	
			$\forall_x(P_x \vee \neg P_x)$	(0)
(1)	$?_n$	0	$P_x \vee \neg P_x$	(2)
(3)	$?$	2	$\neg P_n$	(4)
(5)	P_n	4	$\otimes$	
(3′)	$?$	2	P_n	(6)

P wins.

Remarks concerning the examples:

Here, as in the following, very simple examples are chosen, so that with the help of just one dialogue it is easy to see whether **P** has a winning strategy for the formula in question or not. For example 1 it makes no difference whether you use SR 4i or SR 4c, but the formula in example 2 is only valid in classical logic.

Explication of the notation: The moves of **O** are written down in the **O**-column, the ones of **P** in the **P**-column. The numbers in brackets on the left and right margin represent the order in which the moves were made. Move number 0 is the thesis that is argued about in the dialogue. Attacks are characterised by numbers without brackets that indicate which move of the partner is attacked. Defences are always written down in the same line as the corresponding attacks. Such pairs of attacks and corresponding defences are called rounds.

(As you can see in example 2, when playing according to the classical rule, it is possible for **P** to defend himself again against an attack that has already been answered before. To note down this renewed defence, we repeat the corresponding attack, but please keep in mind, that this is not a move in the dialogue, but only a notational convention, which is indicated by an apostrophe as in (3') of example 2.)

7.2 Prejudices Against Dialogical Logic

Dialogical Logic is generally regarded as exotic and sometimes even completely unknown. Here, three prejudices that – among other things – have led to the fact that the dialogical approach is in this unfortunate situation will be formulated and then rejected.[7]

7.2.1 'Dialogical Logic is a Constructivistic Logic'

It is indeed correct that Dialogical Logic was developed in the context of the constructivist program of the so-called school of Erlangen, and that it was used in these surroundings to defend intuitionistic logic. But it is totally wrong to identify Dialogical Logic with intuitionistic or constructivistic logic. Instead, Dialogical Logic represents a general framework[8] within logical methodology, comparable to, say, Gentzen's sequent-calculus formulations, with the help of which classical, intuitionistic, and many other logics can be examined, just by using different dialogue rules. It seems that among the successors to the constructivistic school of Erlangen there is now a tendency to see Dialogical Logic as an inappropriate tool for the foundation (*Begründung*) of logic (see Hartmann [10]).

[7]There might be other prejudices against Dialogical Logic. For instance, it should not be concealed that dialogical logicians made some mistakes when working out and presenting their approach. Naturally these mistakes have had a negative influence on the reception of Dialogical Logic (see Felscher [6]), but mistakes can often be corrected and in a lot of cases this has already been done.

[8]'Framework' is here used in a non-technical sense, of course; I don't wish to propose Dialogical Logic as rival to, say, LF or ALF.

7.2.2 'Dialogical Logic is Limited to Classical and Intuitionistic Logic'

It is right that with some exceptions[9] the dialogical approach to logic was for a long time only worked out for classical and intuitionistic logic.[10] But in the last two years, together with Shahid Rahman, I have made several proposals to extend it to other logics, too. We have developed dialogical free, paraconsistent, modal, relevance and connexive logics.[11] We have shown that results that were reached within a model-theoretic framework, can also be obtained dialogically. But it is even more interesting that, using dialogical methods, it has been possible to treat of certain notions for which there was no perspicuous semantics, examples being certain systems of paraconsistent, relevance and connexive logics.

It is evident that these few papers about non-classical logics formulated within the dialogical framework cannot compete with the immense literature about non-classical logics treated with the help of model theory. But this does not imply that it would also be impossible to reach a comparable amount of interesting results with the dialogical approach,[12] if one invested as much time, work and money in such a kind of logical research.

7.2.3 'Dialogical Logic Complicates Things Unnecessarily'

It is correct that there are several distinctions in Dialogical Logic that cannot be found in other approaches to logic. But these distinctions do not complicate simple logical procedures essentially (for example the test whether a formula is valid in a certain logic still is a trivial matter in most cases), but they offer conceptual possibilities for certain purposes.

---

[9]Fuhrmann [7] for example presents a dialogical reconstruction of Anderson/Belnap's First Degree Entailment Logic and in Lorenzen [16] some steps towards dialogical modal logics can be found.

[10]Fuhrmann [7], p. 51 writes: "Die Diskussion um die Dialogische Logik ist bisher ausschließlich aus dem Blickwinkel klassischer bzw. konstruktiver Positionen geführt worden. Relevanzlogiken und parakonsistente Logiken sind nicht angemessen in Betracht gezogen worden."

[11]See Rahman/Rückert/Fischmann [31], Rahman/Carnielli [25], Rahman/Rückert [26], [27] and [29].

[12]One early interesting technical result obtained by using dialogical methods is Lorenz' proof of functional completeness of the intuitionistic connectives (Lorenz [15]), that differs considerably from the model-theoretic proof of McCullough [18]. A comparision of Lorenz' result with the proof-theoretic completeness theorems of Prawitz [20] and Zucker/Tragesser [35] might be of interest.

The impression that Dialogical Logic is unnecessarily complicated probably arises when one is not used to the dialogical approach. But with some training it is easy to see that playing dialogues and checking formulas for winning strategies is as easy as writing down truth-tables or Beth-tableaux. For some time students at Saarbrücken learned the dialogical approach simultaneously with the common model-theoretical approach to logic, and it is remarkable that at least when treating quantifiers most of them had less trouble whith the dialogical approach.

7.3 Advantages of Dialogical Logic

In Dialogical Logic there are several distinctions that are not available in other frameworks, for example in the model-theoretic approach. These distinctions offer interesting possibilities for logical research. In the sequel I present some examples.

7.3.1 The Distinction between General and Formal Truth

The standard defintion of logical truth or validity reads as follows: "A proposition A is logically true iff it is true under *all* interpretations." Thus, validity is usually seen as a generalisation of truth. It is also called 'formal truth', because it depends only on the logical form of the proposition in question and not on the interpretation of its constituents:

"The logical truths, then, are those true sentences which involve only logical words *essentially*. What this means is that any other words [...] can be varied at will without engendering falsity." (Quine [21], p. 110)

Now, if we turn to Dialogical Logic the concept of logical truth or validity can be split into two conceptually different notions, namely 'general truth', corresponding to the common conception, and 'formal truth', where 'formal' is understood in a strict sense.

Validity as General Truth

In Dialogical Logic we should think of truth as the existence of a winning strategy for **P**. To formulate validity as 'general truth' within the dialogical framework, we have to introduce so-called material dialogues by adding the following structural rule that replaces the formal structural rule:

SR 6 (rule for material dialogues):
Atomic formulas standing for true propositions may be uttered, atomic formulas standing for false propositions must not be uttered.

With the help of the following definition we have reached a dialogical reformulation of the common view of validity:

Validity as general truth (definition):
A formula is valid iff there is a winning strategy for **P** in every material dialogue about this formula. This means that **P** must have a winning strategy for this formula for each possibility of assigning truth-values to the atomic formulas.

Here, it makes no difference whether using the intuitionistic or the classical structural rule. In any case the resulting logic will be the classical one.[13] Please notice that when playing material dialogues it is always presupposed that all elementary propositions have a definite truth-value, namely 'true' or 'false'.

Validity as Formal Truth

This is different when we turn to the usual definition of validity in Dialogical Logic, namely validity as formal truth:

Validity as formal truth (definition):
A formula is valid iff there is a *formal* winning strategy for **P** in a dialogue about this formula. This means that **P** must have a winning strategy when the formal structural rule is in use.

This way of seeing validity differs conceptually from the common way, because here validity is not just general truth, validity does not just require the existence of winning strategies for **P** for a certain totality of dialogues, but the existence of a winning strategy for **P** in a certain kind of dialogue game, namely in a formal dialogue for the formula in question.

[13] Besides using the classical structural rule or working with material dialogues, there is a third possibility to reconstruct classical logic in the dialogical approach: A formula is valid in classical logic iff **P** has a formal winning strategy for it in intuitionistic dialogues with additional *tertium non datur* hypotheses.

Also, it is not presupposed that all elementary propositions have a truth-value, are either true or false. Thus, the dialogical concept of formality is stricter than the usual one: the form is not only independent of the truth or falsity of the elementary propositions, but it is even independent of whether the elementary propositions have truth-values.[14]

The fruitfulness of the distinction between formal and general truth still needs to be worked out in detail, but it should be obvious that it offers an interesting conceptual instrument for logical research.

7.3.2 The Distinction between the Level of Games and the Level of Strategies

The distinction between the level of dialogue games where questions of meaning and sense are located and the level of strategies where questions about truth and validity are located is not available in other semantic logical approaches. Usually the meaning of the connectives is defined by using concepts of correctness such as 'true' and 'false', for example. In dialogues it is possible that the players make moves that are bad moves from a strategic point of view, and a player may even lose who could have won if he had played in a different way. This acceptance of strategically bad moves on the level of games seems to be unnecessary, but this is not the case. The level of games is important, too, and stands in its own right.

As an example I will try to show that the distinction between the level of games and the level of strategies allows an almost trivial proof of the disjunctive property for dialogical intuitionistic logic. Usually this proof is rather complicated for Gentzen sequent-calculi that allow more than one formula on the right-hand side of a sequent, but when using dialogical methods it is not.

The disjunctive property of intuitionistic logic says that $A \vee B$ is valid iff A is valid or B is valid:

$$\models A \vee B \quad \Leftrightarrow \quad \models A \text{ or } \models B$$

The proof from the right to the left is unproblematic. If **P** has a formal winning strategy for A or for B, it is evident that he has a winning strategy for $A \vee B$: **P** starts the dialogue by stating the thesis $A \vee B$, and **O** attacks it with '?'. In order to win **P** then just has to choose the disjunct he has a winning strategy

[14] Thus with respect to the elementary propositions it is not required that there is either a winning strategy for **P** or for **O**. What is required is that there is a way of arguing about the elementary propositions. This means, they must have sense or meaning, but not necessarily a truth-value. (For the possibility in Dialogical Logic of separating the senses or meanings of propositions from their having truth-values see the next section.)

for. If he has a winning strategy for A (or B) he has to choose A (or B respectively) to answer **O**'s attack.

The proof from the left to the right seems much more difficult, but it also becomes almost trivial in Dialogical Logic, because of the distinction between the level of games and the level of strategies. On the level of games intuitionistic logic is characterised by the so-called intuitionistic structural rule:

(SR 4i) (intuitionistic rule):
In any move, each player may attack a (complex) formula asserted by his partner or he may defend himself against the last attack that has not yet been answered.

The crucial point of this rule with regard to the present argumentation is that **P** is not allowed to defend himself against an attack of **O** he has already answered, unless **O** renews his attack. In our example this means that **P** is not allowed to defend himself again with B (or A) against the attack '?' on $A \vee B$ if he has already defended himself with A (or B respectively).

Now we go to the level of strategies and recall thc definition of validity in the dialogical approach: A formula is valid iff **P** has a formal winning strategy for it. Thus, from the left to the right the metatheorem of the disjunctive property says, that if **P** has a winning strategy for $A \vee B$ he also has a winning strategy for at least one of the two disjuncts. And to have a winning strategy means for **P** that he is able to win the dialogue no matter how **O** plays.

If we look at the beginning of a dialogue with the thesis $A \vee B$, it is clear that the first move of **O** has to be the attack '?' and that **P** has to reply A (or B) in the second move. Now, the dialogue continues with an argumentation about A (or B respectively) alone, if **O** does not renew his attack on $A \vee B$. Consequently, if **P** has a winning strategy for $A \vee B$, he must also have a winning strategy for at least one of the two disjuncts alone, *quod erat demonstrandum.*

So we see that with the help of Dialogical Logic the proof of the disjunctive property of intuitionistic logic becomes almost trivial. It results directly from combining the intuitionistic structural rule on the level of games with the definition of validity that is formulated on the level of strategies. Here it is irrelevant whether we use the symmetric or the asymmetric structural rule. As strategy tableau-systems (i.e. decision methods for checking whether **P** has a formal winning strategy or not) for symmetric dialogues correspond to intuitionistic semantic tableau-systems for Gentzen sequent-calculi in which more than one formula on the right-hand side of a sequent is allowed, we have obtained – by using dialogical methods – a very easy proof of the disjunctive property, and, modulo the equivalence-proof concerning tableaux and dialogue-formulations, also for the Gentzen systems mentioned above.[15]

7.3.3 The Distinction between the Particle Rules and the Structural Rules

In Dialogical Logic the rules are divided into particle rules and structural rules. The particle rules determine for each logical particle how the corresponding formulas can be attacked and defended. The structural rules determine the general course of a dialogue.[16]

Now it is very interesting to see that you can get to different logical systems by only changing the set of structural rules while retaining the same set of particle rules. For example, dialogical classical and intuitionistic logic differ only in one structural rule, and you can get to a paraconsistent or a free logic by adding certain structural rules. Thus, the differentiation between particle rules and structural rules makes it very simple to generate new logics by combining certain structural rules.

The division into particle and structural rules is an essential feature also of Display Logic.[17] In Display Logic the idea that alternate systems are to be obtained by modifying structural rules against the background of a fixed set of connective rules is sometimes referred to as *Došen's Principle*:

"[T]he rules for the logical operations are never changed: all changes are made in the structural rules." (Došen [5], p. 353)

Thus, the proof-theoretic approach of Display Logic working with modifications of Gentzen style sequent-calculi and Dialogical Logic apply the same methodology for presenting non-classical logics and combinations of them. In this respect both could be seen as parts of a common enterprise. In any case, a detailed comparison of Dialogical Logic and Display Logic remains an interesting task.

Here, I will first present the main ideas of dialogical free, paraconsistent, modal and relevance logics, and then I will discuss the possibilities of combining

---

[15] This argumentation is worked out in detail in Rahman/Rückert [28]. This paper also includes a discussion of the philosophical background and consequences.

[16] Thus every rule governing a dialogue game that is no particle rule is called a structural rule. Perhaps it is appropriate to refine the category of structural rules, for example the class of formal rules (for atomic formulas, for attacking negations or for introducing new constants) seems to be of particular interest.

[17] Display Logic was inaugurated by Belnap [2]. Further work has been done for example by Wansing [33].

them.[18]

Dialogical Free Logic

The main idea of dialogical free logic is to make the quantifiers stronger so that they carry existential import: if a player in a dialogue uses a certain constant to defend an existential quantifier or to attack a general quantifier he simultaneously admits that this constant denotes an existing object. As in formal dialogues **P** is only allowed to use information that **O** has admitted first, we can add the following structural rule to our usual set of rules to define free (and inclusive) formal dialogue games:

SR 7 (formal rule for constants):
Only **O** may introduce constants. (A constant is introduced iff it is used for the first time to defend an existential quantifier or to attack a general quantifier.)

With the help of this rule we get a basic dialogical system of free logic.[19] A simple example shows that in the so defined dialogical free logic fewer formulas are valid than in non-free logics:

Example 3 (free logic):

	O		**P**	
			$P_n \to \exists_x P_x$	(0)
(1)	P_n	0	$\exists_x P_x$	(2)
(3)	?	2		

O wins.

P loses because he is not allowed to defend himself against the attack in move (3): no constant has been introduced so far. (Note that n has not been introduced even if it appears in the dialogue.)

[18] Dialogical connexive logic is not appropriate for my present purpose, because there not only the structural rules but also the particle rules, at least for the subjunction, have to be extended (see Rahman/Rückert [29]).

[19] This basic system is similar to some versions of so-called outer domain systems of free logic (see Bencivenga [3]), but it is inclusive, i.e. it allows the universe of discourse to be empty. It is also possible to invent more sophisticated dialogical free logics, for example with an indefinite number of pairs of quantifiers (see Rahman/Rückert/Fischmann [31]).

Dialogical Paraconsistent Logic

The main point concerning paraconsistent logics is that not every contradiction should make the whole system trivial. This means *ex falso sequitur quodlibet* should not be valid in general. In Rahman/Carnielli [25] several proposals for extending Dialogical Logic are made that lead to this effect. An interesting idea is that only contradictions on the atomic level should be excluded from implying anything.[20] For this purpose we have to add the following structural rule:

SR 8 (formal rule for negative literals):
P is allowed to attack the negation of an atomic formula iff **O** has attacked the same formula before.

Example 4 (paraconsistent logic):

	O			**P**	
				$(a \wedge \neg a) \to b$	(0)
(1)	$a \wedge \neg a$	0			
(3)	a		1	$?L$	(2)
(5)	$\neg a$		1	$?R$	(4)

O wins.

P loses because he is neither allowed to defend himself with b (because of SR 2) nor to attack $\neg a$ with a because **O** has not done the same before.

Dialogical Modal Logic

To get to dialogical modal logics it is not sufficient to change the set of structural rules, but here we have to introduce new particle rules for the modal operators 'necessary' and 'possible'. The new concept of a dialogue context

[20]One way to defend this approach is to distinguish between two sorts of negations, a negation *de re* and a negation *de dicto* (see Sinowjew [32]). If there is a contradiction with a negation *de dicto* (possible only on the atomic level), the system does not become trivial, because in dialogical paraconsistent logics such a contradiction gets isolated in a certain sense, so that it cannot be used to infer anything (see Rahman[24]). Wittgenstein is a precursor of such an idea: "You might get $p. \sim p$ by means of Frege's system. If you can draw any conclusion you like from it, then that, as far as I can see, is all the trouble you can get into. And I would say, "Well then, just don't draw any conclusions from a contradiction."" (Diamond [4], p. 220)

also has to be introduced.[21] In dialogical modal logics a dialogue game is played by stating formulas in different dialogue contexts. If a player states 'necessary-p' in a dialogue context n he commits himself to state p in all dialogue contexts that are admissible from n. Correspondingly, if a player states 'possible-p' he commits himself to defend p in at least one admissible dialogue context.

Particle Rules for the Modal Operators

$\Box$, $\Diamond$	Attack	Defence
$\Box A$ (in dialogue context α)	? (in an admissible dialogue context β, chosen by the attacker)	A (in β)
$\Diamond A$ (in dialogue context α)	? (in α)	A (in an admissible dialogue context β, chosen by the defender)

For each modal logic system we must determine by supplementary structural rules which dialogue contexts are admissible. In Rahman/Rückert [26] the dialogical approach to modal logics has been worked out for classical and intuitionistic versions of *T*, *B*, *S4* and *S5*. It should not be very difficult to reconstruct other modal logic systems by mere modifications of the structural rules.[22]

Dialogical Relevance Logic

In Rahman/Rückert [27] we have made a proposal for a very strict dialogical relevance logic (even uniform substitution is no longer valid).[23] In this case

[21] Dialogue contexts are the dialogical counterparts to possible worlds in model-theoretic modal semantics.

[22] Nortmann [19] presents a dialogical version of the modal logic system *G*.

[23] The name 'dialogical relevance logic' is perhaps misleading, because our system differs considerably from the usual systems called relevance logic. Our system is rather a formal

we get to this non-classical logic not by changing the set of rules on the level of dialogue games, but by formulating a criterion that the winning strategy of **P** has to fulfil: the winning strategy should contain no redundant parts.

Relevant validity (definition):
A formula is relevantly valid iff there is a formal winning strategy for **P** that contains no redundant parts (this means that **P** would have no winning strategy left if he didn't have all of his possible move choices at his disposition).

Example 5 (relevance logic):

	O			**P**	
				$(a \wedge b) \to b$	(0)
(1)	$a \wedge b$	0		b	(4)
(3)	b		1	$?R$	(2)

P wins (but not relevantly).

Even if **P** has a formal winning strategy for this formula, it is not relevantly valid, because he does not need to use the attack '?L' against move (1) of **O** to win.

Combinations of Logics

In dialogical free and paraconsistent logic only the set of structural rules was changed, in dialogical modal logic new particle rules and new structural rules had to be added and in relevance logic a new definition of relevant validity was introduced. But it is decisive for the possibility of combining different non-classical dialogical logics, that the changes are all at different locations in the dialogical framework, so that it is no problem at all to combine them. The ideas presented here already offer two in the fifth possibilities for different dialogical systems (please keep in mind that you can always choose between the intuitionistic and classical structural rule), for example intuitionistic non-free modal relevance logic or classical free non-modal relevance logic.

It is clear that not all of these different possibilities are equally interesting.

---

logical version of the well-known Gricean maxims for conversation (Grice [9]). It still needs to be examined whether commonly known systems of relevance logic can be formulated in dialogical terms by changing the set of structural rules. One step in this direction was taken by Fuhrmann [7].

Perhaps some of them do not have a field of application at all. But at least some of them seem to be very interesting: in Rahman [23] a combination of free and paraconsistent logics is proposed to treat fictional entities. This idea is worked out in more detail in Rahman [24], where a further combination with intuitionistic and classical features is developed: the players can argue classically with regard to existing objects but have to use the intuitionistic structural rule concerning fictions.

7.4 Concluding Remarks

With this paper I intended to defend the dialogical approach to logic in a general way rather than work out one dialogical logic system extensively. Thus a more detailed examination of every example and step in the argumentation was not possible. If the reader has the impression that many themes have not been treated in detail, he should have a look at the corresponding articles referred to in the text. In this paper it was my goal to correct some prejudices concerning Dialogical Logic and to stimulate more interest in it by presenting some possibilities for logical research that the dialogical approach offers.[24]

HELGE RÜCKERT
University of Saarbrücken, Institute of Philosophy
66041 Saarbrücken, Germany
E-mail: heru0001@stud.uni-sb.de

[24] I wish to thank Shahid Rahman (Saarbrücken), Goeran Sundholm (Leiden) and an anonymous referee for helpful suggestions, and Karl Hudson for correcting my English.

Bibliography

[1] Barth, E. and Krabbe, E., *From Axiom to Dialogue: A Philosophical Study of Logics and Argumentation*, Berlin, New York, 1982.

[2] Belnap, N., Display Logic, *Journal of Philosophical Logic*, 11 (1982), p. 375-417.

[3] Bencivenga, E., Free logics, in [8], p. 373-426.

[4] Diamond, C. (ed.), *Wittgenstein's Lectures on the Foundations of Mathematics*, Cornell University Press, 1976.

[5] Došen, K., Sequent Systems and Groupoid Models I, *Studia Logica*, 47 (1988), p. 353-389.

[6] Felscher, W., Dialogues as a Foundation for Intuitionistic Logic, in [8], p. 341-372.

[7] Fuhrmann, A., Ein relevanzlogischer Dialogkalkül erster Stufe, *Conceptus* XIX, Nr. 48 (1985), p. 51-65.

[8] Gabbay, D. and Guenthner, F. (eds.), *Handbook of Philosophical Logic*, Vol. III, Dordrecht, 1983.

[9] Grice, H., *Studies in the Way of Words*, Cambridge, 1989.

[10] Hartmann, D., Kulturalistische Logikbegründung, in [11], p. 57-128.

[11] Hartmann, D. and Janich, P. (eds.), *Die Kulturalistische Wende*, Frankfurt a. M., 1998.

[12] Hintikka, J., What is Elementary Logic? Independence-Friendly Logic as the True Core Area of Logic, in *Selected Papers, Vol. 3: Language, Truth and Logic in Mathematics*, Dordrecht, Boston, London, 1998, p. 1-27.

[13] Hintikka, J., Niiniluoto, I. and Saarinen, E. (eds.), *Essays on Mathematical and Philosophical Logic*, Reidel, Dordrecht, 1978.

[14] Krabbe, E., Formal Systems of Dialogue Rules, *Synthese*, Nr. 63 (3) (1985), p. 295-328.

[15] Lorenz, K., Dialogspiele als semantische Grundlage von Logikkalkülen, in [17], p. 96-162.

[16] Lorenzen, P., *Lehrbuch der kostruktiven Wissenschaftstheorie*, Mannheim, Wien, Zürich, 1987.

[17] Lorenzen, P. and Lorenz, K., *Dialogische Logik*, Darmstadt, 1978.

[18] McCullough, D., Logical Connectives for Intuitionistic Propositional Logic, *The Journal of Symbolic Logic*, Vol. 36 (1), 1971, p. 15-20.

[19] Nortmann, U., How to Extend the Dialogical Approach to Provability Logic, in [30], p. 95–103.

[20] Prawitz, D., Proofs and the Meaning and Completeness of the Logical Constants, in [13], p. 25-40.

[21] Quine, W., Carnap and Logical Truth, in *The Ways of Paradox and Other Essays* (revised and enlarged edition), Harvard University Press, 1976, p. 107-132.

[22] Rahman, S., *Über Dialoge, Protologische Kategorien und andere Seltenheiten*, Frankfurt a. M., 1993.

[23] Rahman, S., Hugh MacColl on Symbolic Existence: A Possible Reconstruction, *The Nordic Journal of Philosophical Logic*, Vol. 4 (2), 1999.

[24] Rahman, S., On Frege's Nightmare. A Combination of Intuitionistic, Free and Paraconsistent Logics, in [34], p. 55–80.

[25] Rahman, S. and Carnielli, W., The Dialogical Approach to Paraconsistency, *Synthese*, Nr. 125 (1/2) (2000), p. 201–232.

[26] Rahman, S. and Rückert, H., Dialogische Modallogik (für *T*, *B*, *S4* und *S5*), *Logique et Analyse*, in print.

[27] Rahman, S. and Rückert, H., Dialogische Logik und Relevanz, *FR 5.1 Philosophie, Universität des Saarlandes*, Memo Nr. 27, December 1998.

[28] Rahman, S. and Rückert, H., Die pragmatischen Sinn- und Geltungskriterien der Dialogischen Logik beim Beweis des Adjunktionssatzes, *Philosophia Scientiæ*, (3) 3, 1998-1999, p. 145-170.

[29] Rahman, S. and Rückert, H., Dialogical Connexive Logic, in [30], p. 105–139.

[30] Rahman, S. and Rückert, H. (eds.), *New Perspectives in Dialogical Logic,Synthese*, Nr. 127 (1/2) (2001).

[31] Rahman, S., Rückert, H. and Fischmann, M., On Dialogues and Ontology. The Dialogical Approach to Free Logic, *Logique et Analyse*, 167 (1997), p. 357–374.

[32] Sinowjew, A., *Komplexe Logik*, Berlin, 1970.

[33] Wansing, H., *Displaying Modal Logic*, Kluwer, 1998.

[34] Wansing, H. (ed.), *Essays on Non-Classical Logic*, World Scientific, Singapore, London, 2001.

[35] Zucker, J. and Tragesser, R., The Adequacy Problem for Inferential Logic, *Journal of Philosophical Logic*, 7, 1978, p. 501-516.

Chapter 8

Semantics for Constructive Negations

Yaroslav Shramko

"Was überhaupt die Welt bewegt, das ist der Widerspruch, und es ist lächerlich zu sagen, der Widerspruch lasse sich nicht denken" (G.W.F. Hegel)

I propose a new method of semantic analysis for intuitionistic logic in terms of intuitionistic state-descriptions. I consider a possibility of contradictory state-descriptions and show that such state-descriptions may be of use in defining a negation of an intuitionistic type. On this basis I develop a general Kripke-style semantic construction for a collection of systems for various kinds of constructive negation.

8.1 Preliminaries. A Hierarchy of Negations

I start with the positive logic **P** that has the following axiom schemes and a rule:

A1. $A \supset (B \supset A)$

A2. $(A \supset B) \supset ((A \supset (B \supset C)) \supset (A \supset C))$

A3. $A \supset (B \supset (A \& B))$

A4. $A \& B \supset A$

A5. $A \& B \supset B$

A6. $A \supset A \vee B$

A7. $B \supset A \vee B$

A8. $(A \supset C) \supset ((B \supset C) \supset ((A \vee B) \supset C))$

MP $A \supset B, A/B$.

The following extra schemes are needed for the other logics:

PL $((A \supset B) \supset A) \supset A$

RAA $(A \supset B) \supset ((A \supset \sim B) \supset \sim A)$

EFQ $\sim A \supset (A \supset B)$

TND $A \vee \sim A$

DNE $\sim\sim A \supset A$.

Curry in [3], chap. 6 considers five systems of *constructive* (as he says) negation. He characterizes negation in each system using the terms *refutability* and *absurdity*[1] (see [3], p. 261):

System **M** = **P** + RAA: minimal negation, or *simple refutability*;

System **I** = **M** + EFQ: intuitionistic negation, or *simple absurdity*;

System **D** = **M** + TND: strict negation, or *complete refutability*;

System **E** = **M** + PL: *classical refutability*;

System **C** = **M** + DNE: classical negation, or *complete absurdity*.

The system **M** was proposed by Johansson [8] as well as the system **D**. As to the system **E** (do not confuse it with a system of relevance logic **E** *of entailment*),

[1] My account of Curry's original consideration is modified in respect that Curry considers the Gentzen-style L-formulations of the systems, whereas I deal with Hilbert-style axiomatic formulations.

the story is more intricate. Došen (see [4] p. 27) refers to it as "Curry's system **E**". However, this expression is not quite accurate. According to Curry ([3], p. 306), the system was suggested by Bernays in his review [1]. Then, the H-formulation of this system was studied by Kanger in [9]. And, finally, Kripke made "an extensive study of it from the standpoint of an L-formulation" ([3], p. 306). Curry maintains that the labels "**LE**" and "classical refutability" are also due to Kripke, namely to his paper "The system LE" which seems to remain unpublished. Segerberg (see [13] p. 46) also points out that this system was treated by Kanger, and that the corresponding paper of Kanger contains a reference to an earlier discussion of the system by Bernays. He remarks that Kanger's reason for considering **E** is that "it constitutes a weakened classical calculus in the same sense as the minimal calculus is weakened intuitionistic calculus".

Thus, we arrive at a pretty nice picture: **M** is a weakening of **I** (in some sense of the term); **E** is a weakening of **C** (*in the same sense*); and **D** takes an intermediate position. That is, if to consider classical negation as the "utmost" (or "degenerate") case of a constructive negation (as Curry does), systems **M** - **C** constitute a collection of systems for various kinds of constructive negation. The connections between these systems can be described as follows: $\mathbf{M}_T \subset \mathbf{I}_T$, $\mathbf{I}_T \subset \mathbf{C}_T$, $\mathbf{M}_T \subset \mathbf{D}_T$, $\mathbf{D}_T \subset \mathbf{E}_T$, $\mathbf{E}_T \subset \mathbf{C}_T$, $\mathbf{D}_T \cap \mathbf{I}_T \neq \emptyset$, $\mathbf{E}_T \cap \mathbf{I}_T \neq \emptyset$. ($\mathbf{S}_T$ is the set of theorems of the corresponding system.)

8.2 Introduction. "Kripke-Approach" to Semantic Analysis

When Kripke [10] proposed his famous world-semantics for a collection of modal logics, one elegant peculiarity of this semantics drew general attention. The point of Kripke's semantic analysis is that the basic (normal) modal logic - the system **K** - has the most general model structure, and semantics for other systems are simply obtained by adding extra conditions to the **K**-model structure (on the binary relation R). This allows one to elucidate some essential features of these systems. The Routley-Meyer semantics for a collection of relevant logics can be constructed so that it also would enjoy the same elegant property (see, e.g., [12]). The model structure for the basic relevant logic **B** has in this case no conditions - as well as the model structure for **K** - and semantics for other relevant systems (**R**, **E**, etc.) can be "obtained by adding extra conditions on the ternary relation R". ([12], p. 217)

The aim of the present paper is to spread the "Kripke-approach" to semantic analysis on the above collection of systems of constructive negation. To this effect, I construct a special semantic structure, and it appears that the corresponding model for minimal logic has *no* conditions, whereas all the other systems can be obtained by adding some extra conditions (and these conditions are in harmony both with a general intuitionistic intuitive understanding of negation and with Curry's "refutability-absurdity" characterizations of negations in the corresponding systems).

My analysis correlates with the ones of [13] and [4]. It has, however, an essentially distinctive feature. Namely, it is based on a new semantic concept of ***intuitionistic state-description.*** Introducing this concept results in a new semantic construction which enjoys both a good intuitive background and a technical transparency. In the last section I shall clarify briefly the relationships between my approach and the ones of Segerberg and Došen.

8.3 Formal Definitions of Construction Negation and Informal Understanding of Negation in Intuitionism

A *Kripke-model* for intuitionistic logic (introduced in [11], a detailed account see also in [5]) is a triple $\langle W, R, \Vdash \rangle$, where W is a non-empty set of "possible worlds", R is *reflexive* and *transitive* relation on W, and $\Vdash$ is a *forcing relation* between worlds and sentences of the language satisfying the following condition (for $a, b \in W$ and p_i being a propositional variable):

Truth-preservation for atomic propositions :

$a \Vdash p_i$ and $Rab \Rightarrow b \Vdash p_i$.

For the purposes of the present paper the definition of forcing relation *for negation* is of especial interest. In the standard Kripke-model it is defined as follows:

Definition 8.3.1 $a \Vdash {\sim}A \Leftrightarrow \forall b(Rab \Rightarrow b \nVdash A)$.

Now consider a usual informal interpretation of the above Kripke-model. Taking into account Heyting's remark that intuitionistic logic is a *logic of knowledge*, it is quite natural to interpret sets of possible worlds as sets of theoretical constructions ("pieces of information" - if to use Urquhart's term from [21]).

In conformity with the "spirit of intuitionism", $a \Vdash A$ is to be understood as "A is constructively proved in the framework of theoretical construction a" (= "A is intuitionistically true"). Relation R is interpreted as a (possible) time-relation between theoretical constructions. That is Rab means that theoretical construction b is a result of a possible development of theoretical construction a.[2] In view of this interpretation the informal sense of definition 8.3.1 can be spelled out as follows: " $\sim A$ is proved in the framework of a iff in the framework of every possible construction b (which is a result of some development of the construction a) A is not proved, i.e. iff *A can never be proved*".[3]

But usual intuitionistic intuition about negation is not *exactly* this! It is very well-known that in intuitionism ~A is considered as true, if and only if assumption that A is true leads to a contradiction. For example, Heyting, considering intuitive understanding of mathematical (intuitionistical) propositions, writes:

> "In mathematical assertions ... 'not' has always the strict meaning. 'The proposition p is not true', or 'the proposition p is false' means 'If we suppose the truth of p, we are led to a contradiction'. ([7], p. 18)

And then:

> "Every mathematical assertion can be expressed in the form 'I have effected the construction A in my mind'. The mathematical negation of this assertion can be expressed as 'I have effected in my mind a construction B, which deduces a contradiction from the supposition that the construction A were brought to an end"'. ([7], p. 19)

Thus, one can assert that the Kripke-style definition for negation (definition 8.3.1) *does not reproduce* the usual intuitionistic informal understanding of negation-operator (although one can easily show that it is compatible with it). Therefore, one can consider some possible improvements (modifications) of this definition. One such modification has been suggested by Veldman in [22]. The main feature of his construction consists in introducing a notion of an *exploded world*: a is an exploded world, if and only if $a \Vdash \bot$ ($\bot$ satisfies the

[2] Cf. also the interpretation given by Fitting, who considered an intuitionistic model as a quadruple $\langle G, R, \models, P\rangle$: "$G$ is a collection of possible states of knowledge; any $\Gamma \models G$ may be considered to be a collection of physical facts. $\Gamma R \Delta$ means if now we know Γ, later we might know Δ ... $\Gamma \models X$ means that from the facts Γ we may deduce X." ([6], p. 220)

[3] By Fitting: " ... from the facts G we may conclude X if and only if from no possible additional facts can we conclude X". ([5], p. 21)

condition $\bot \supset A$ for every formula A). The negation in Veldman's semantic construction can be defined by

Definition 8.3.2 $a \Vdash {\sim}A \Leftrightarrow \forall b(Rab \Rightarrow (b \Vdash A \Rightarrow b \Vdash \bot))$.

Veldman uses his modification for an intuitionistic proof of the completeness-theorem. Exploded worlds are also investigated in [19], [20] and elsewhere.

Let mc interpret an exploded world as a contradictory theoretical construction (piece of information). Then it becomes clear that Veldman's modification is not only a "technical device" (as Veldman writes himself - see [22], p. 159), but an adequate reproduction of intuitionistic informal understanding of negation. Moreover, the point of the present paper is to show that the Veldman-style approach to defining negation together with construction semantics in terms of ***intuitionistic state-descriptions*** allows us to built up a general semantic structure for an intuitionistic collection of systems (up to classical logic) which, as I believe, has a natural intuitive background.[4]

8.4 State-Descriptions as a Method of Semantic Analysis. A Model for Positive Logic

State-descriptions as a method of semantic analysis have been proposed by Carnap for classical and modal logics. The method finds its sources in the Leibniz's idea of "possible worlds" on the one hand, and some ontological ideas of *Tractatus Logico-Philosophicus* on the other hand. As is well-known, the notion of fact is among the main notions of Tractatus. Facts form a structural basis of the World:

> "1 The world is everything that is the case.
> 1.1 The world is the totality of facts, not of things.
> 1.11 The world is determined by the facts, and by these being all the facts.
> 1.12 For the totality of facts determines both what is the case, and also all that is not the case.
> 1.13 The facts in logical space are the world.

[4]V. Markin drew my attention to the fact that the right-hand side of the definition 8.3.2 is equivalent to $\forall b(b \nVdash \bot \Rightarrow (Rab \Rightarrow b \nVdash A))$. That is, definitions 8.3.1 and 8.3.2 are equivalent with respect to normal worlds. However, if we allow non-normal (exploded) worlds, the things become different.

> 1.2 The world divides into facts.
>
> 1.21 Any one can either be the case or not be the case, and everything else remain the same."

This structure finds its quite precise reflection in the logical structure of our language, so that for every fact there is an (atomic) proposition which corresponds to this fact.

Carnap's state-descriptions is supposed to be a description of the world on the level of facts. Moreover, if we take into account a possibility of alternative developments of the world, we come to the idea of a set of possible state-descriptions. Now consider a definition of state-description which is "canonical" in the literature:

> "A state-description is a conjunction containing for every atomic statement either it or its negation but not both, and no other statements." ([2], p. 224)

A state-description is defined here as a *conjunctive sentence* of the form $\tilde{p}_1 \& \tilde{p}_2 \& \ldots \& \tilde{p}_n$ (where $\tilde{p}_i$ is a propositional variable or its negation).

It is not entirely clear what is the status of state-descriptions in Carnap's theory. On the one hand, Carnap evidently considered state-descriptions among "concepts and methods suitable for semantical analysis" ([2], p. 8). On the other hand, state-descriptions explicitly belong to the syntactical level of the language. Therefore, Carnap resorts to "multiplication of entities". He introduces the notion of "holding" side by side with "truth". Then he states: "a sentence holds in a state-description means ... that it would be true, if the state-description ... were true." ([2], p. 9) One can try to avoid this unwelcome multiplication and directly consider state-descriptions semantical entities. In this case the above definition would be incorrect from the methodological point of view, as by this definition state-descriptions include some elements of object language (e.g., conjunction). The usage of entities of object language as ingredients of semantic constructions evidently violates the demand of division between object language and metalanguage. A definition of the truth-conditions for conjunction would contain then a circle (as the state-descriptions that occur in the right-hand side of the definition include object-language conjunctions).

It is worth to mention that Carnap has proposed also another definition of state-descriptions:

> "A class of sentences ... which contains for every atomic sentence either this sentence or its negation, but not both, and no other sentences, is called a state-description..." ([2], p. 9)

The latter variant of definition has certain advantages in comparison with the former one. A state-description is defined here as a *set of sentences*. The object-language conjunction disappears in this way from the state-descriptions - a metalanguage comma is used instead. However, a questionable point remains here, which consists in the object-language *negation* that is still used by construction of state-descriptions. The critical remarks that have been made above concerning conjunction, can be reproduced also with regard to negation.

This means that even by the second definition, state-descriptions are not fully semantic constructions. If we wish to consider state-descriptions as a pure *semantic* background (foundation) for some logic, we have to eliminate all the object-language connectives from them.

The first suggestion that could be made, is to expel all the negations from the state-descriptions. In fact, this suggestion suits *positive logic* quite well. Let V^+ be the set of propositional variables $\{p_1, p_2, ..., p_n, ...\}$. Then *positive state-description* is a non-empty subset of V^+. A model for the positive logic **P** (**P**-model) is then a triple $\langle W, R, \Vdash \rangle$, where W is a non-empty set of positive state-descriptions, and R can be simply defined as set-theoretical inclusion ($\subseteq$).

Lemma 8.4.1 *The following hold for every* ***P****-model* $\langle W, R, \Vdash \rangle$ *and for every* a, b, *from* W:

(i) $p_i \in a$ *and* $Rab \Rightarrow p_i \in b$;

(ii) Raa;

(iii) Rab *and* $Rbc \Rightarrow Rac$.

The proof of this lemma is quite trivial.

Definition 8.4.2 $a \Vdash p_i \Leftrightarrow p_i \in a$;

Definition 8.4.3 $a \Vdash A\&B \Leftrightarrow a \Vdash A$ *and* $a \Vdash B$;

Definition 8.4.4 $a \Vdash A \vee B \Leftrightarrow a \Vdash A$ *or* $a \Vdash B$;

Definition 8.4.5 $a \Vdash A \supset B \Leftrightarrow \forall b(Rab \Rightarrow (b \Vdash A \Rightarrow b \Vdash B))$.

A is *verified* in a **P**-model $\langle W, R, \Vdash \rangle$ iff $a \Vdash A$ for all $a \in W$. A is **P**-*valid* iff A is verified in all **P**-models.

Theorem 8.4.6 *For every formula A: $a \Vdash A$ and $Rab \Rightarrow b \Vdash A$.*

The proof is easy, by induction on A.

8.5 Intuitionistic State-Descriptions. Models for Negation

As long as we stay within positive logic, we may easily ignore any negations - in or out of state-descriptions. Things become different, however, if we pass over to any of the systems **M** - **C** described above, for now we cannot simply avoid the problem of negation. Moreover, according to Wittgenstein's ideas, negation is an essential ingredient of the world's description on the level of facts. Hence, to be a complete description of the world, a state-description has to contain some kind of negation. Combining this point with the demand of division between metalanguage and object language, we arrive at the idea of using some sort of *metalanguage negation* within state-descriptions.

To realize this idea, I make use of Heyting's distinction between "mathematical" and "factual" negations. As this differentiation is extremely important in context of the present paper, I will wholly reproduce the corresponding passage from Heyting's work, although it will contain some repetitions of what was already said above (all italics are mine):

> "Strictly speaking, we must well distinguish the use of 'not' in mathematics from that in explanations which are not mathematical, but are expressed in ordinary language. In mathematical assertions no ambiguity can arise: 'not' has always the strict meaning. 'The proposition p is not true', or 'the proposition p is false' means 'If we suppose the truth of p, we are led to a contradiction'. But if we say that the number-generator ρ which I defined a few moments ago is not rational, this is not meant as a mathematical assertion, but as a *statement about a matter of facts*; I mean by it that as yet no proof for the rationality of ρ has been given. As it is not always easy to see whether a sentence is meant as a

> mathematical assertion or as a statement about the present state of our knowledge, it is necessary to be careful about the formulation of such sentences. Where there is some danger of ambiguity, we express the mathematical negation by such expressions as 'it is impossible that', 'it is false that', 'it cannot be', etc., while the *factual negation* is expressed by 'we have no right to assert that', 'nobody knows that', etc.
>
> There is a criterion by which we are able to recognize mathematical assertions as such. Every mathematical assertion can be expressed in the form: 'I have effected the construction A in my mind'. The mathematical negation of this assertion can be expressed as 'I have effected in my mind a construction B, which deduces a contradiction from the supposition that the construction A were brought to an end', which is again of the same form. On the contrary, the *factual negation* of the first assertion is: 'I have not effected the construction A in my mind'; this statement has not the form of a mathematical assertion." ([7], pp. 18-19).

To sum up: the *mathematical* negation is by Heyting the intuitionistic negation proper which can occur in intuitionistic theories. The *factual* negation is a metalanguage negation that belongs to a metalanguage used for describing intuitionistic theories. This *meta*language and its expressions can be non-constructive - as opposed to the expressions of an intuitionistic *object* language.

Consider some sentence A belonging to an intuitionistic theory. The informal intuitionistic interpretation of the sentence is - "A is (constructively) proved" (within the theory). The object-language (intuitionistic) negation of such a proposition has to be expressed in the form "A is refuted", or - as was noticed above - "assertion of A leads to a contradiction". A metalanguage (factual) negation of the proposition is, as against, simply "A is not proved" (or "I have not effected the construction A in my mind").

This distinction between two sorts of negation constitutes the basis of the notion of *intuitionistic state-description* which I propose.[5] Let me mark the intuitionistic negation with "$\sim$", and the factual negation with "$\neg$". Let V^+ be as in section 4, and let V^- be the set of the propositional variables taken with factual negations $\{\neg p_1, \neg p_2, ..., \neg p_n, ...\}$. Then an *intuitionistic state-description* (i.s.d.) a is a subset of $V^+ \cup V^-$, satisfying the following condition: for every p_i

[5]What I call here "intuitionistic state-description" has been introduced in [17] under the name "real intuitionistic state-description".

$$p_i \in a \text{ or } \neg p_i \in a. \tag{a}$$

If we turn to informal understanding of intuitionistic state-description, it can be interpreted as a partial (on the level of atomic sentences) metadescription of a state of some intuitionistic theory (at some moment). Roughly speaking, expression $p_i \in a$ (a is some i.s.d.) means that p_i is proved in the theory which is determined by a (or in the moment a), and $\neg p_i \in a$ means that p_i is not proved in the corresponding theory (or at the corresponding moment).

Note, that condition (a) demands that i.s.d. must be *complete* with respect to factual negation. Now the problem of inconsistency arises: it is *not* generally required that any i.s.d. has to be *consistent* with respect to factual negation, that is I do not take the condition

$$p_i \notin a \text{ or } \neg p_i \notin a. \tag{b}$$

This may seem to be very strange: taking into account the underlying intuitive interpretation, this means that a situation can appear, when some sentence *is* and *is not* proved simultaneously. How can it be? Some primary intuitive ideas - first of all the law of contradiction - seem to be afforded. I believe, however, that this situation can be explained in an intuitively satisfactory way, and this can be done just in accordance with the Heyting's understanding of intuitionistic (mathematical) and factual negations, and my interpretation proposed above.

Let us first spell out the meaning of the expression $p_i \in a$. It means that a proof of p_i (in theory a) is given, that is - according to the tradition - there is a sequence of sentences such that any sentence from the sequence is either an axiom of a, or is obtained by inference rules, and the last sentence of the sequence is p_i. An intuitionistic theory is inconsistent iff there is a sentence A, such that A is proved in it, and $\sim A$ is proved in it. Consider now a theory which is contradictory *with respect to* p_i. That is, the proofs of p_i and $\sim p_i$ in the theory are given. Hence, there is a sequence of sentences such that any sentence from the sequence is either an axiom of a theory, or is obtained by an inference rule, and the last sentence of the sequence is p_i, *and* there is a sequence of sentences such that any sentence from the sequence is either an axiom of a theory, or is obtained by an inference rule, and the last sentence of the sequence is $\sim p_i$. But the last observation means that *in fact* p_i is not proved, i.e. that the above mentioned "proof" (sequence of sentences) for p_i *proves nothing.* However, this "proof" is *still present* (as long as our theory is contradictory)! Thus, we have in a sense quite ambiguous (meta)theoretical situation - *formally* we *have* a proof of p_i, but this proof does not prove p_i, so, *actually*, we *do not have* a proof of p_i. And this is as it should be, because our theory is contradictory, and we naturally should expect that the corresponding description of the theory somehow reflects this inconsistency. On the level of intuitionistic state-descriptions this situation is presented by a contradictory i.s.d. $\{p_i, \neg p_i\}$, and this i.s.d. perfectly describes the situation we have in the case of contradictory theory: we have a "proof" of p_i, but this *does not mean at all* that p_i is "really" proved.

This argument can be easily reconstructed so that it does not contain any explicit reference to object-language negation. Let us take (as Heyting does) the notion of contradiction as a primitive notion, and let us define a contradictory theory as a theory that includes some self-contradictory sentence (e.g., $1 = 2$) as a theorem. Again, if a sentence p_i is proved in such a theory, then, of course, we do have a formal proof of p_i, but nevertheless, we cannot seriously state, that p_i is really proved (because the theory, where the proof of p_i is given, is contradictory and as such incredible).

We should clearly distinguish between two different meanings of the expression "p_i is proved" - the *formal* one and the *real* one. From a formal point of view to say "p_i is proved" means to say "there is a sequence of sentences such that ... etc." (as above). But if an intuitionist says "p_i is proved" (having in mind a real meaning of the term) she/he means that p_i is *intuitionistically true* (and this of course cannot be the case, when p_i is self-contradictory). These two meanings do not coincide, but they also are not incompatible. Any contradictory i.s.d. provides a construction where both meanings can be combined. If we have $\{p_i, \neg p_i\}$, it simply means: "Although we have a formal "proof" of p_i, nevertheless p_i is not true (because the theory, where the "proof" was given, is contradictory)".

This distinction can also be explicated as a distinction between a *weak* notion of proof (a formal proof in the theory is given), and a *strong* notion of proof (a formal proof in the theory is given, *and* the theory is consistent). Correspondingly, the expression "p_i is not proved" can be used in two senses: either (1) there is no formal proof of p_i in the given theory, or (2) there is no formal proof of p_i in the given theory, *or* the theory is inconsistent[6]. The second meaning reflects an understanding that *any formal proof of p_i in a contradictory theory is not a real proof.* Let me interpret (1) using the terminology of intuitionistic state-descriptions as $p_i \notin a$, and let $\neg p_i \in a$ stands for (2). It is clear that (1) $\Rightarrow$ (2), but not *visa versa*! This is why we take the condition (a) but do

[6]Here, as well as in all the other corresponding places, one has to add "with respect to p_i" so that the strong concept of proof works also in case of logics where EFQ is not valid (e.g. in relevant logics). Sometimes I omit these words for the sake of simplicity of exposition.

not take (b). Now, let me interpret a contradictory i.s.d. so that if we have $\{p_i, \neg p_i\}$, then p_i is taken in the weak sense, but $\neg p_i$ is taken in the strong sense. Combining these two meanings (a proof in the theory is given and [there is no proof of p_i in the given theory, or the theory is inconsistent]) we immediately get a result that the theory is inconsistent! Thus, $\{p_i, \neg p_i\}$ is an adequate representation (on the level of state-descriptions) of a contradictory intuitionistic theory.[7]

One may notice that there is an ambiguity in this interpretation of factual negation. For, when - in the case of contradictory theory - we say that p_i is not proved, we mean something different as a simple absence of the corresponding sequence of sentences. The ambiguity arises as a difference between "formal" and "informal" (or weak and strong) interpretations of the expressions. However, this ambiguity reflects an essential feature of factual negation, and reproduces Heyting's understanding of factual negation. Heyting characterizes the mathematical negation as such that "always has a strict meaning", because "in mathematical assertions no ambiguity can arise" - *contrary to factual negation.* Thus, interpretation of factual negation can involve some ambiguity[8] (especially in the case, when our theory is inconsistent!).

One may also say that *in fact* contradictory intuitionistic state-descriptions under such an interpretation are not contradictory at all. Yes, they are not. I would like to stress that "contradictory" intuitionistic state-descriptions are not contradictory themselves, they only represent the contradictory theories. An i.s.d. a would have been *really* contradictory, if we would have $p_i \in a$ and $p_i \notin a$. But this is impossible, because the whole semantic construction would have turned then into nonsense. Introduction of factual negation helps to solve a sophisticated technical problem - to represent inconsistent theories in a non-contradictory way. In other words, the factual negation proves to be a very suitable technical tool for representing inconsistent theories on the semantic level.

Notice that the interpretation of factual negation given above perfectly corresponds to Heyting's understanding of the factual negation. Heyting writes that factual negation can be expressed as "we have no right to assert that". But this is exactly the case (2) described above - we have no right to assert p_i iff either no proof of p_i is given or a proof is given in a contradictory theory.

A *general model for negation* (**G**-model) is a **P**-model constructed on the basis of intuitionistic state-descriptions, and can be defined as a triple $\langle W, R, \Vdash \rangle$, where W is a non-empty set of intuitionistic state-descriptions, and R is a

[7]For more detailed explanations on this matter see in [16]

[8]This is a kind of "systematic ambiguity" (cf. [18], p. 33).

binary relation on W defined as follows:

Definition 8.5.1 $Rab \Leftrightarrow a^+ \subseteq b^+$ *[a^+ (b^+) is the "positive" part of a (b), i.e. a^+ (b^+) is that and only that part of a (b) which consists of the variables without factual negations].*[9]

It easy to see that lemma 8.4.1 holds for **G**-models as well. Let me adopt the definitions 8.4.2 - 8.4.5 above. Then the theorem 8.4.6 also holds.

8.5.1 The System M

Now I am in a position to introduce the notion of a *contradictory i.s.d. a* ($con(a)$) formally. This may be done by means of the following definition:

Definition 8.5.2 $con(a) \Leftrightarrow \exists p_i (p_i \in a$ *and* $\neg p_i \in a)$.[10]

M-model can be obtained by adding to **G**-model a valuation clause for negation:

Definition 8.5.3 $a \Vdash {\sim}A \Leftrightarrow \forall b(Rab \Rightarrow (b \Vdash A \Rightarrow con(b)))$.

By means of definition 8.5.3 a minimal negation (simple refutability, in Curry's terms) is defined, and this definition *literally* reproduces the intuitive sense of this negation: ${\sim}A$ is true iff an assumption that A is true leads us to *some* contradiction. It is easy to see that ${\sim}A \supset (A \supset B)$ is not **M**-valid, whereas ${\sim}A \supset (A \supset {\sim}B)$ is.

8.5.2 The System I

The observation above may seem to be a surprise, as we might expect to get the negation of intuitionistic calculus, but got "only" the minimal negation. It

[9] Some deep philosophical considerations demand that condition $b^- \subseteq a^-$ should be added to the right-hand side of this definition. However, it appears that *purely technically* the condition $a^+ \subseteq b^+$ is enough for formulating semantics for constructive negations. Nevertheless, when we wish to continue the analysis of the present paper and to involve also incomplete intuitionistic state-descriptions for developing a *relevant intuitionistic logic*, the condition $b^- \subseteq a^-$ becomes necessary (cf. [15], p. 49).

[10] Heyting writes that "contradiction must be taken as a primitive notion. It seems very difficult to reduce it to simpler notions..." [7], p. 98. However, one can see that constructing semantics in terms of intuitionistic state-descriptions allows to introduce the notion of contradiction by definition.

appears that if we wish to have the real Heyting's "mathematical" negation, we have to introduce the notion of an *absolutely contradictory i.s.d.* a ($abcon(a)$):

Definition 8.5.4 $abcon(a) \Leftrightarrow \forall p_i(p_i \in a \text{ and } \neg p_i \in a)$.

I-model is obtained from **M**-model by adding the following extra condition:

Condition 8.5.5 $\forall a \in W(con(a) \Rightarrow abcon(a))$.

Thus, definition 8.5.3 turns into

Definition 8.5.6 $a \Vdash {\sim}A \Leftrightarrow \forall b(Rab \Rightarrow (b \Vdash A \Rightarrow abcon(b)))$.

This definition corresponds to Curry's characterization of negation of the system **I** as "simple absurdity": if we suppose that A is true, we come to the absurd. Note, that I do not take the so-called "hereditarity condition" for inconsistent worlds as, e.g. Segerberg ([13], p. 20) does, neither for **M**-models, nor for **I**-models. For **M**-models it is not needed at all, for **I**-models its "job" does the theorem 8.5.8 below.

Lemma 8.5.7 *For every **I**-model:* $\forall a \in W(\text{not } con(a) \Leftrightarrow \text{not } abcon(a))$.

Proof is very easy.

Theorem 8.5.8 *For every formula* A*:* $\forall W \forall a \in W(abcon(a) \Rightarrow (\forall b(Rab \Rightarrow abcon(b)) \Rightarrow a \Vdash A))$.

Proof. By an induction on construction of the formula A.

Consider an arbitrary i.s.d. a such that $abcon(a)$ and $\forall b(Rab \Rightarrow abcon(b))$.

Let A be a propositional variable p_i. Then, by definition 8.5.4, $p_i \in a$, and by definition 8.4.2 $a \Vdash p_i$.

If A has the form $B \& C$ or $B \vee C$, proof is easy.

Let A be $B \supset C$, and $a \Vdash B$ and $a \Vdash C$ (Induction Hypotheses). By theorem 8.4.6 (which holds for **I**-models too), $\forall b(Rab \Rightarrow b \Vdash B)$ and $\forall b(Rab \Rightarrow b \Vdash C)$. Hence, $\forall b(Rab \Rightarrow (b \Vdash B \text{ and } b \Vdash C))$, hence, $\forall b(Rab \Rightarrow (b \Vdash B \Rightarrow b \Vdash C))$. By definition 8.4.5, $a \Vdash B \supset C$.

Let A be $\sim B$, and $a \Vdash B$ (IH). By theorem 8.4.6, $\forall b(Rab \Rightarrow b \Vdash B)$. But $\forall b(Rab \Rightarrow abcon(b))$. Hence, $\forall b(Rab \Rightarrow (b \Vdash B$ and $abcon(b)))$, hence $\forall b(Rab \Rightarrow (b \Vdash B \Rightarrow abcon(b)))$. By definition 8.5.6 $a \Vdash \sim B$.

■

Thus, whereas minimal logic allows a coexistence of different contradictory theories, this is impossible within intuitionistic logic. In **M**-models two intuitionistic state-descriptions can be contradictory in their different aspects (parts), in **I**-models there can be only one contradictory i.s.d. - the absolutely contradictory one. This is the difference between *a* contradiction and *the* contradiction which reflects some important intuitive motivations that underlies minimal and intuitionistic logics.

8.5.3 The System D

D-model is obtained from **M**-model by adding

Condition 8.5.9 $\neg p_i \in a$ *and* $Rab \Rightarrow \neg p_i \in b$.

Valuation Clause for **D**-negation (complete *refutability*) is definition 8.5.3.

In system **D** (as well as in **M** and **I**) formula $\sim\sim p_1 \supset p_1$ (DNE) is not a theorem. DNE can be refuted, e.g. in the following **M** and **I**-model:

$W' = \{a, b\}$; $a = \{\neg p_1\}$, $b = \{p_1\}$.

Then $a \nVdash \sim\sim p_1 \supset p_1$. But this is not a **D**-model, because condition 8.5.9 requires that b should be $\{p_1, \neg p_1\}$. Unfortunately, in this case $a \Vdash \sim\sim p_1 \supset p_1$. However, there exists a **D**-model in which DNE is refuted:

$W'' = \{a\}$; $a = \{\neg p_1, p_2, \neg p_2\}$.

Then $a \nVdash \sim\sim p_1 \supset p_1$. It will be shown bellow that TND is valid in all **D**-models.

Lemma 8.5.10 *For all* **D**-*models:* Rab *and not* $con(b) \Rightarrow Rba$.

Proof. Let Rab and not $con(b)$. Suppose not Rba, i.e. $b^+ \subsetneq a^+$, i.e. $\exists p_i(p_i \in b$ and $p_i \notin a)$. If $p_i \notin a$, then, by condition (a), $\neg p_i \in a$. By condition 8.5.9, $\neg p_i \in b$. Hence, b is contradictory. A contradiction.

■

Thus, we can see that in **D**-models relation R is not only reflexive and transitive, as in **M** and **I**-models (lemma 8.4.1), but also symmetric *subject to the condition that accessible world is not contradictory.*

Theorem 8.5.11 *For every formula A: $a \nVdash A$ and Rab and not $con(b) \Rightarrow b \nVdash A$.*

Proof. Consider an arbitrary A such that $a \nVdash A$, and Rab, and not $con(b)$. By the lemma 8.5.10, Rba. Suppose $b \Vdash A$. Then, by theorem 8.4.6 $a \Vdash A$. A contradiction. Hence, $b \nVdash A$.
■

8.5.4 The System E

There is an interesting question, whether the absolutely contradictory world can have another usage except of definition for negation of Heyting's system **I**. This question can be answered in the affirmative.

E-model is obtained from **M**-model by adding

Condition 8.5.12 *$a \neq b$ and $Rab \Rightarrow abcon(b)$.*

In **E**-models the condition 8.5.5 is not taken, and the negation of system **E** is defined by the definition 8.5.3. Thus, system **E** represents a logic of *stable knowledge.* The informal sense of condition 8.5.12 is the following: there is no possibility for the knowledge development, because any attempt of such a development collapses into an absolutely contradictory theoretical construction.[11] But negation in **E** is still nonclassical and intuitionistic-type, because DNE is refuted in the above **D**-model W'' which is an **E**-model as well.

Lemma 8.5.13 *For all **E**-models: $abcon(a)$ and $Rab \Rightarrow abcon(b)$.*

Proof. Obviously follows from condition 8.5.12 and lemma 8.4.1(2).
■

Lemma 8.5.14 *For all **E**-models: Rab and not $abcon(b) \Rightarrow Rba$.*

[11] Further informal considerations of the intuitive foundations of the system **E** as well as of some other systems can be found in [14].

Proof. Let Rab and not $abcon(b)$. Suppose not Rba. That is, there exists a propositional variable p_i , such that $p_i \in b$ and $p_i \notin a$. Thus, a differs from b, hence, by condition 4.11, $abcon(b)$. A contradiction. Hence, Rba.

■

Notice, that for **E**-models lemma 8.5.10 is easily proved without using condition 8.5.9, for not $con(b) \Rightarrow$ not $abcon(b)$. Thus, the set of **D**-models is a subset of the set of **E**-models.

Theorem 8.5.15 *For all* **E***-models, for every formula A:* $abcon(a) \Rightarrow a \Vdash A$.

Proof. Induction on A. Cases when A is a propositional variable, or has the form $B\&C$, or $B \vee C$, or $B \supset C$ are the same as in theorem 8.5.8. Consider the case, when A is $\sim B$ and $a \Vdash B$ (Induction Hypotheses). By lemma 8.5.13 $\forall b(Rab \Rightarrow abcon(b))$, and by theorem 8.4.6 $\forall b(Rab \Rightarrow b \Vdash B)$. But $abcon(b) \Rightarrow con(b)$ (by definitions 8.5.2 and 8.5.4). Hence, $\forall b(Rab \Rightarrow (b \Vdash B \Rightarrow con(b)))$, i.e. $a \Vdash \sim B$.

■

8.5.5 The System C

Remember the remark of Segerberg that the system **E** is a weakened classical calculus *in the same sense* as the minimal calculus is weakened intuitionistic calculus. This remark gives us a key for obtaining a model for the system **C**.

C-model = **E**-model + condition 8.5.5.[12]

Thus, within **C**-models we do not have simple contradictory worlds and the valuation clause for classical negation is definition 8.5.6 (classical absurdity!). It is easy to see that lemma 8.5.7 and theorem 8.5.8 hold for all **C**-models.

8.5.6 Propositional Constants

To conclude the section, I would like to point out that the above construction allows us to give an interesting interpretation of some well-known propositional constants. Minimal and intuitionistic logics are often formulated by means of introducing a constant "falsity" or "absurdity" ($\bot$) as a primitive notion, and defining negation as $\sim A \Leftrightarrow A \supset \bot$. However, not many authors make a clear

[12]Another way to get **C**-model is **I**-model + condition 8.5.9.

distinction between the notions of falsity and absurdity (and the corresponding constants), using them as synonyms.

Now, let **f** be the propositional constant of falsity, and $\bot$ - of absurdity. The truth-conditions for these constants can be defined as follows:

Definition 8.5.16 $a \Vdash \mathbf{f} \Leftrightarrow con(a)$.

Definition 8.5.17 $a \Vdash \bot \Leftrightarrow abcon(a)$.

These definitions show what the difference between the constants consists of, and explain their informal meanings. These constants represent different kinds of contradictory theories: **f** stands for simple contradictory theoretical constructions, and $\bot$ - for the absolutely contradictory one. Then by $\sim A \Leftrightarrow A \supset \mathbf{f}$ the minimal negation (refutability) is defined, and by $\sim A \Leftrightarrow A \supset \bot$ - the intuitionistic negation (absurdity).

8.6 Soundness

Theorem 8.6.1 *If formula A is (**M**, **I**, **D**, **E**, **C**)-theorem, then it is valid in the corresponding (**M**, **I**, **D**, **E**, **C**)-model.*

Proof. All the axiom schemes A1 - A8 are valid in **G**-model (hence, in (**M**, **I**, **D**, **E**, **C**)-models) and *modus ponens* preserves **G**-validity (hence, (**M**, **I**, **D**, **E**, **C**)-validity).

Consider RAA. Suppose it is not **M**-valid. Then $\exists W \exists a \in W$ such that $a \nVdash (A \supset B) \supset ((A \supset \sim B) \supset \sim A) \Leftrightarrow \exists W \exists a \in W \exists b(Rab$ and $b \Vdash A \supset B$ and $b \nVdash (A \supset \sim B) \supset \sim A \Leftrightarrow \exists W \exists a \in W \exists b(Rab$ and $\forall c(Rbc \Rightarrow (c \Vdash A \Rightarrow c \Vdash B))$ and $\exists c(Rbc$ and $c \Vdash A \supset \sim B$ and $c \nVdash \sim A)) \Leftrightarrow \exists W \exists a \in W \exists b(Rab$ and $\forall c(Rbc \Rightarrow (c \Vdash A \Rightarrow c \Vdash B))$ and $\exists c(Rbc$ and $\forall d(Rcd \Rightarrow (d \Vdash A \Rightarrow \forall g(Rdg \Rightarrow (g \Vdash B \Rightarrow con(g)))))$ and $\exists d(Rcd$ and $d \Vdash A$ and not $con(d)))$. Consider these b, c and d. Since Rbc and Rcd, by lemma 8.4.1, Rbd. Hence, $d \Vdash A \Rightarrow d \Vdash B$. Since Rdd (lemma 8.4.1) we have $d \Vdash B \Rightarrow con(d)$. We have $d \Vdash A$, hence, $con(d)$. A contradiction. Hence, RAA is **M**-valid, so, it is (**I**, **D**, **E**, **C**)-valid.

Consider EFQ. Suppose it is not **I**-valid. That is, $\exists W \exists a \in W(a \nVdash \sim A \supset (A \supset B))$. That is, $\exists W \exists a \in W \exists b(Rab$ and $b \Vdash \sim A$ and $b \nVdash A \supset B) \Leftrightarrow \exists W \exists a \in W \exists b(Rab$ and $\forall c(Rbc \Rightarrow (c \Vdash A \Rightarrow abcon(c)))$ and $\exists c(Rbc$ and $c \Vdash A$ and $c \nVdash B))$. Consider these a, b and c. We have $c \Vdash A \Rightarrow abcon(c)$ and

$c \Vdash A$ and $c \nVdash B$. Consider an arbitrary d such that *Rcd*. By theorem 8.4.6 $d \Vdash A$. By lemma 8.4.1(3) *Rbd*. Hence, *abcon*(d), i.e. $\forall d$(*Rcd* $\Rightarrow$ *abcon*(d)). We have *abcon*(c), hence, by theorem 8.5.8, for every formula B, $c \Vdash B$. A contradiction. Thus, EFQ is **I**-valid.

Consider TND. Suppose, it is not **D**-valid. That is, $\exists W \exists a \in W(a \nVdash A \vee {\sim}A) \Leftrightarrow \exists W \exists a \in W(a \nVdash A$ and $a \nVdash {\sim}A) \Leftrightarrow \exists W \exists a \in W(a \nVdash A$ and $\exists b$(*Rab* and $b \Vdash A$ and not *con*(b))). Consider these a and b. By lemma 8.5.10, *Rba*. By theorem 8.4.6 $a \Vdash A$. A contradiction. Hence, TND is **D**-valid.

Consider PL. Suppose it is not **E**-valid, i.e. $\exists W \exists a \in W(a \nVdash ((A \supset B) \supset A) \supset A)$. Hence, $\exists W \exists a \in W \exists b$(*Rab* and $b \Vdash (A \supset B) \supset A$ and $b \nVdash A$). But $b \Vdash (A \supset B) \supset A \Leftrightarrow \forall c$(*Rbc* $\Rightarrow$ ($c \Vdash A \supset B \Rightarrow c \Vdash A$)). By lemma 8.4.1(2) $b \Vdash A \supset B \Rightarrow b \supset A$. Hence, $b \nVdash A \supset B$, i.e. $\exists c$(*Rbc* and $c \Vdash A$ and $c \nVdash B$). By theorem 8.5.15 c is not absolutely contradictory. Hence, by lemma 8.5.14, *Rcd*, and then, by theorem 8.4.6, $b \Vdash A$. A contradiction. Hence, PL is **E**-valid.

Consider DNE. Suppose, it is not **C**-valid. That is, $\exists W \exists a \in W(a \nVdash {\sim}{\sim}A \supset A \Leftrightarrow \exists W \exists a \in W \exists b$(*Rab* and $b \Vdash {\sim}{\sim}A$ and $b \nVdash A$)). By theorem 8.5.8, either $\exists c$(*Rbc* and not *abcon*(c)), or not *abcon*(b). Consider the first case: by theorem 8.4.6, $c \Vdash {\sim}A$, i.e. $\forall d$(*Rcd* $\Rightarrow$ ($d \Vdash {\sim}A \Rightarrow$ *abcon*(d))). By lemma 8.4.1(2), *Rcc*, hence, $c \Vdash {\sim}A \Rightarrow$ *abcon*(c). So, we have $c \nVdash {\sim}A$, i.e. $\exists d$(*Rcd* and $d \Vdash A$ and not *abcon*(d)). By lemma 8.5.14, *Rdc*, hence, by theorem 8.4.6, $c \Vdash A$. Again, by lemma 8.5.14, *Rcb*, hence, by theorem 8.4.6, $b \Vdash A$. A contradiction. Consider the second case: by lemma 8.5.14, *Rba*, hence, by theorem 8.4.6, $a \Vdash {\sim}{\sim}A$, i.e. $\forall b$(*Rab* $\Rightarrow$ ($b \Vdash {\sim}A \Rightarrow$ *abcon*(b)), i.e. $\forall b$(not *abcon*(b) $\Rightarrow$ (*Rab* $\Rightarrow b \nVdash {\sim}A$)). Hence, $b \nVdash {\sim}A$, i.e. $\exists c$(*Rbc* and $c \Vdash A$ and not *abcon*(c)). By lemma 8.5.14, *Rcb*, and by theorem 8.4.6, $b \Vdash A$. A contradiction. Hence, DNE is **C**-valid.

■

8.7 Completeness

Let **S** be one of the systems **M**, **I**, **D**, **E** or **C**.

Definition 8.7.1 *A non-empty set of formulas x is **S**-theory iff for all formulas A and B:*

$A \in x$ *and* $\vdash_S A \supset B \Rightarrow B \in x$.

Definition 8.7.2 ***S**-theory x is prime iff $A \vee B \in x \Rightarrow A \in x$ or $B \in x$.*

Definition 8.7.3 *S-theory x is contradictory iff there exists a formula A such that $A \in x$ and $\sim A \in x$.*

Definition 8.7.4 *S-theory x is absolutely contradictory iff $x = F(\mathbf{S})$ (where $F(\mathbf{S})$ is the set of all the formulas of the language of* **S***).*

Definition 8.7.5 *The* **S***-canonical collection of sets of formulas (***S***-can) is the greatest set of sets of formulas satisfying the conditions:*

(i) $\forall x \in$ **S***-can* x *is prime* **S***-theory;*

(ii) $\forall x \in$ **S***-can* $\forall y \in$ **S***-can* $(var(x) \subseteq var(y) \Rightarrow x \subseteq y)$, *($var(x)$ is the set of all propositional variables of x).*

Lemma 8.7.6 *For every* **S***-theory x the following hold:*

(i) The set of **S***-theorems belongs to x;*

(ii) $A \in x$ *and* $B \in x \Rightarrow A\&B \in x$;

(iii) $A \in x$ *and* $A \supset B \in x \Rightarrow B \in x$.

Proof. Consider an arbitrary **S**-theory x:

(i) x is not empty, i.e. some formula A belongs to x. But $A \supset L$ is **S**-theorem (where L is an arbitrary **S**-theorem). Hence, by 8.7.1, $L \in x$.

(ii) Holds by 8.7.1 and the fact that $A \supset (B \supset (A\&B))$ is **S**-theorem.

(iii) Let $A \in x$ and $A \supset B \in x$. Hence, by lemma 8.7.6(2), $A\&(A \supset B) \in x$. But $(A\&(A \supset B)) \supset B$ is **S**-theorem. Thus, by 8.7.1, $B \in x$.

Thus, (1)-(3) hold for any **S**-theory.
■

Lemma 8.7.7 *Let $\mathbf{M}_T$ and $\mathbf{I}_T$ be the sets of* **M***-theorems and* **I***-theorems respectively. Then $M_T \in$* **M***-can and $I_T \in$* **I***-can.*

Proof. Since **M** and **I** have *modus ponens* as a rule of inference, $\mathbf{M}_T$ is **M**-theory and $\mathbf{I}_T$ is **I**-theory. Moreover, they are prime due to well-known

disjunction property. Then, $var(\mathbf{M}_T) = \emptyset$ as well as $var(\mathbf{I}_T)$. Hence, for every $x \in \mathbf{M}$-can $var(\mathbf{M}_T) \subseteq x$ and for every $y \in \mathbf{I}$-can $var(\mathbf{I}_T) \subseteq y$. By lemma 8.7.6(1), $\mathbf{M}_T \subseteq x$ and $\mathbf{I}_T \subseteq y$. Hence, definition 8.7.5(2) holds for $\mathbf{M}_T$ and $\mathbf{I}_T$ as well.
■

Lemma 8.7.8 *Every prime **I**- and **C**-theory x is contradictory iff x is absolutely contradictory.*

Proof. $\Leftarrow$: trivially;

$\Rightarrow$: by lemma 8.7.6(2) and the fact that $A\& \sim A \supset B$ is **I**- and **C**-theorem.
■

Definition 8.7.9 ***M**-structuralised collection of sets (**M**-s.c.s) X is a collection of sets of formulas satisfying the following conditions for every $x \in X$:*

(i) $A\&B \in x \Leftrightarrow A \in x$ *and* $B \in x$;

(ii) $A \vee B \in x \Leftrightarrow A \in x$ *or* $B \in x$;

(iii) $A \supset B \in x \Leftrightarrow \forall y \in X(var(x) \subseteq var(y) \Rightarrow (A \in y \Rightarrow B \in y))$;

(iv) $\sim A \in x \Leftrightarrow \forall y \in X(var(x) \subseteq var(y) \Rightarrow (A \in y \Rightarrow y$ *is contradictory*$))$.

Definition 8.7.10 ***I**-structuralised collection of sets (**I**-s.c.s) is obtained from **M**-s.c.s. by adding*

5. If x is contradictory, then x is absolutely contradictory.

Definition 8.7.11 ***D**-structuralised collection of sets (**D**-s.c.s) is obtained from **M**-s.c.s. by adding*

6. $var(x) \subseteq var(y)$ *and y is noncontradictory* $\Rightarrow var(y) \subseteq var(x)$.

Definition 8.7.12 ***E**-structuralised collection of sets (**E**-s.c.s) is obtained from **M**-s.c.s. by adding*

7. $var(x) \subseteq var(y)$ *and y is not absolutely contradictory* $\Rightarrow var(y) \subseteq var(x)$.

Definition 8.7.13 *C-structuralised collection of sets (**C**-s.c.s) is obtained from **E**-s.c.s. by adding condition (5) from definition 8.7.10.*

Lemma 8.7.14 ***S**-can is **S**-s.c.s.*

Proof. Consider **M**-can and arbitrary x, y from **M**-can.

(i) (a) Let $A\&B \in x$. Since $\vdash_M A\&B \supset A$ and $\vdash_M A\&B \supset B$, by 8.7.1, $A \in x$ and $B \in x$.

(b) Let $A \in x$ and $B \in x$. By lemma 8.7.6(2) $A\&B \in x$.

(ii) (a) Let $A \vee B \in x$. Since x is prime, $A \in x$ or $B \in x$.

(b) Let $A \in x$ or $B \in x$. Since $\vdash_M A \supset A \vee B$ and $\vdash_M B \supset A \vee B$, $A \vee B \in x$.

(iii) (a) Let $A \supset B \in x$. Then $\forall y \in \mathbf{M}-can(x \subseteq y \Rightarrow A \supset B \in y)$. Suppose $A \in y$. By lemma 8.7.6(3) $B \in y$. Hence, $\forall y \in \mathbf{M} - can(x \subseteq y(A \in y \Rightarrow B \in y)$. By definition 8.7.5(2), $\forall y \in \mathbf{M} - can(var(x) \subseteq var(y) \Rightarrow (A \in y \Rightarrow B \in y))$.

(b) Suppose $A \supset B \notin x$. Since $\vdash_M B \supset (A \supset B)$, $B \notin x$. Consider the set of **M**-theories $T \subseteq$ **M**-can, such that $\forall y \in T(x \subseteq y$ and $A \supset B \notin y$ and $B \notin y)$. The set T is ordered by the set- theoretical inclusion, and every chain from T has the upper bound (the union of chain's sets). Hence, by Zorn's lemma, there is a maximal element $G \in T$. Assume $A \notin G$. Consider a theory $[G, A]$ which is a set of formulas D, such that there exists a formula $C \in G$ such that $C\&A \supset D \in G$.

$[G, A]$ really is **M**-theory. (Suppose some $D \in [G, A]$ and $\vdash_M D \supset E$. By lemma 8.7.6(1) $D \supset E \in G$. Using transitivity (which is valid in **M**), we obtain $C\&A \supset E \in G$. Hence, by definition of $[G, A]$, $E \in [G, A]$.)

$[G, A]$ is prime. (Suppose $E \vee F \in [G, A]$. Then $C\&A \supset E \vee F \in G$. G is prime, hence, $C\&A \supset E \in G$ or $C\&A \supset F \in G$. Thus, $E \in [G, A]$ or $F \in [G, A]$.)

$[G, A] \in$ **M**-can, because $G \subseteq [G, A]$ and G is maximal element of T $(\forall x \in T : x \subseteq G)$. Since G is maximal and $[G, A]$ is nontrivial extension of G, $B \in [G, A]$ or $A \supset B \in [G, A]$. That is $C\&A \supset B \in G$ or $C\&A \supset (A \supset B) \in G$. Consider the first case. $C\&A \supset B$ is equal to $C \supset (A \supset B)$, hence, $C \supset (A \supset B) \in G$. Since $C \in G$, $A \supset B \in G$. A contradiction. Consider the second case.

If $C\&A \supset (A \supset B) \in G$, then $C \supset (A \supset (A \supset B)) \in G$, so, $C \supset (A \supset B) \in G$ (for $(A \supset (A \supset B)) \supset (A \supset B)$ is **M**-theorem). Since $C \in G$, $A \supset B \in G$. A contradiction. Hence, our assumption was wrong, and $A \in G$. Thus, $\exists y(x \subseteq y$ and $A \in y$ and $B \notin y)$, and by definition 8.7.5(2), $\exists y(var(x) \subseteq var(y)$ and $A \in y$ and $B \notin y)$.

(iv) (a) Let $\sim A \in x$. Consider an arbitrary $y \in$ **M**-can, such that $x \subseteq y$. Let $A \in y$. Then $\sim A \in y$ and $A \in y$. Hence, by definition 8.7.3 (using also definition 8.7.5(2)), $\forall y \in \mathbf{M} - can(var(x) \subseteq var(y) \Rightarrow (A \in y \Rightarrow y$ is contradictory)).

(b) Suppose $\sim A \notin x$. x is noncontradictory, because $B\&\sim B \supset \sim A$ is **M**-theorem. Consider the set of **M**-theories $T \subseteq$ **M**-can, such that $\forall y \in T(x \subseteq y$ and $\sim A \notin y$ and y is noncontradictory). The set T is ordered by the set- theoretical inclusion, and every chain from T has the upper bound (the union of chain's sets). Hence, by Zorn's lemma, there is a maximal element $G \in T$, such that $\sim A \notin y$ and y is noncontradictory. Assume $A \notin G$. Consider a theory $[G, A]$ defined as above. Using the same argument, we obtain $\sim A \in [G, A]$ or $[G, A]$ is contradictory. That is $C\&A \supset \sim A \in G$ or there exists a formula B, such that $C\&A \supset (B\&\sim B) \in G$. Consider the first case. We have $C \supset \sim A \in G$ or $A \supset \sim A \in G$. If $C \supset \sim A \in G$, then $\sim A \in G$. If $A \supset \sim A \in G$, then $\sim A \in G$ as well (because $\vdash_M (A \supset \sim A) \supset \sim A$). A contradiction. Consider the second case. Using the fact that $\vdash_M B\&\sim B \supset \sim A$, we are led to the same contradiction. Hence, our assumption was wrong, and $\exists y(x \subseteq y$ and $A \in y$ and y is noncontradictory). By definition 8.7.5(2), $\exists y(var(x) \subseteq var(y)$ and $A \in y$ and y is noncontradictory).

Thus, **M**-can really is **M**-s.c.s.

Consider **I**-can. It is necessary to prove additionally that definition 8.7.10(5) is fulfilled for **I**-can. And it really is by lemma 8.7.8. Hence, **I**-can is **I**-s.c.s.

Consider **D**-can. Consider an arbitrary x and y from **D**-can. Let $var(x) \subseteq var(y)$ and y is non-contradictory. Suppose $var(y) \subsetneq var(x)$. That is, there is a propositional variable p_i, such that $p_i \in y$ and $p_i \notin x$. Since $p_i \vee \sim p_i$ is **D**-theorem, then by lemma 8.7.6(1) $p_i \vee \sim p_i \in x$. x is prime, hence, $p_i \in x$ or $\sim p_i \in x$. But $p_i \subsetneq x$, hence, $\sim p_i \in x$. But $x \subseteq y$ (by definition 8.7.5(2)), hence $\sim p_i \in y$. Thus, y is contradictory. A contradiction. Hence, $y \subseteq x$, and then $var(y) \subseteq var(x)$. Definition 8.7.11(6) is fulfilled.

Consider **E**-can. Consider arbitrary x and y from **E**-can. Let $var(x) \subseteq var(y)$ and y is not absolutely contradictory. By definition 8.7.5(2) $x \subseteq y$. Suppose there exists a formula B such that $B \in y$ and $B \notin x$. For $\vdash_E ((B \supset A) \supset B) \supset B$, $(B \supset A) \supset B \notin x$. By the case 3(b) in the proof of this lemma above, $\exists z(x \subseteq z$ and $B \supset A \in z$ and $B \notin z)$. But it can be also proved that for arbitrary prime **E**-theories x, y, $z(x \subseteq y$ and $x \subseteq z \Rightarrow y \subseteq z$ or $z \subseteq y)$. Indeed, let $x \subseteq y$ and $x \subseteq z$. Suppose neither y is a subset z, nor z is a subset of y. That is, there is a formula A, such that $A \in y$ and $A \notin z$, and there exists a formula B such that $B \in z$ and $B \notin y$. $((A \supset B) \supset A) \supset A$ is **E**-theorem as well as $((B \supset A) \supset B) \supset B$. Hence, $(A \supset B) \supset A \notin z$ and $(B \supset A) \supset B \notin y$. That is, $\exists m(z \subseteq m$ and $A \supset B \in m$ and $A \notin m)$ and $\exists n(y \subseteq n$ and $B \supset A \in n$ and $B \notin n)$. But $B \in m$ and $A \in n$ (because $z \subseteq m$ and $y \subseteq n$). By lemma 8.7.6(3) $B \supset A \notin m$ and $A \supset B \notin n$. $B \supset A \notin x$ and $A \supset B \notin x$. But $(B \supset A) \vee (A \supset B)$ is **E**-theorem. Hence, by lemma 8.7.6(1), $(B \supset A) \vee (A \supset B) \in x$. Since x is prime we are led to a contradiction. Hence, $y \subseteq z$ or $z \subseteq y$. But $y \subseteq z$ is impossible because $B \in y$ and $B \notin z$. Hence, $z \subseteq y$. That is $B \supset A \in y$. By lemma 8.7.6(3) $A \in y$. Notice that A is an arbitrary formula, hence, y is absolutely contradictory. A contradiction. Hence, $y \subseteq x$, and then $var(y) \subseteq var(x)$. Definition 8.7.12 is fulfilled for **E**-can.

Consider **C**-can. First show that definition 8.7.12(7) holds for it. Let $var(x) \subseteq var(y)$ and y is not absolutely contradictory. By definition 8.7.5(2) $x \subseteq y$. Suppose, $y \subsetneq x$, i.e., there exists a formula A such that $A \in y$ and $A \notin x$. Since $\vdash_K A \vee \sim A$ and x is prime, $\sim A \in x$. Then $\sim A \in y$. By lemma 8.7.6(2) $A \& \sim A \in y$. For $\vdash_K A \& \sim A \supset B$, $B \in y$ (where B is an arbitrary formula). Hence, y is absolutely contradictory. A contradiction. Hence, $y \subseteq x$, and then $var(y) \subseteq var(x)$. Definition8.7.10(5) is fulfilled for **C**-can by lemma 8.7.8.
■

Lemma 8.7.15 *For every* **S**-*s.c.s.* X *there exists a* **S**-*model* $\langle W, R, \Vdash \rangle$, *such that* $\forall x \in X \exists a \in W(A \in x \Leftrightarrow a \Vdash A)$.

Proof. Consider an arbitrary **S**-s.c.s. X. Let us transform every $x \in X$ as follows:

(i) pick out all the variables from x;

(ii) if $x \neq F(\mathbf{S})$, then for every p_i such that $p_i \notin var(x)$ add $\neg p_i$ to $var(x)$ - then we obtain some i.s.d. which we call a^x;

(iii) if $x = F(\mathbf{S})$, then add to $var(x)$ all the propositional variables with factual negations - a^x is in this case absolutely contradictory;

(iv) if $x \neq F(\mathbf{S})$ but x is contradictory, then add to $var(x)$ $\neg p_i$ for some $p_i \in x$ - then a^x is simple contradictory.

In this way we obtain some set of i.s.d. W', and this set is just the **S**-model which we are looking for. Let me prove this fact.

At first notice that $var(x)$ is just a^{x+}. Hence, by definition 3.1,

$$var(x) \subseteq var(y) \Leftrightarrow Ra^x a^y \qquad (*)$$

Now, let A be a propositional variable. Then lemma is true due to definition 8.4.2.

Let A be $B\&C$. Then $B\&C \in x \Leftrightarrow B \in x$ and $C \in x$ (8.7.9(1)) $\Leftrightarrow a^x \Vdash B$ and $a^x \Vdash C$ (Induction Hypotheses) $\Leftrightarrow a^x \Vdash B\&C$ (definition 8.4.3).

Let A be $B \vee C$. Then $B \vee C \in x \Leftrightarrow B \in x$ or $C \in x$ (8.7.9(2)) $\Leftrightarrow a^x \Vdash B$ or $a^x \Vdash C$ (IH) $\Leftrightarrow a^x \Vdash B \vee C$ (definition 8.4.4).

Let A be $B \supset C$. Then $B \supset C \in x \Leftrightarrow \forall y(var(x) \subseteq var(y) \Rightarrow (B \in y \Rightarrow C \in y))$ (8.7.9(3)) $\Leftrightarrow \forall a^y \Vdash (Ra^x a^y \Rightarrow (a^y \Vdash B \Rightarrow a^y C))$ (IH and (*)) $\Leftrightarrow a^x \Vdash B \supset C$ (definition 8.4.5).

Let A be $\sim B$. Then $\sim B \in x \Leftrightarrow \forall y(var(x) \subseteq var(y) \Rightarrow (B \in y \Rightarrow y$ is contradictory)) (8.7.9(4)) $\Leftrightarrow \forall a^y(Ra^x a^y \Rightarrow (a^y \Vdash B \Rightarrow con(a)))$ (IH, (*) and conditions of construction of a^x) $\Leftrightarrow a^x \Vdash \sim B$ (definition 8.5.6).

Hence, if X is **M**-s.c.s., then W' is **M**-model.

Now, if X is **I**-s.c.s., then W' is **I**-model due to definition 8.7.10; if X is **D**-s.c.s., then W' is **D**-model due to definition 8.7.11; if X is **E**-s.c.s., then W' is **E**-model due to definition 8.7.12; if X is **C**-s.c.s., then W' is **C**-model due to definition 8.7.13.

■

Lemma 8.7.16 *If A is not **S**-theorem, then there exist $x \in$ **S**-can, such that $A \notin x$.*

Proof. If **S** is **M** or **I**, the lemma is true by lemma 8.7.7. Let **S** be **D**, **E** or **C**. Let $\mathbf{S}_T$ be the set of theorems of **D**, **E** or **C** accordingly. So, $A \notin \mathbf{S}_T$. $\mathbf{S}_T$ is **S**-theory. Now consider a set of all **S**-theories Z, such that $\forall y \in Z$: $A \notin y$. Z is ordered by set-theoretical inclusion, hence, by Zorn's lemma, there exists a maximal element $T \in Z$. Suppose $B \vee C \in T$ and $B \notin T$

and $C \notin T$. Let us define **S**-theory $[T, B]$ as the set of all formulas D such that there exists a formula $F \in T$, such that $F\&B \supset D$; and **S**-theory $[T, C]$ as the set of all formulas D such that there exists a formula $Q \in T$, such that $Q\&C \supset D$. $[T, B]$ and $[T, C]$ really are **S**-theories. Since they are also nontrivial extensions of T, then, by maximality of T, $A \in [T, B]$ and $A \in [T, C]$. That is $F\&B \supset A \in T$ and $Q\&C \supset A \in T$. By lemma 8.7.6(2), $(((F\&B) \supset A)\&((Q\&C) \supset A)) \in T$, and since $((H \supset A)\&(P \supset A)) \supset ((H \vee P) \supset A)$ is **S**- theorem, $((F\&B) \vee (Q\&C)) \supset A \in T$. Hence, using distributivity & and $\vee$, $((F \vee Q)\&(B \vee Q)\&(F \vee C)\&(B \vee C)) \supset A \in T$, and then $A \in T$. A contradiction. Thus, T is prime, and hence, $T \in$ **S**-can.

■

Theorem 8.7.17 *If* $\nvdash_S A$, *then* $\nvDash_S A$.

Proof. Let A is not **S**-theorem. Then, by lemma 8.7.16, there exists $x \in$ **S**-can, such that $A \notin x$. By lemma 8.7.14, x is **S**- s.c.s. Hence, by lemma 8.7.15, there exists a **S**-model $\langle W, R, \Vdash \rangle$, there exists $a \in W$, such that $a \nVdash_S A$. Hence, $\nvDash_S A$.

■

8.8 Generalizations

Constructing semantics in terms of intuitionistic state-descriptions has merit. It elucidates the intuitive sense of the notion "exploded world",[13] and makes it possible to distinguish between various kinds of such worlds. Moreover, it also makes it possible to *define* relation R and the forcing relation in such a way that one can *prove* all their further properties (e.g., reflexivity and transitivity of R, and the condition of truth-preservation of $\Vdash$).

Of course, it is possible to formulate more general semantics without using the concept of intuitionistic state-description and factual negation, but in that case

[13]Moreover, it allows us to avoid, e.g., the following, almost mystic, account of such worlds: "A modified Kripke-model can be thought of as a Kripke-model in the usual sense, extended by some strange "exploding" points (points at which $\perp$ is valid). The usual condition for validity of a negative sentence $\neg A$ is replaced by a stronger one: Formerly one said: the formula $\neg A$ is valid in a, is not valid at any (non-exploding) successor of a. Now we say: the formula $\neg A$ is valid in a if all successors of a, at which A is valid, explode." ([22], p. 166) Of course, it could seem quite strange, when a world suddenly "explodes". But, as I tried to show in the paper, the appropriate semantic construction which allows us to define such worlds as inconsistent theoretic constructions makes their intuitive sense clearer and more comprehensive. There is nothing "strange", when our theories appear to be inconsistent (although this situation could be considered "bad", or even "non-normal").

one has to *postulate* all the necessary properties of relation R and the forcing relation (and, if necessary, other semantical concepts). Such general semantics have been constructed for **M**, **I**, and a number of their extensions in [13] and [4]. The analysis of the present paper enables, however, to simplify and order these constructions, in particular for Curry's collection of systems, as well as to elucidate their intuitive background. Thus, although my generalized **M**-model will be essentially the same as in [13] (with some small distinctions), I will propose other models for **I**, **D**, **E**, and **C**, taking into account the results of the above analysis.

Consider a model $\langle W, R, \Vdash\rangle$, where W is a non-empty set, R is a binary relation on W subject to the following:

Condition 8.8.1 *Raa;*

Condition 8.8.2 *Rab and Rbc* $\Rightarrow$ *Rac;*

and $\Vdash$ satisfies the following (for every propositional variable p_i):

Condition 8.8.3 $a \Vdash p_i$ *and* $Rab \Rightarrow b \Vdash p_i$.

Then **M**-model is a quadruple $\langle W, R, N, \Vdash\rangle$, where W, R, are as above, and $N \subseteq W$ (N perhaps empty). Valuation clause for negation is the following:

Definition 8.8.4 $a \Vdash {\sim}A \Leftrightarrow \forall b(Rab \Rightarrow (b \Vdash A \Rightarrow b \in N))$.

The set N just represents the set of contradictory theories, i.e. it is the set of Veldman's "exploded worlds". In [13] this set has been introduced under the letter "Q" which stands for the term "queer worlds". Perhaps the reading, e.g., "non-normal worlds" which can be found in the same paper is more suitable: the situation, when a theory proves contradictory, is rather non-normal than queer. Definition 8.8.4 reflects Heyting's ideas of reducing intuitionistic negation to the notion of contradiction.

I-model is a 4-tuple $\langle W, R, n, \Vdash\rangle$, where W, R are as above, and $n \in W$ satisfying the following double condition:

Condition 8.8.5 $\forall p_i(b \Vdash p_i) \Leftrightarrow b = n$.

I-negation is defined by the following

Definition 8.8.6 $a \Vdash \sim A \Leftrightarrow \forall b(Rab \Rightarrow (b \Vdash A \Rightarrow b = n))$.

In **I**-models n is *the only* contradictory "world" which represents the "absolutely contradictory theory". "Partially contradictory" worlds (as in **M**-model) are impossible within intuitionistic logic.

Lemma 8.8.7 *For every b: $Rnb \Rightarrow b = n$.*

Theorem 8.8.8 *For every **I**-model, for any formula A: $n \Vdash A$.*

D-model is obtained from **M**-model by adding

Condition 8.8.9 *Rab and $b \in N \Rightarrow Rba$.*

E-model is a 5-tuple $\langle W, R, N, n, \Vdash \rangle$, where W, R, N are as in **M**-model, and $n \in N$ satisfying the condition 8.8.5 and the following

Condition 8.8.10 *$a \neq b$ and $Rab \Rightarrow b = n$.*

E-negation is defined by means of definition 8.8.4! That is, although **E**-model includes n, it is not used for definition of **E**-negation, which is still defined in style of minimal negation (using N). The world n plays, however, a very important restricting role within **E**-models.

C-model is **E**-model without the set N.

Acknowledgements. The paper was written in 1996-1998 during my research stay at the Humboldt University (Berlin) which was supported by the **Alexander von Humboldt Foundation**. I am grateful to the Foundation for providing excellent working conditions and to Prof. Horst Wessel and Dr. Uwe Scheffler for hospitality, encouragement and helpful comments. It was also due to my research stay at the Uppsala University in the Fall 1997 (supported by the **Swedish Institute**) and fruitful discussions with Prof. Krister Segerberg and other colleagues that allowed me to develop some important philosophical argumentation of the paper.

YAROSLAV SHRAMKO
Department of Philosophy, State Pedagogical University
50086 Kryvyi Rih, Ukraine
E-mail: kff@kpi.dp.ua

Bibliography

[1] Bernays, P. Review of Curry, *Journal of Symbolic Logic*, 18, 1953, pp. 266-268

[2] Carnap, R. *Meaning and Necessity. A Study in Semantics and Modal Logic.* Second edition, Chicago and London (The University of Chicago Press), 1988 (First edition - 1947)

[3] Curry, H. B. *Foundations of Mathematical Logic*, McGrow-Hill Book Company, New York, 1963

[4] Došen, K. Negation as a modal operator, *Reports on Mathematical Logic*, 29, 1986, pp. 15-27

[5] Fitting, M. C. *Intuitionistic Logic. Model Theory and Forcing.* North-Holland, Amsterdam - London, 1969

[6] Fitting, M. C. Intuitionistic model theory and the Cohen independence proofs, *Intuitionism and Proof Theory.* North-Holland, Amsterdam - London, 1970

[7] Heyting, A. *Intuitionism an Introduction.* Studies in Logic and Foundations of Mathematics, Amsterdam, 1956

[8] Johansson, I. Der Minimalkalkül, ein reduzierter intuitionistischer Formalismus, *Compositio Math.*, 4, 1936, pp. 119-136

[9] Kanger, S. A note on partial postulate sets for propositional logic, *Theoria*, 21, 1955, pp. 99-104

[10] Kripke, S. A. Semantic analysis of modal logic I. Normal modal propositional calculi, *ZMLGM*, 9, 1963, pp. 67-96

[11] Kripke, S. A. Semantic analysis of intuitionistic logic I., *Formal Systems and Recursive Functions*, Amsterdam, 1965, pp. 92-129.

[12] Priest, G. and Sylvan, R. Simplified semantics for basic relevant logics, *Journal of Philosophical Logic*, 21, 1992, pp. 217-233

[13] Segerberg, K. Propositional logics related to Heyting's and Johansson's, *Theoria*, 34, 1968, pp. 26-61

[14] Shramko, Y. Time and Negation, in: Faye, J., Scheffler, U., and Urchs, M. (eds.) *Perspectives on Time*. Dordrecht / Boston / London (Kluwer Academic Publishers), 1997, pp. 399-416

[15] Shramko, Y. *Intuitionismus und Relevanz*. Logos-Verlag, Berlin, 1999

[16] Shramko, Y. Semantic representation of inconsistent intuitionistic theories, *Logical Studies*, No. 2, 1999 (Online Journal, ISBN 5-85593-128-5, http://www.logic.ru/LogStud/02/LS2.html)

[17] Shramko, Y. State-descriptions as a method of semantic analysis for intuitionistic logic, in: Julian Nida-Rümelin (ed.) *Rationality, Realism, Revision* , Perspectives in Analytical Philosophy, v. 23, Walter de Gruyter, Berlin-New York, 1999, pp. 110-118

[18] Suszko, R. Ontology in the *Tractatus* of L. Wittgenstein, *Notre Dame Journal of Formal Logic*, v. IX, 1968, pp. 7-33

[19] Swart de, H. Another intuitionistic completeness proof, *Journal of Symbolic Logic*, 41, 1976, pp. 644-662

[20] Troelstra, A. S. Completeness and validity for intuitionistic predicate logic, *Colloq. int. log.* Clermont-Ferrand, Paris, 1977, pp. 35-98

[21] Urquhart, A. Semantics for relevant logics, *Journal of Symbolic Logic*, 37, 1972, pp. 159-169

[22] Veldman, W. An intuitionistic completeness theorem for intuitionistic predicate logic, *Journal of Symbolic Logic*, 41, 1976, pp. 159-166

Chapter 9

Recent Trends in Paraconsistent Logic

MAX URCHS

Ten years ago an important collection, containing logical and philosophical essays on the inconsistent, was finally published ([43]). Within these ten years one might have observed energetic efforts directed towards a comprehensive self-organisation of the field of so-called paraconsistent logic. Two years ago, the First World Congress on Paraconsistent Logic was held in Gent/Belgium. Last year a large conference in Thorn/Poland was devoted above all to Jaskowski's heritage in this field. The Second World Congress on Paraconsistent Logic will take place in Brazil in May 2000. Evidently, paraconsistent logic reveals a strong tendency to develop into an autonomous area of logical research. It seems that at present a new homogeneous field of research in non-classical logic is emerging, accompanied by a number of well-founded and important applications.

Therefore I think it appropriate to take a closer look at the main tendencies in paraconsistent logic, and to ask, how this research programme relates to other topics in logic, as well as to methodological and philosophical issues.[1]

[1]I thank André Fuhrmann for helpful discussions.

9.1 Philosophical and Historical Background

Paraconsistent logic is the part of non-classical logic that tries to cope with reasoning from inconsistent sets of premisses in a logically controlled way.

9.1.1 A Few Historical Remarks

Aristotle was allegedly the first to question the principle of excluded contradiction and attempt a justification. His analysis, however, claimed this principle together with tertium non datur, the most certain of all principles. The ultimate certainty of tertium non datur was not especially durable in the history of logic. The principle of excluded contradiction, however, ruled almost undivided in logic for the next 2000 years. As Rescher put it, *horror contradictionis* has been endemic among rigorous thinkers. This was mostly due to specific properties of classical logic: every formula is derivable from a contradiction[2] Therefore, in view of a contradiction everything is true. That would be the end of any logical investigation.

Needless to say that such an opinion, as any other opinion one could think of, met no unanimity outside logic. Philosophical discussion from its very beginning left space for alternative treatment of sentences conflicting each other. The best known representative of a more leaned-back attitude towards contradictions was Heraklit, perhaps.

Later on such a dialectical perspective found many followers, in particular in classical German philosophy. As it is well know, that kind of philosophical reflection was of great influence in various fields of the humanities. In philosophy, however, it was largely discredited by the new project of neo-positivism. Also beginning analytic philosophy felt not much sympathy with dialetheas. Only within the last decades we observe new activities in philosophical treatment of inconsistencies by means of modern analytic philosophy, including the apparatus of logic.

The concept of an inconsistency is by no means a sharp one. Besides logical contradictions there are refutations, collisions of thesis and antithesis, incoherences, antinomies, contrasts, oppositions, self-defeating assertions, there is "contradictio-in-adiecto", paradoxical pronouncement, not to forget oxymorons and a number of other cases. Furthermore, there are dozens of adjectives intended to denote in a very subtle and refined way the slightest shades in meaning of various forms of inconsistencies. In German, I counted more than

[2]For example by means of disjunctive syllogism: from H follows $H \vee G$, therefore by $\neg H$ we obtain G.

50, and – I take it – it is not very different in English. Actually, this reservoir of terminological material is still largely ignored in philosophy. In this paper, I do not aim at a classification either. Instead I just take the word "inconsistency" to be a generic term for all kinds of incompatibility and polarity.

Assuming such a broad conception of inconsistency, it is easy to motivate considerable interest in the issue. There is really no lack in examples of inconsistencies in sciences. The situation is best documented, perhaps, in modern physics (for examples see e.g. [56]). The upshot is that a large number of serious scientists have a relaxed attitude towards inconsistencies.

For a philosopher, the question of the status of inconsistencies is to be raised immediately: are they in some cases true descriptions of phenomena out there in reality, or are they rather of epistemic nature? The first position is called strong paraconsistency. It takes at least some inconsistencies to be true (so-called dialetheas). The moderate position is referred to as weak paraconsistency. All the above examples from the sciences illustrate this kind of paraconsistency. Weak paraconsistency seems to be acceptable also for, how Bryson Brown once put it (cf. [11], 490), conservative thinkers who are merely sensitive to our epistemic limits, and prepared to acknowledge the need to reason, from time to time, with premises that cannot all be true, without having them explode in a puff of logic.

9.1.2 The Principle of Contradiction

Now the crucial question, at least from my point of view, is: should we be afraid of contradictions? My answer is: We certainly should! It is not only a matter of Western cultural tradition – contradictions indeed indicate a deviation from normality, from the usual standards of rationality. Therefore it seems perfectly in order to assume the *ex contradictione quodlibet sequitur* principle. This principle leads to explosion of the system whenever one single contradiction occurs.

Graham Priest defines the paraconsistency of a calculus by its lacking the *ex falso quodlibet principle*. I agree with his definition in letter, but not in spirit. From a philosophical position, the decisive point is to differentiate between the principle of *ex contradictione quodlibet* and a similar, but different principle called *ex falso quodlibet*. We should accept the first one as the keystone of all Western rationality and yet dismiss the second one. Imagine that you have to take down a discussion. Suddenly, somebody claims A and some other participant opposes, claiming *A is not true*, or *non–A* for short. On your sheet of paper you wrote down scrupulously A and *non–A*. And now you observe a remarkable fact: The discussion goes on and may become quite exiting – but no one of the participants panics! None of them feels constrained to accept any claim as true. Both claiming a thesis and then attacking it by claiming its negation are quite popular events in any course of a discussion. This does not cause the discussion to break down because of abundance of information. It is impossible that both *A* and *non–A* are true. In the realm of two-valued logic one of them must be false. So (at least) one thesis on your sheet of paper is false. Nevertheless, this fact seems to be not dangerous at all.

Let us now assume – as a second case – that some of the participants claims both *A* and *non–A* at the same time. This causes quite a different situation! What is the difference? One can precisely describe the conditions under which inconsistent claims may occur in the minutes. Assume that the quarrel goes about *A*. Some of the participants have reason to claim that *A* is true while the other ones disagree: according to them *A* is not true. And there is no possibility to persuade one of those groups by logical reasons only to give up their position. As far as there is no new empirical evidence accepted by all participants each of them has a defense: "We are right and the others are wrong!" But now assume that one and the same speaker claims that *A is true* and at the same time he disagrees and claims that *A is not true*. Then there are purely logical reasons which should persuade him to change his mind. One can remind him of the common use of the words *and* and *not* from which follows that his claim makes no sense. Obviously, the above defense strategy should not be used in this case. Otherwise the speaker would characterize himself as intellectually somewhat embarrassed. That means, if there occurs a contradictory claim in the minutes (not merely claims which are inconsistent with each other) then the person who claimed it either does not use the common language of all of the other participants (and is therefore not a rational *speaker*) or he is mentally puzzled (whence, not a *rational* speaker). In any case it seems the best to exclude him from a rational discussion. The reason is, that at least I would expect just everything from somebody who claims obvious contradictions like *A et non–A*. In this sense it seems quite reasonable to assume that anything follows from *A et non–A* – a rational discussion becomes trivial by a contradictory claim. The principle *ex contradictione quodlibet* is therefore in keep with discursive logic:

From *A et non–A* follows anything.

On the other hand we had observed that from a false claim made in discussion not everything follows. That means, in a logical framework appropriate for formalizing the discussion the following *ex falso quodlibet* is not a permissible rule:

From A follows anything or from *non*–A follows anything;

in other words

From A *and non*–A follows anything.

Therefore it seems reasonable to dismiss the *ex falso quodlibet* principle in discussive logic – and insofar I agree with Priest. At the same time, I think that we have good reason not to dismiss the *ex contradictione quodlibet principle.* If there are some dark and slightly mysterious areas in paraconsistent logic – and I am quite sure that such areas do exist – then right in between both principles runs the borderline separating rational paraconsistent logic from the paralogical part.

9.2 Harnessing Paraconsistency

Although rapidly growing in the last few years, the literature on paraconsistent logic is relatively not too numerous. Searching in mathematical databases or in the internet, one obtains a ratio of publications in paraconsistent logic and relevant logic of about 2:3, intuitionistic or deontic logic gives already 1:5, and modal logic is well above 1:20. That leads to the supposition that paraconsistent logic is still a somewhat exotic field of research. The more so that many distinguished logicians seem to feel much discomfort with the very notion of paraconsistent logic. Admittedly, often statements about the importance of inconsistency-tolerant reasoning are based on bad philosophy. There is muddled reference to Eastern myths and religion or wild speculation on dialectics. However, there are also fruitful and important applications. We will mention some of them.

9.2.1 Mathematics

Usually, applications in mathematics are the most prominent examples for the advantages of paraconsistent logic. Robert K. Meyer's relevant arithmetic $R^\sharp$ was a first example ([37]), followed by a whole class of inconsistent arithmetical theories ([38]). Moreover, the protagonists for a paraconsistent foundation of mathematics may call on prominent advocates, first of all Wittgenstein who defended this view in the early 30s and upheld it despite of very substantial criticism by Turing.

> You might get $p \wedge \neg p$ by means of Frege's System. If you can draw any conclusion you like from it, then that, as far I can see, is all the trouble you can get into. And I would say, 'Well then, just don't draw any conclusion from a contradiction'. ([63], 220)

Wittgenstein's famous "So what"-attitude towards mathematical inconsistencies reappears throughout his work, most strikingly perhaps in the laconic confession, made in a discussion with Moritz Schlick:

> There will be mathematical investigations of calculi containing contradictions, and people will actually be proud of having emancipated themselves from consistency. (quoted after [62], 139)

I doubt whether this will be so indeed. It seems to me that in some sense this line of research is an abuse of paraconsistent logic. The reason is that paraconsistency, at least in its philosophically unproblematic, i.e. weak form, goes together with vague, insufficiently precise, not fully explicated language. All this is not especially typical of the situation in mathematics. Maybe the role of paraconsistent logic in mathematics will be rather that of a tool for deeper analysis of a previously apparently homogeneous concept, namely for the concept of formal contradiction. This concept then might split up into a manifold of precisely defined different concepts – a case we experienced with the notion of infinity. Paraconsistent reasoning might discover another hidden structure in mathematics. But I don't think Paraconsistent logic has a future as a methodological basis of mathematics in the way intuitionistic logic has. There is no need of a mechanism that allows to cope with paradoxes in arithmetic, the goal is an arithmetic free of paradoxes.

The matter is more complicated to judge, if set theory or semantics is at issue. But again, if someone feels no sympathy for strong paraconsistency, then the well-known paradoxes in foundations of mathematics and in formal semantics need another cure than a paraconsistent treatment.

9.2.2 Automated Reasoning

Consider a computer running a large database. While the computer stores the information, it is also used to operate on it, and, most importantly, to infer from it. Now it is quite common for the database to contain inconsistent information, because of mistakes by the data entry operators or because of multiple sourcing. This is certainly a problem for database operations with theorem-provers, and so has drawn much attention from computer scientists.

Techniques for removing inconsistent information have been investigated. Yet all have limited applicability, and, in any case, are not guaranteed to produce consistency. Hence, even if one may get get rid of contradictions when they are found, an underlying paraconsistent logic is desirable if hidden contradictions are not to generate surprising answers to queries. Moreover, according to an old conjecture of Dunn, a paraconsistent background logic might proof superior to classical logic for program development. For instance, in that way infertile paths in search routines could be recognized earlier.

In artificial intelligence, particularly in automated reasoning, paraconsistent ideas therefore play an important role. One of the first, fully implemented Theorem-Provers was the program KRIPKE developed in the 80s at the ANU (see [52]). It implemented the relevant logic **LR** (**R** without distribution of $\wedge$ over $\vee$). An overview of the recent state of work in this field is contained in the second volume of the Handbook of defeasible reasoning ([8]). More material is contained in [58].

Two positions are distinguished here. The first one, the so-called actual contradictions view investigates inference mechanisms designed to cope with actual inconsistencies in a non-trivial way. The second option, the potential contradictions view, assumes mechanism to resolve conflicts. This is mostly done in the field of defeasible reasoning. The two perspectives occur in artificial intelligence in both proof-theoretic and in semantical-based form. A survey of almost twenty semantics for more or less comfortable handling of program inconsistency is presented by Damasio and Pereira in [16]. In the last years, logic programming has been applied to central topics of Artificial Intelligence such as updates and belief revision. Therefore it is only natural that the logic programming community became interested in paraconsistency. The basic idea is to accept inconsistent information and to perform reasoning tasks that take it into account. The crucial point, however, was a mechanism for explicitly declaring the falsity of propositions. Such an explicit non-classical negation, besides the usual default one, is available only recently.

The prevailing position is that contradictions are captured by an auxiliary notion, namely that of negation. Of course, an appropriate connective $\neg$ must be contained in the language. If H is a formula, then so is $\neg H$, denoting a statement denying the statement H. Independently of the underlying consequence operation, any logic adhering to the N–scheme includes $H \wedge \neg H$ as a contradiction, and usually it treats $\{H, \neg H\}$ as contradiction as well. This schema apparently prevails in artificial reasoning.

However, the "true" notion of negation is by no means evident. It makes a big difference, for instance, whether one takes negation as incompatibility or as a contradiction forming functor. For instance, the volumes edited by Wansing ([59]) and Wansing and Gabbay ([23]) contain an impressive list of various concepts of negation as a logical connective. Taking into consideration the vast manifold of possible expressions of incoherent propositions, one might well assume that there are many more possible kinds of negation still undefined in a formal framework.

Oversimplified treatment of negation by some authors provokes easy criticism. For instance, Slater argues that whenever a logic turns out to be paraconsistent, then the connective called "negation" is no real negation (cf. ([50]). Or, to put it more moderately, paraconsistent logicians need to explain their use of negation. Recently, an answer to Slater is given by Brown. Brown shows that the above argument cannot possibly be directed against paraconsistent logic in general, since an important class of paraconsistent systems – so-called preservationist logics – are not subject to Slater's criticism ([11]). In a more general perspective, it is not obvious why exclusively to blame negation. Maybe one should give a second thought to the role of conjunction in these calculi. And maybe even the mode of assertion should be reconsidered.

9.2.3 Belief Revision

In artificial intelligence research, belief revision is the study of rationally revising bodies of belief in the light of new evidence. Notoriously, people have inconsistent beliefs. They may even be rational in doing so. For example, there may be apparently overwhelming evidence for both something and its negation. There may even be cases where it is in principle impossible to eliminate such inconsistency. For example, consider Makinson's paradox of the preface ([31]). A rational person, after thorough research, writes a book in which she claims $A_1, \ldots, A_n$. But she is also aware that no book of any complexity contains only truths. So she rationally believes $\neg(A_1 \wedge \ldots \wedge A_n)$ too. Therefore, principles of rational belief revision should work on inconsistent sets of beliefs.

Within a foundationalist approach to belief change, there are basically two ways of handling revision of belief. You may, in so-called horizontal perspective ([48]), consider consequences classically inferred from a basis of beliefs. Then, in order to operate on your basis, i.e. to remove sentences or to recover from false beliefs, you have to invent very sophisticated procedures that are sometimes not easy to interpret. Or you take, in vertical perspective, rather natural change operations on your information bases and complete them by a refined consequence operation for drawing inferences from that basis. Such a consequence operation should obviously be a paraconsistent one. (For an explicit construction of a paraconsistent inference relation in terms of the so-called merge operation see [20], 91 ff. and also [21])

9.2.4 Philosophy and Methodology

Paraconsistency has clear philosophical motives. However, some of them may not be agreeable to everyone. In particular dialethism – i.e. the view that there are true contradictions – is a position that initiates very mixed feelings. I do not intend to scrutinize the philosophical aspects of paraconsistency. Nor do I want to make use of paraconsistent logic as a tool in investigating philosophical questions. Rather I would like to turn to methodology of empirical sciences here. There are some very careful methodological case studies of concrete scientific discoveries. For instance Joel Smith, who thoroughly analyzed the role of inconsistency in scientific reasoning in general ([51]). Yoke Mehus' analysis of Rudolf Clausius creation of modern thermodynamics shows convincingly that an inconsistency-tolerating logical basis is not only the appropriate tool for scientific progress, it moreover is a necessary condition for proper understanding what really happened in Clausius' case. The methodologically troubling point is, as Mehus convincingly argues, that the choice of an inadequate logical background prevents us even from proper understanding of the discovery of Clausius ([33]).

The emergence of inconsistencies in science can be brought about by the hard choice between the expressive power of the language under consideration on the one hand, and the efficiency of the mathematical apparatus which is used to control this language on the other hand. Let me state this thought more explicitly. Doubtless, there are inconsistencies in scientific theories. This does not decide, whether we are condemned to endure inconsistencies in eternity. I am convinced that in the long run, we can get rid of inconsistencies in the body of any theory. Short term, however, the elimination of inconsistencies might be achievable only at unreasonably high costs or it may be plainly impossible to eliminate them. That may lead us to a dilemma: to exclude inconsistencies altogether is not the appropriate way for a methodology that respects the practice of empirical sciences. But to admit contradictions seems to be inconceivable to an even higher degree. This way is blocked by the principle of contradiction. And this principle is, as I said, justly assumed to be the keystone of the venerable vault of Western rationality. So we better don't shake it.

Often a more precise language will make the inconsistencies go away. But you won't get a better language for free. In terms of Artificial Intelligence, this illustrates the usual trade-off between a comfortable and precise (and therefore very extended) language on the one hand and the limited as well as expensive resources necessary for processing the linguistic material on the other hand. Sometimes it may pay off to work with a modest but not complicated language that needs little memory and low calculation capacity, as well as short calculation time. Of course, in order to do so you need to have the right inference engine. In this case it should be an inconsistency-tolerating one. Here paraconsistent logic appears to be the appropriate methodological background.

Let me add just one pragmatic argument for temporarily remaining with inconsistencies. Sometimes, it is not even desirable to resolve inconsistencies in an early development stage, because they themselves are a resource of information. In economy, for instance, it may happen that a decision in favor of the first best option turns out to be less optimal than to go for the second best option. This could be so, because the second best option allows to react more flexibly in the further course of events and to finally arrive consequently at a better position. In other words, under specific circumstances, it may pay off to hold open decisions as long as possible. Similarly in empirical sciences: coping with conflicting working hypotheses, one might wish not to decide which hypothesis to dismiss, until new evidence occurs. In the meantime, one has to tolerate inconsistencies. How exactly to perform this in a formal way?

9.3 Main Tendencies in Paraconsistent Logic

As I mentioned at the outset, there are many different approaches to be found in the literature. We therefore have to concentrate on the most important. For further reference, [43] is still a valuable source.

9.3.1 Da Costa's Systems

Newton C.A. da Costa is one of the pioneers in paraconsistent logic. In particular, the study of non-truth-functional systems was initiated by da Costa. Assisted by Ayda Arruda, he produced several kinds of such systems, among them the hierarchy of so-called "positive-plus" systems C_i, where $1 \leq i \leq \omega$ satisfying the following conditions (cf. [13]):

(i) the principle of contradiction, $\neg(H \wedge \neg H)$, is not valid in general.;

(ii) in each of these systems, from two contradictory propositions, H and $\neg H$, it is not possible in general to deduce every proposition;

(iii) each system in the hierarchy $C_1, C_2, \ldots, C_\omega$ is strictly stronger than the following ones;

(iv) all classical theorems are valid for "well-behaved propositions" (H behaves well in C_n, if $H^1 \wedge H^2 \wedge \ldots \wedge H^n$ is a theorem of C_n, where $H^0 = H^1 = \neg(H \wedge \neg H)$ and $H^{n+1} = (H^n)^0$;

(v) the systems should contain as many classical theorems as possible.

The main idea here was to maintain the apparatus of some positive logic, say classical or intuitionistic, but to allow negation to behave non-truth-functionally. Thus, take an interpretation to be a function which maps formulas to 1 or 0; $\wedge$, $\vee$, and $\rightarrow$ behave in the usual (classical) way. Therefore the construction has to block explosion by a specific negation. This basic idea is that the value of $\neg H$ is independent of that of H. In particular, both may take the value 1.

$$v(H) = 0 \Rightarrow v(\neg H) = 1 \text{ and } v(\neg\neg H) = 1 \Rightarrow v(H) = 1$$

Negation has no further significant properties under these semantics. Acceptance and consequence operation are defined as usual. Various properties of negation may be obtained by adding further constraints on interpretations. C_ω is obtained by adding to positive intuitionist logic the requirements that, for any H, either H or $\neg H$ must take the value 1 and that whenever $\neg\neg H$ is 1, so does H. If we assume H^o for $\neg(H \wedge \neg H)$ then there is a natural interpretation of H^o as the consistency of H. Further postulates concerning H^o make the difference between the systems C_i, for finite i.

All systems $C_1, C_2, \ldots, C_\omega$ are non-trivial and all but C_ω are also what he calls finitely trivializable: there is a formula F such that $C_n \cup F$ is trivial. The above hierarchy can be extended to a hierarchy of first-order calculi with or without identity, $C_i^\star$ and $C_i^=$ for $1 \leq i \leq \omega$, respectively. Furthermore, there is a hierarchy of calculi of descriptions $D_1, D_2, \ldots, D_\omega$ and an outline of paraconsistent set theories $NF_1, NF_2, \ldots, NF_\omega$.

Since 1964, da Costa's systems and related calculi are widely studied in and out of Brazil.

9.3.2 Many-Valued and Relevant Logic

One way of generating a paraconsistent logic is to use a logic with more than two truth values. The formulae which hold in a many-valued interpretations are those which have a designated value. A many-valued logic will therefore be paraconsistent if it allows both a formula and its negation to be designated.

The simplest strategy, perhaps, is to use only two truth values and to allow propositions to have both of them. A formula has a designated truth value: *true (only)* or *both truth and false* (which, naturally, is a fixed point for negation). This is the approach of the paraconsistent logic of Asenjo's Calculus of Antinomies ([3]). Adding a fourth possible combination, *neither true nor false*, which behaves in an appropriate way, one obtains Nuel Belnap's Useful Four-Valued Logic for properly thinking computers ([1], 506 ff.). Similar ideas yield a construction of Dana Scott's ([49]) or Michal Dunn's semantics for First Degree Entailment ([17]). Some results of da Costa and Jerzy Kotas let think about deep connections with Łukasiewicz's many-valued logics ([15]). If one takes the truth values to be the real numbers between 0 and 1, with a suitable set of designated values, the upshot is a paraconsistent fuzzy logic.

Relevance logics[3] were pioneered by Alan Anderson and Belnap. World-semantics for them were developed first independently, then jointly by the Routleys and Robert Meyer. In an interpretation for such logics, conjunction and disjunction behave in the usual way. Then, as before, negation requires a non-classical truth condition. In the early 1970s, Richard and Val Routley invented their "star operator" to treat negation. For each world, w, there is an associate world, $w^\star$. Dunn ([18]) interprets the Routley star in terms of a binary relation, C, on worlds. Cwx means that x is compatable with w. $w^\star$, then, is the maximal world (the world containing the most information) that is compatable with w.

$\neg H$ is true at w iff H is false, not at w, but $w^\star$. Thus, if H is true at w, but false at $w^\star$, $H \wedge \neg H$ is true at w. To obtain the standard relevant logics (with both double negation principles), one needs to add the constraint that $w^{\star\star} = w$. There are other semantics for negation as well.

In the first line, relevant logic is concerned not with negation or conjunction, but with the study of entailment, i.e. with a conditional connective, $\rightarrow$ (satisfying modus ponens). One may therefore say that paraconsistency is merely a side-effect for systems of relevant logic. Semantics for $\rightarrow$ are obtained by supplementing each interpretation with a ternary relation, $\mathcal{R}$. $H \rightarrow G$ is true at w iff at all worlds where H is true, G is true. If w is non-normal, $H \rightarrow G$ is true at w iff for all x, y, such that $\mathcal{R}wxy$, if H is true at x, then G is true at y. (Validity is defined as truth preservation over normal worlds.) This gives the basic relevant logic **B**. Stronger logics, such as **R**, are obtained by adding further requirements on the ternary relation.

[3] They are called 'relevance logics' in North America and 'relevant logics' in Britain and Australasia.

9.3.3 Inconsistency Adaptive Logic

The conception of so-called inconsistency-adaptive logic (in former times: dynamic dialectical logic) was developed by Diderik Batens in the mid eighties ([4]). Batens leaned on philosophical ideas of Leo Apostel. Today this approach is most dynamically developed by a group of young logicians and philosophers in Belgium, centered around Batens and Jean Paul van Bendegem (see, e.g., [5]).

The construction was originally designed for the logical reconstruction of the following paradigm case: A theory T, based on classical logic, and hence intended to be consistent, turns out to be inconsistent. If T is considered to be interesting, one will want to replace T by a consistent theory T'. Batens correctly observes that T itself is heuristically important under the circumstances: we want a large number of theorems of T, actually all 'good' ones, to be theorems of T'. However, we can only make sense of this requirement if we know which sentences are theorems of T. Unfortunately, if we stick to classical logic, all sentences are theorems of T. If we substitute some of the traditional paraconsistent systems for classical logic in T, the resulting set of theorems turns out to be too poor.

As Batens argues, in the last case the problem is that these systems restrict the rules of inference globally; for instance, they take disjunctive syllogism to be incorrect in general. In order to specify the 'good' theorems of T, we need a logic that localizes inconsistencies and modifies the rules of inference in view of these. That exactly is what inconsistency-adaptive logic does: in the neighborhood of inconsistencies, they go paraconsistent; everywhere else, classical logic is applied in its full strenght. Inconsistency-adaptive logics 'oscillate' between a (poor) paraconsistent logic and classical logic, and they do so in view of the specific inconsistencies of the theory. In that sense, inconsistency-adaptive logics have a dynamic proof-procedure. The precise explication is a bit tricky. However, simplified dynamic proof formats for adaptive logic will be available soon. For the time being, there is an axiomatic system with both unconditional – i.e. classical – and with conditional rules. The crucial point is the notion of consistent behaviour of a formula H in a proof. This notion is introduced recursively taking into account the structure of the specific proof.

The semantic clause for negation is established by the completeness requirement: if $v_M(A) = 0$, then $v_M(\neg A) = 1$). The valuation function v_M determined by a model M is defined as follows:

$$v_M(\neg A) = 1 \text{ iff } v_M(A) = 0 \text{ or } v(\neg A) = 1$$

CLuN, a weak paraconsistent logic, is the full positive part of classical logic, extended with $A \vee \neg A$. Many negation properties from classical logic are lost: both directions of Double Negation, de Morgan properties, etc. But no contradiction $A \wedge \neg A$ entails any other contradiction in **CLuN**.

On that basis Batens considers two inconsistency-adaptive logics. Both have classical logic as their 'upper limit' logic (the logic that defines logical normality), and **CLuN** as their 'lower limit' logic (this defines the consequences that obtain unconditionally). They differ from each other in the assumed strategy how to interpret the phrase 'as consistently as possible'. This strategy determines the conditions under which an inference, that holds according to classical logic but does not hold according to **CLuN**, may be applied to specific members and consequences of the premises. In case of his **ACLuN1**, the underlying idea is *reliability*. All rules derivable in **CLuN** are used without any restriction, whereas derivable rules of **CL** are applied "provisionally" and on the condition that certain formulae behave consistently, i.e. the are reliable. Roughly, that amounts to rejecting any suspicious premises altogether. **ACLuN2** uses *minimal abnormality*, a slightly bolder strategy that allows to obtain more inferences (for details see [5]). In the meantime, a group of adaptive logics has been explained and studied. Some of them are not paraconsistent, but tolerate other logical abnormalities ([6]).

The main intuition of inconsistency-adaptive logic is to isolate contradictions, in order to prevent them from spreading around and infecting the whole theory. But there is another clear intuition available what is also philosophically deep and logically appealing, since it leads to very elegant formal calculi. The central idea is this: What is really dangerous is not inconsistency as such, but contradictions. Thus one should hinder inconsistencies to condense into contradictions. Thesis and anti-thesis bouncing together bring about an explosion - analoguously, as two subcritical masses detonate when they jointly cross the critical limit.

9.3.4 Non-Adjunctive Systems

The non-adjunctive way in paraconsistent logic set out with Jaśkowski's construction of a propositional calculus for inconsistent deductive systems ([24], [25], English translation: [26]). Another contribution to this tradition is Rescher and Brandoms approach towards a logic of inconsistency ([47]). Also Lewis ([30]) is suggestive of a non-adjunctive approach to accommodating contradiction.

Jaśkowski's construction of discussive logic is probably the best bashed project in the field. There is no room to correct all unfair or objectionable criticism concerning this approach. In my opinion, it is one of the most interesting and promising approaches in inconsistency-tolerant reasoning. Moreover, it has an excellent philosophical motivation. Numerous classical ideas by Leibniz or Kant can be restated within this setting. Discussive logic is evidently motivated by the weak approach to paraconsistency. According to a proposal by Perzanowski, the philosophical background of Jaśkowski's system and related calculi should be called "para*in*consistency".

Jaśkowski was the first to observe that it makes sense to differentiate contradictory logical calculi from so called over-crowded ones (cf. [26]).

Definition 9.3.1 *A logical calculus L is contradictory in the formal language FOR [symb.: $L \notin Cons$]* $\Longleftrightarrow_{df} \exists\, H \in FOR : H, \neg H \in L$.

If a contradictory system is based on classical logic, then every formula is a thesis of the system. But, not so in general. Any system in which every formula is a tautology is called over-crowded, over-filled, or else: trans-complete.

Definition 9.3.2 *A logical calculus L is over-complete in the formal language* $FOR \Longleftrightarrow_{df} FOR = L$.

Here is Jaśkowski's original comment on the matter:

> This deviates from the terminology accepted so far: in the methodology of the deductive sciences such systems have so far been called contradictory, but for the purpose of the analysis presented in this paper it is necessary to make a distinction between two different meanings of the term "a contradictory system", and to use it only in one sense, as specified above. The over-complete systems have no practical significance: no problem may be formulated in the language of an over-complete system, since every sentence is asserted in that system. Accordingly, the problem of the logic of contradictory systems is formulated here in the following manner: the task is to find a system of the sentential calculus which: 1) when applied to contradictory systems would not always entail their over-completeness, 2) would be rich enough to enable practical inference, 3) would have an intuitive justification. Obviously, these conditions do not univocally determine the solution, since they may be satisfied in varying degrees, the satisfaction of condition 3) being rather difficult to appraise objectively." ([26], 145)

The essential point in Jaśkowski's construction is a slightly more sophisticated attempt to conjunction – in fact we have two of them: an inner one and an external. Here is a short definition[4] of Jaśkowski's system D_2: Let FOR_d be the set of all formulas freely generated from a denumerable set of propositional variables by means of some Boolean complete set of propositional functors and two additional two-argument "discussive" connectives: the discussive conjunction $\wedge_d$ and the discussive implication $\rightarrow_d$. Next we explain a translation $t : FOR_d \longrightarrow FOR_m$ from FOR_d to propositional modal language FOR_m . t leaves unchanged propositional variables as well as the Boolean connectives. Let $\Diamond$ be the $S5$-possibility. Then we establish:

(1)	$t(H)$	$=_{df}$	H	, for $H \in AT$;
(2)	$t(\neg H)$	$=_{df}$	$\neg t(H)$;	
(3)	$t(H \wedge G)$	$=_{df}$	$t(H) \wedge t(G)$;	
(4)	$t(H \wedge_d G)$	$=_{df}$	$t(H) \wedge \Diamond t(G)$;	
(5)	$t(H \rightarrow_d G)$	$=_{df}$	$\Diamond t(H) \rightarrow t(G)$.	

Definition 9.3.3 $D_2 =_{df} \{H \in FOR_d; \Diamond t(H) \in S5 \}$.

The above classical construction can be generalized considerably. It is possible to use a large class of modal systems, among them even non-normal ones, to obtain interesting discussive calculi. Let S be any regular modal logic containing $S3$. According to Polish tradition it seems quite natural to understand discussive logic as a logical system (i.e. a consequence operation in a formal language) rather than as a set of formulas. For every modal calculus S containing $S3$ we are able to define a consequence operation Cn_S in the discussive language FOR_d and to give a direct semantical characterization for the system $\langle FOR_d, Cn_S \rangle$ thus obtained. With every such S we correlate a discussive system S_d, i.e. a consequence operation Cn_S in the discussive language FOR_d.

Definition 9.3.4 *Let $H \in FOR_d$. H is d-valid in a point of the model $\mathcal{M}$ [symbolically: $\mathcal{M} \models_d H[x]$] $\Longleftrightarrow_{df} \exists y \in R(x) : \mathcal{M} \models t(H)[y]$.*

The notion of d–validity in a point of a model is extended to models, frames, and classes of frames, as usual. In natural way the acceptance property in S leads to an inference relation Cn_S.

[4]It would be possible, and perhaps easier as well, to explain D_2 as a conservative extension of standard modal logic. Nevertheless, as we are forced to put the emphasis on subtleties of the formal language, I prefer to choose the "save" definition.

Definition 9.3.5 *Let $\mathcal{K}_S$ be the class of all Kripke-frames for S and let $X \subseteq FOR_d$. $Cn_S(X) =_{df} \{H \in FOR_d : \forall \mathcal{F} \in \mathcal{K}_S(\mathcal{F} \models_d X \Longrightarrow \mathcal{F} \models_d H)\}$.*

We state without proof the following lemmata and theorems:

Lemma 9.3.6 *Cn_S is a consequence operation in FOR_d.*

For all calculi S containing the modal system *S3* the following deduction theorem is true:

Theorem 9.3.7 $\forall S \quad \forall X \subseteq FOR_d \quad \forall H, G \in FOR_d :$
$(H \rightarrow_d G) \in Cn_S(X) \Longleftrightarrow G \in Cn_S(X \cup \{H\})$.

Usually we interpret the deduction theorem as a characterization of the implication within the considered system. But now it goes the other way round: the discussive implication possesses the expected properties of a discussive inference. By theorem 1 they are transmitted to the consequence relation. Moreover, we have the following theorem:

Theorem 9.3.8 $Cn_{S5}(\emptyset) = D_2$.

The above theorem shows that the consequence version of Jaśkowski's discussive calculus D_2 belongs to the class of logical systems $\{\langle FOR_d, Cn_S\rangle; S3 \subseteq S\}$. For that reason and because of the properties emerging from the Deduction Theorem we call the calculi $\langle FOR_d, Cn_S\rangle$ *discussive Jaśkowski-systems.*

What happens, if we change the modal logic underlying the construction of discussive calculi? It turns out that Jaśkowski's construction is stable with respect to changing the underlying modal logic[5]. A first result was obtained by Furmanowski ([22]:

Theorem 9.3.9 $\forall S4 \subseteq S \subseteq S5$: *M–S = M–S5*

As Błaszczuk and Dziobiak found ([9]), *S4* is not the least system that obtains this property.

Theorem 9.3.10 $T^\star := T \oplus \Diamond\Diamond H \setminus \Diamond H$ *is the least system which* M*–counterpart equals M-S5.*

[5]For details concerning the following material see [55].

Perzanowski had shown in [40] that no normal system below D ($D := K \oplus \Diamond(H \to H)$) gives rise to non-trivial discussive Jaśkowski-style systems. What, then, about non-normal based systems? Kotas and da Costa expressed the conjecture that such systems would be too weak to be interesting ([14]). Yet there is good reason to take a closer look on discussive calculi based on non-normal modal systems. To that purpose, let us slightly generalize the notion of M–counterpart: for $k \geq 1$, let $M^k\text{–}S = \{H \in FOR_m; \Diamond H \in M^{k-1}\text{–}S\}$ ($M^0\text{–}S = S$). Dziobiak was the first to observe that $M^2\text{–}S3 = M\text{–}S5$. This property is typical for the investigated systems. Let S_N be the "normal variant" of S, i.e. its closure w.r.t. $H \setminus \Diamond H$.

Theorem 9.3.11 *$\forall S3 \subseteq S$: $M^2\text{–}S = M\text{–}S_N$.*

However, the assumption in the above theorem is essential: it does not work for *S2*.

Theorem 9.3.12 *$\forall S3 \subseteq S \subseteq S5$: $M^{k+2}\text{–}S = M\text{–}S5$, for all $k \in \omega$.*

Consequently the manifold of discussive systems based on regular systems between *S3* and *S5* collapses into D_2 for higher dimensions. What happens on the first level? Here is a partial answer:

Theorem 9.3.13 *$\forall S \subseteq S3.5$: $M^{k+2}\text{–}S \neq M\text{–}S$, for all $k \in \omega$.*

It thus seems that Jaśkowski's construction of discussive logic on the basis of modal calculi is amazingly stable. A lot of interesting semantical questions can be stated. Anyway, we shall turn to syntactical considerations again.

Once being given discussive implication, discussive conjunction suggests itself: conjunction of A and non-F is negated if H, then F. So what we get is the following definition[6]:

$$H \wedge_d F =_{df} \neg(\Diamond H \to \neg F)$$

So discussive conjunction turns out to be just $\Diamond H \wedge F$. That is apparently anything but acceptable: symmetry is the least one should demand of conjunction. How could we possibly interpret such a connective? A way out suggests by the discussive interpretation of Jaśkowski's approach. A well founded assumption of cognitive linguistics says that, usually, the more important an information is, the more forward it is transmitted. Now, suppose we already have some H. Subsequently, F comes up somehow. Therefore we have $F \wedge_d H$. However, F

[6]This is not Jaśkowski's original discussive conjunction from [24]. However, it is logically – and ideologically – very close.

is new information. So it might be a good idea to accept it under proviso only. That, perhaps, sufficiently motivates the slanted conjunction.

But it is easy enough to find a symmetric version of $\wedge_d$. Let us first recall that the discussive implication is not very intuitive, either. Its main motivation was a purely technical one: just find a connective that meets modus ponens. By chance, $\rightarrow_d$ was the first appropriate one that came along.

In order to proceed more systematically, one might try an interpretation in terms of practical discurs, again. Discussive implication plays the part of hypothesis testing, i.e. to answer the question, whether or not we should accept some F. One might reason as follows: well, we if would assume F to be true (hence $\Diamond F$), then G turns out to occur (hence G). Therefore, $\Diamond F \rightarrow G$, in other words $F \rightarrow_d G$.

Then, however, one might think about a slightly stronger version of hypothesis testing: if would assume F to be true (hence $\Diamond F$), then we would need to accept also G (hence $\Box\Diamond G$). That would amount to the following definition:

$$F \rightarrow_{d_1} H = \Diamond F \rightarrow \Diamond\Box H$$

The new connective is not worse than the original one, since – as well as $\rightarrow_d$ – it also meets modus ponens. Moreover, it is correlated with the following discussive conjunction:

$$F \wedge_{d_1} H 0_{df} \neg(F \rightarrow_{d_1} \neg H) \equiv \Diamond F \wedge \Diamond H.$$

So we have a discussive conjunction that is symmetric. What about its further properties? First of all, adjunction holds for $\wedge_{d_1}$:

$$H, F / H \wedge_{d_1} F.$$

And, as before, $H \wedge_{d_1} \neg H \rightarrow_{d_1} F$ is not a theorem of D_2. Therefore, $\wedge_{d_1}$ does not sabotage the system: it does not turn inconsistencies into contradictions.

On the other hand, since both classical negation and alternative are in D_2, classical conjunction can be constructed in the system. However, as before, adjunction does not hold for $\wedge$. Therefore irrelevant triviality, $H \wedge \neg H \rightarrow F$, is no threat.

According to what was said at the beginning about rational paraconsistent logic and irrational paralogic, discussive logic is at the safe side. How far away, let us nevertheless ask, are these systems from collapsing in view of inconsistencies? It turns out that any discussive calculus explodes, if there occurs a pair of inconsistent necessary sentences. The reason is that for necessary sentences adjunction holds:

$$\Box H, \Box F / \Box(H \wedge F)$$

Therefore the safety of discussive calculi apparently only hinges on the possibility (or rather: impossibility) to define necessary discussive contradictions. That, however, is easily done. In case of $\wedge_{d_1}$ it suffice to take $\neg(\neg H \wedge_{d_1} \neg H)$ that equals $\neg(\Diamond\neg H \wedge \Diamond\neg H)$, hence $\Box H$. For $\wedge_d$ the following is appropriate $\neg(\neg H \wedge_d (F \vee \neg F))$. Both cases could be explicitly excluded by pointing, again, to the basic methodological setting: there is no need introduce superfluous elements like repeated identical conjuncts or tautological elements. But this defense would hardly be an elegant one. However, maybe there is no real danger by the mere possibility to cope with necessary formulae. What is needed is a pair of inconsistent necessary formulae. But it is by no means obvious that there are such entities like contingent absoluta. Quite to the contrary, there seem to be good philosophical reason to refute such a variant.

There is one closely related observation. In his original paper, Jaśkowski refuted $\rightarrow_{d_1}$ as inappropriate discussive implication, because a formula $H \rightarrow_{d_1} G$ together with its negation would yield triviality. (By the way, the same is true for $\wedge_{d_1}$.) Jaśkowski was interested in "rich calculi", i.e. rich in theorems. Therefore the above observation gave sufficient reason to dismiss the defined symmetric connectives. Yet it seems to me that they are interesting after all. Taking into account Jaśkowski's original interpretation of discussive logic in terms of scientific or any other rational discourse, there is an important difference between inconsistent elementary propositions, that represent just observations or opinions or the like on the one hand, and inconsistent complex formulae on the other hand. The latter would indicate that there is something wrong within the system, i.e. with the form of reasoning of the system. In other words – in this case the consequence operation would seem to be defective. Unfortunately, Jaśkowski ignored this path and so did his followers until recently. It seems that this observation will raise interesting questions concerning the relative stability of discussive logics with respect to inconsistencies. I will not further the issue here.

Let me end with a more general reflection. The reason for preferring discussive logic as the most promising approach in paraconsistency is not only because of its formal elegance and deep philosophical motivation. Besides, discussive logic represents an ideology that is, I take it, the most appropriate one for paraconsistency. To put it informally: at the very core of paraconsistency lies not negation, but conjunction. The paradigm for paraconsistency, I take it, is scientific discourse. For any logical formalization, the observer's perspective is the only appropriate one. Hence, when creating a paraconsistent logic we have typically to assume the position of a keeper of the minutes of scientific discussion. Why should we then insinuate that a person who claims a negated sentence has in mind some exotic kind of negation? Such an assumption could be justified only by referring to the overall consistency of the ongoing discussion. That motive, however, cannot be attributed to the person who made the claim. Writing down her claim in terms of non-classical negation thus means to systematically distort it. We therefore should better concentrate on conjunction. With respect to inconsistency tolerating calculi, this connective seems to be the most important one – at least for those approaches which are directed towards application.

9.3.5 Other Approaches

As I said at the beginning, many other approaches are investigated by various authors. Some non-classical logics are paraconsistent in letter, but not in spirit. An example is Johannson's minimal logic ([29]). From an inconsistent set of premisses not every formula can be inferred. But: one can infer every negated formula! Something similar holds for a family of systems $J_1, \ldots J_4$ by da Costa and Arruda ([2]): every implication follows from an inconsistency ([53]). By the way, that led Igor Urbas to the definition of strict paraconsistency ([53] – too strong a concept, as I showed elsewhere ([54]). Let me mention only a few more ideas.

Reverse trouble with paraconsistency suffers Sinowjew and Wessel's so-called strict inference system. Wessel has an improved system ($A \vdash B$ holds iff $A \to B$ is a classical tautology, the variables in B are contained in A, and A is no contradiction, nor is B a tautology[7], see [61], 144 f.) that actually, "when applied to contradictory systems would not always entail their over-completeness", though Wessel vigorously – and not without reason – denies that it is paraconsistent ([60]). Perhaps Priest is right, who supposes that Wessel does not differentiate between paraconsistency and dialethism ([42]).

Chellas' minimal logic **D** provides a tool to handle moral dilemmas (such as inconsistent norms) in a rational way ([12]). There are various systems in epistemic logic, e.g. by Halpern, that serve the same goal. More results are obtained by Jaspers (fusion logic, [27], [28]), Fagin (the logic of local reasoning, [19]), van der Hoek and Meyer (local reasoning for incoherent belief, e.g. [34], [35]; default reasoning, [36]). The most radical way to deal with incoherent knowledge is probably Rantala's (very) impossible world semantics ([46]).

By contrast, perhaps the most conservative way – from a classical point of view – is contained in Fuhrmann's [21]. He shows how to use the theory of belief change to classically extract a maximal ammount of information from possibly inconsistent premisses.

[7]A similar idea is developed in [57]. Both proposals are instances of the so-called filter-approach in paraconsistency.

Another example is the Logic of Paradox by Graham Priest ([41]). This logic is based on Kleene's strong three-valued truth tables. The third truth value is read as "unknown". On the basis of Graham priest's ideas, Manuel Bremer investigates calculi that are, as the author claims, distinguished by their intuitive semantic interpretation as well as by their almost classical proof-theory ([10]). There is also a paraconsistent variant of intuitionistic logic by Nelson ([39]). (Let me add that in a standard procedure discussive calculi may be augmented by any other non-classical system that is described in terms of relational semantics. Thus there is intuitionistic discussive logic, causal discussive logic, and so forth.)

Furthermore, there is a lot of work in progress, still unpublished or only available via the internet. Here one can mention, to begin with, Arina Britz' new semantics for Priests Logic of Paradox. This leads to the definition of the notion of pathologicality, as a dual to paraconsistency. Kleene Logic and the Logic of First Degree Entailments are presented as examples of pathological logics. Don Faust has a framework (called Evidence Logic) that can tolerate what he calls substantial evidential conflict while not allowing contraditions. Of course, also the approach by functor variables, known for its unusual flexibility, fits for paraconsistent modelling. This is elaborated in Ingolf Max' work ([32]). Shahid Rahman, first together with Walter Carnielli and later by himself, works at paraconsistent dialogical approaches in Jaśkowski's as well as in Lorenzen's and Lorenz's tradition (the permissive and the non-ontological commitment interpretation of paraconsistency, [45], [44]). The proceedings of the Gent Congress on Paraconsistency as well as the material of the Toruń Meeting will contain lots of further proposals.

9.3.6 Will There be a Unification?

The answer, I think, suggests itself: there are further and further approaches, new ideas emerge and more and more techniques of modern logic are put to work in paraconsistency. Of course, there are results concerning relations between different approaches. For instance, Diderik Batens shows that adaptive logic is closely connected with inconsistency tolerant inference mechanism in terms of maximal consistent subsets of the premises, even at the predicative level ([7]). Another very remarkable attempt is recently undertaken by Bryson Brown, who tries to give a general framework for a classification of paraconsistent calculi in terms of consequence operation ([11])

However, keeping in mind that paraconsistency is by no means a homogeneous field and that it has very diverse applications, there seems to be little hope, as well as little need for speedy unification.

MAX URCHS
Fachgruppe Philosophie
Universität Konstanz
E-mail: max.urchs@uni-konstanz.de

Bibliography

[1] A. Anderson, N. Belnap, and M. Dunn, *Entailment. The Logic of Relevance and Necessity*, vol. 2, Princeton University Press, Princeton, 1992.

[2] A. Arruda and N. da Costa, *Sur le schema de la seperation*, Nagoya Mathematical Journal **38** (1970), 71–84.

[3] F. Asenjo, *A Calculus of Antinomies*, Notre Dame Journal of Formal Logic **16** (1966), 103–105.

[4] D. Batens, *Dynamic dialectical logics*, vol. Paraconsistent Logic. Essays on the Inconsistent, pp. 187–217, Philosophia Verlag, Munich, 1989.

[5] D. Batens, *Inconsistency-adaptive logics*, vol. Logic at Work. Essays dedicated to the Memory of Helena Rasiowa, pp. 445–472, Physica Verlag (Springer), Berlin, 1998.

[6] D. Batens, *A survey of inconsistency-adaptive logics*, in print.

[7] D. Batens, *Towards the Unification of Inconsistency Handling Mechanisms*, Logic and Logical Philosophy **7** (to appear), xxx.

[8] P. Besnard and A. Hunter, *Reasoning with actual and potential contradictions*, Handbook of defeasible reasoning and uncertainty managment systems, vol. 2, Kluwer, Dordrecht, 1998.

[9] J. Błaszczuk and W. Dziobiak, *An axiomatization of M^k-counterparts for some modal calculi*, Reports on Mathematical Logic **6** (1976), 3–6.

[10] M. Bremer, *Wahre Widersprüche. Einführung in die parakonsistente Logik*, Academia, Sankt Augustin, 1998.

[11] B. Brown, *Yes, Virginia, there really are paraconsistent logics*, JPL **28** (1999), 489–500.

[12] B. Chellas, *Modal Logic. An Introduction*, Cambridge University Press, Cambridge, 1980.

[13] N.C.A. da Costa, *Sistemas formais inconsistentes*, Ph.D. thesis, Universidade Federal do Parana, 1963.

[14] N.C.A. da Costa and J. Kotas, *On some modal logical systems defined in connexion with Jaśkowski's problem*, vol. Non-Classical Logics, Model Theory and Computability, pp. 57–73, North-Holland, Amsterdam, 1977.

[15] N.C.A. da Costa and J. Kotas, *On the problem of Jaśkowski and the logics of łukasiewicz*, vol. Mathematical Logic. Proceedings of the first brazilian conference, pp. 127–139, Dekker, New York, 1978.

[16] C. Damasio and L. Pereira, *A survey of paraconsistent semantics for logic programs*, vol. Handbook of defeasible reasoning and uncertainty managment systems, pp. 241–320, Kluwer, Dordrecht, 1989.

[17] M. Dunn, *Intuitive Semantics, for First Degree Entailment and Coupled Trees*, Philosophical Studies **29** (1976), 149–168.

[18] M. Dunn, *Star and Perp*, Philosophical Perspectives **7** (1993), 331–357.

[19] R. Fagin and J. Halpern, *Belief, awareness and limited reasoning*, Artificial Intelligence **34** (1988), 39–76.

[20] A. Fuhrmann, *An Essay on Contraction*, Studies in Logic, Language and Information, CSLI, Stanford University, 1997.

[21] A. Fuhrmann, *When hyperpropositions meet*, JPL **28** (1999), 1–16.

[22] T. Furmanowski, *Remarks on discussive propositional calculus*, Studia Logica **34** (1975), 39–43.

[23] D. Gabbay and H. Wansing (editors), *What is negation?*, Kluwer, Dordrecht, 1999.

[24] S. Jaśkowski, *Rachunek zdań dla systemów dedukcyjnych sprzecznych*, Studia Societatis Scientiarum Torunensis **1** (1948), no. 5, 57–77.

[25] S. Jaśkowski, *O konjunkcji dyskusyjnej w rachunkach zdań dla systemów dedukcyjnych sprzecznych*, Studia Societatis Scientiarum Torunensis **1** (1949), no. 8, 171–172.

[26] S. Jaśkowski, *Propositional calculus for contradictory deductive systems*, Studia Logica **24** (1969), 143–160.

[27] J. Jaspars, *Fused modal logic and inconsistent belief*, vol. Proc. WOCFAI'91, pp. 267–275, Paris, 1991.

[28] J. Jaspars, *Logical omniscience and inconsistent belief*, vol. Diamonds and Defaults, pp. 129–146, Kluwer, Dordrecht, 1993.

[29] I. Johannson, *Der Minimalkalkül, ein reduzierter intuitionistischer Formalismus*, Compositio Mathematica **4** (1936), 119–136.

[30] D. Lewis, *Logic for equivocators*, Nous **16** (1982), 431–441.

[31] D. Makinson, *The Paradox of the Preface*, Analysis **25** (1964), 205–207.

[32] I. Max, *Mehrdimensionalität und Widerspruch. Logische Untersuchungen zur Philosophie, Wissenschaftstheorie und Linguistik*, 1998, Habilitationsschrift, Leipzig University.

[33] J. Mehus, *Adaptive logic in scientific discovery: the case of Clausius*, Logique et Analyse **143–144** (1993), 359–391.

[34] J. Meyer and W. van der Hoek, *A modal logic for nonmonotonic reasoning*, vol. Non-Monotonic Reasoning and Partial Semantics, pp. 37–77, Elis Horwood, Chichester, 1992.

[35] J. Meyer and W. van der Hoek, *A cumulative default logic based on epistemic states*, vol. Symbolic and Quantitative Approaches to Reasoning and Uncertainty, pp. 265–273, Springer, Berlin, 1993.

[36] J. Meyer and W. van der Hoek, *Epistemic Logic for AI and Computer Science*, Cambridge University Press, Cambridge, 1995.

[37] R. Meyer, *Relevant arithmetic*, Bulletin of the Section of Logic of the Polish Academy of Sciences **5** (1976), 133–137.

[38] R. Meyer and C. Mortensen, *Inconsistent models for relevant arithmetics*, The Journal of Symbolic Logic **49** (1984), 917–929.

[39] D. Nelson, *Negation and separation of concepts in constructive mathematics*, vol. Constructivity in Mathematics, pp. 208–225, North-Holland, Amsterdam, 1957.

[40] J. Perzanowski, *On M-fragments and L-fragments of normal propositional logics*, Reports on Mathematical Logic **5** (1976), 63–72.

[41] G. Priest, *Logic of paradox*, JPL **8** (1979), 219–241.

[42] G. Priest, *Gegen Wessel*, Philosophische Beiträge **2** (1989), 109–120.

[43] G. Priest and R. Routley, *Paraconsistent Logic. Essays on the Inconsistent*, Philosophia, Munich, 1989.

[44] S. Rahman, *Dual intuitionistic paraconsistency without ontological commitments*, Contribution to the Congress on Analytic Philosophy, Spain, December 1999, 1999.

[45] S. Rahman and W. Carnielli, *The dialogical approach to paraconsistency*, 1998, FR 5.1 Philosophie, Universität des Saarlandes, Bericht Nr. 8, (appears also in: D. Krause [2000]: The work of Newton da Costa, Río de Janeiro, Kluwer).

[46] V. Rantala, *Impossible world semantics and logical omniscience*, Acta Filosofica Fennica **35** (1982), 105–115.

[47] N. Rescher and R. Brandom, *The logic of inconsistency. A study in non-standard possible-world semantics and ontology*, Blackwell, Oxford, 1980.

[48] H. Rott, *Making Up One's Mind. Foundations, Coherence, Nonmonotonicity*, 1996, Habilitationsschrift, Konstanz.

[49] D. Scott, *Continuous lattices*, Lecture Notes in Mathematics 274, vol. Toposes, algebraic geometry and logic, pp. 97–136, Springer, Berlin, 1972.

[50] B. Slater, *Paraconsistent logics?*, JPL **24** (1995), 451–454.

[51] J. Smith, *Inconsistency and scientific reasoning*, Studies in History and Philosophy of Science **19** (1988), 429–445.

[52] P. Thistlewaite, M. McRobbie, and R. Meyer, *Automated Theorem-Proving in Non-Classical Logics*, Research Notes in Theoretical Computer Science, Pitman, London, 1988.

[53] I. Urbas, *Paraconsistency*, Studies in Soviet Thought **39** (1990), 343–354.

[54] M. Urchs, *Paraconsistency: 'strict' is too strong*, vol. Logica91, pp. 15–20, Svoboda and Zapletal, Praque, 1991.

[55] M. Urchs, *Handling Inconsistent Information. Towards a Logic of Rational Discourse*, vol. Perspectives in Analytical Philosophy, Logic and Mathematics 5, pp. 269–284, de Gruyter, Berlin, 1995.

[56] M. Urchs, *Complementary Explanations*, Synthese (1999), 137–149.

[57] G. Wagner, *Ex contradictione nihil sequitur*, vol. Proc. IJCAI'91, Morgan Kaufmann, 1991.

[58] G. Wagner (editor), *Handling Inconsistency in Knowledge Systems*, Journal of Applied Non-classical Logics **7** (1997), no. 1–2.

[59] H. Wansing (editor), *Negation. A Notion in Focus*, Perspectives in Analytical Philosophy, vol. 7, de Gruyter, Berlin, 1996.

[60] H. Wessel, *Logische, dialektische und mystische Widersprüche*, Philosophische Beiträge **2** (1989), 121–127.

[61] H. Wessel, *Logik*, Logische Philosophie, Logos, Berlin, 1998.

[62] L. Wittgenstein, *Wittgenstein und der Wiener Kreis*, Ludwig Wittgenstein. Schriften, vol. 3, Suhrkamp, Frankfurt/M., 1967.

[63] L. Wittgenstein, *Wittgenstein's Lectures on the Foundations of Mathematics*, Ithaca, 1976.

Chapter 10

Obligations, Authorities, and History Dependence

HEINRICH WANSING

The paper is about certain methodological issues in deontic logic.[1] It argues for three recommendations: 1. not to rely on quantification over obligations in the metalanguage to justify distinctions between normative concepts, 2. to formally represent not only the addressees of norms but also the authorities who obligate, permit or forbid, and 3. not to accept formal representations of normative discourse in which the truth of normative statements does not depend on histories.

10.1 Introduction

Over the last decade, deontic logic has undergone substantial development. This significant advancement of deontic logic has chiefly come about through applications of deontic logic in Computer Science and Artificial Intelligence. Whereas previously, originating with the work of G.H. von Wright (1951), deontic logic was conceived of mainly as a branch of normal modal logic or

[1]This paper is a revised version of my contribution to the electronic Festschrift dedicated to Johan van Benthem on the occasion of his 50th birthday in 1999. I would like to thank Mark A. Brown for detailed critical comments that helped me clarifying my opposing views.

a branch of non-normal classical modal logic (Chellas 1980), in recent years subareas like dynamic deontic logic (Meyer 1988) and defeasible deontic logic (Nute 1997) have led to new applications of deontic logic, as well as hitherto neglected complex phenomena and subtleties of normative discourse being addressed. In such a development, methodology plays an important role in determining both the conceptual foundations and the formal framework(s) to be investigated and applied.

The present note deals with the methodology of deontic logic. It takes as its starting point and background a detailed discussion of methodological issues in deontic logic by one of the leading researchers in this field, namely Mark A. Brown's "Conditional and Unconditional Obligation for Agents In Time" (2001).

10.2 Identification of Obligations

In ordinary normative discourse, we sometimes quantify over obligations.[2] We may, for example, say that a person has fulfilled all or none of her obligations. However, from the mere fact that quantifying over obligations is grammatical and idiomatic, it neither follows that

(i) in order to formally represent normative discourse a first-order object language with individual variables ranging over obligations ought to be used, nor that

(ii) quantifying over obligations in the metalanguage is illuminating for a clear understanding of normative discourse, for drawing distinctions between normative notions, or for developing a system of deontic logic, nor that

(iii) parts of certain semantic structures may or ought to be regarded as semantic counterparts of obligations.

Whereas deontic logicians who agree with (i) will probably also agree with (ii) and (iii), endorsing (ii) and (iii) need not be accompanied by a commitment to (i). Brown (2001), for instance, suggests representing normative discourse in a multi-modal propositional language and uses quantification over obligations in the metalanguage to motivate a distinction between two types of deontic operators. Moreover, Brown models obligations as sets of branches of time in certain semantic structures. Obviously, two obligations understood as sets

[2] Most of what is said in this paper about obligation *mutatis mutandis* also applies to permission and prohibition.

of branches are identical if and only if they have the same elements. The identity conditions for obligations reified by quantification in the metalanguage in order to motivate and guide the design of a formal object language are more problematic. It seems to me that the obligations that are quantified over in ordinary discourse are always obligations under a description. What I mean by this is that we do not name these obligations but refer to them or groups of them using definite descriptions of the form "the obligation to do Q", "agent α's obligation to do Q", or "α's many obligations", etc.[3] Suppose John has agreed upon a contract by which I obligate him to return my copy of *The Genealogy of Disjunction* within one month. What does the definite description "John's obligation to return my copy of *The Genealogy of Disjunction* within one month" refer to? What kind of entity am I placing John under, by placing him under this obligation? If one assumes that the obligation arises from the contract, then the contract is distinct from the obligation it gives rise to. If the obligation to do Q and the obligation to do Q' were identical if and only if they arise from the same contract or contractual agreement, i.e., the same abstract linguistic entity or speech act, there would not be much reason to distinguish between obligations and certain linguistic entities or speech acts.

Brown seems to suggest that two obligations are identical if and only if they have the same fulfillment conditions. The distinction Brown draws is between Type 1 unary deontic modalities [1] satisfying either the rule

$$(RM) \quad \text{If} \vdash p \supset q, \text{ then } \vdash [1]p \supset [1]q$$

or the rule

$$(RM)_c \quad \text{If} \vdash p \supset q, \text{ then } \vdash [1]q \supset [1]p$$

and Type 2 operators [2] satisfying the weaker rule

$$(RE) \quad \text{If} \vdash p \equiv q, \text{ then } \vdash [2]p \equiv [2]q$$

but defying (RM) and $(RM)_c$. There is nothing wrong with the distinction between Type 1 and Type 2 operators. However, I do not agree with the motivation Brown gives for this distinction. According to Brown, there is a difference between fully specifiable and only incompletely specifiable obligations. We need a Type 2 operator to express a fully specified obligation and a Type 1 operator to draw attention to a prominent feature of a not completely specified obligation. Brown (2001, Section 1) writes:

At least two distinct types of modal operator ... are needed to express ordinary unconditional claims of obligation, because we make (and *need* to be able to make) such claims sometimes with lesser, sometimes with greater, specifity as to the exact

[3]Clearly, we cannot refer to obligations using non-anaphoric deictic expressions.

nature of the obligation. A deontic operator [1] of Type 1 will indicate an obligation by citing one salient consequence of its fulfillment, with [1]p interpreted to mean that the (tacit) agent has some (not fully specified) obligation or other whose fulfillment will necessitate the truth of p. However the truth of p will in general be no guarantee of the fulfillment of the obligation which underlies the claim that [1]p. In short, the truth of p will be a necessary, but not a sufficient, condition for the fulfillment of some otherwise unspecified obligation. ... An operator of Type 2 will be used to state (up to logical equivalence) precisely what the obligation itself is, with [2]p interpreted to mean that the (tacit) agent has an obligation for whose fulfillment the truth of p is not only a *necessary*, but also a *sufficient* condition.

Let us consider an example. Suppose a legislator requires every citizen to support the country's secret service, and that therefore agent α is obligated to support the secret service. Is this obligation to be represented by a Type 1 or by a Type 2 operator? Does the sentence "[1]α supports the secret service" cite one salient consequence of the fulfillment of α's obligation to support the secret service or one consequence of some otherwise unspecified obligation? Or should we use a Type 2 operator to state precisely what α's obligation is? What α is obligated to do is not very specific; she may support the secret service in plenty of different ways. Suppose the legislator (or rather one of the legislator's executives) is more concrete and requires α to provide the secret service with a certain document. Still, this does not amount to a substantially more specific obligation insofar as α may see to it in very many different ways that the secret service obtains the document in question. It is conceivable, for instance, that α fails to discharge her obligation if she asks the press to pass the document to the secret service after publication.

It may be objected that Brown is interested only in "simply dischargeable obligations" (Brown 1996) that arise from making promises or entering contractual arrangements. Whereas such obligations cease to exists after being fulfilled, α's obligation to support the secret service appears to be a standing obligation. Without entering a discussion of a further classification of obligations, the problem of distinguishing between fully specified simply dischargeable obligations and not completely specified simply dischargeable obligations remains. Brown (2001) gives some further explanation:

We do sometimes wish to be understood as expressing the precise content of an obligation. This will, ideally, be the case whenever we agree on some contractual arrangement, for example. On the other hand, it may well be that many of our obligations are too subtle and complex for us to be able to give any simple sentence which captures necessary and sufficient conditions for their fulfillment. In such cases, we are accustomed to direct attention to the obligation using sentences which merely indicate salient consequences of fulfilling the obligation, i.e. we have recourse to Type 1 operators. In short, both types are needed for a full treatment of ordinary discourse about obligations.

According to Brown, Type 1 operators "permit us to allude to an obligation without identifying it precisely". Of course we can talk about the obligation whose necessary and sufficient conditions of fulfillment consist in providing the secret service with a certain document. However, what are the identity conditions of not completely specified obligations?[4] In ordinary normative discourse, reified obligations come as obligations under some description, and, at least theoretically, it is not clear when such a description is only partial or complete. If we say that a description of an obligation is complete, whenever the description states necessary and sufficient conditions for the fulfillment of the obligation, then we need to distinguish between necessary and both necessary and sufficient fulfillment conditions of obligations that are not presented to us under a description but are somehow given directly. However, in the absence of criteria for distinguishing between necessary and sufficient fulfillment conditions and only necessary fulfillment conditions of obligations, in my view, quantification over obligations and identifying them through fulfillment conditions is not a convincing basis for drawing the distinction between Type 1 and Type 2 operators. There seems to be no indication in ordinary discourse about obligations revealing whether or not α's obligation to support the secret service, or her obligation to provide the secret service with a certain document, or her obligation to deposit the document in a certain wastebasket is identified precisely by the description employed or merely alluded to without being identified precisely. Since it is unclear whether and how such a distinction can be drawn, it is everything but clear that we *really* need two types of obligation operators to properly represent normative discourse.

Moral 1: Refrain from quantification over obligations in order to motivate distinctions in deontic logic.

10.3 Authorities and Addressees of Norms

I couldn't agree more with Brown when he points out that the following considerations are important:

- obligations are obligations of agents;
- an agent's obligations can conflict with one another;
- there is more than one agent in this world;

[4]Moreover, I doubt that there are recipes for identifying salient consequences of fulfilling a reified, not completely specified obligation that is supposed to underly an obligation report.

- one agent's obligations may conflict with those of another agent;
- agents are (presumed to be) free to make choices;
- agents act in time;
- our obligations change over time, partly as the result of our actions and the actions of others.

However, there are further features of norms[5] and normative discourse that are also important in order to obtain an accurate formal representation, namely:

(i) normative operators can be iterated;

(ii) obligations originate from authorities;

(iii) obligations may depend on the future course of events.

Items (i) and (ii) are closely related and will be treated in the present section. Item (iii) will be taken up in the next section.

In Wansing (1998) I have argued to the effect that in representations of normative discourse one ought to specify not only the addresses of the norms under consideration but also the *authorities* who issue these norms. Such authorities are agents or groups of agents, for instance legislators or communities of moral philosophers, who happen to agree upon a certain ethical theory. Specifying the authority is appropriate not only because norms indeed depend on authorities, but also because making explicit the authorities of norms helps the realization that normative concepts can be iterated. It is grammatical and natural to say, for example, that the lawmaker ought to forbid parking on highways or that parents ought to permit that their children climb trees in the garden. The *normal form* of obligation statements is:

Agent α/group Γ obligates agent β/group Δ to see to it that A.

If, like Brown (2001), one is concerned with modeling the *ought-to-do*, i.e., obligating to act, the iteration of normative operators requires representing normative statements as agentive statements. Otherwise obligation reports like "Peter ought to obligate John to refrain from smoking" cannot be formalized. In the seeing-to-it-that (stit) theory of agency put forward by Belnap, Perloff, and Xu (see, for instance, (Belnap and Perloff 1988), (Belnap 1991), (Belnap,

[5]By norms I do not here mean imperatives but the situations resulting from the actions described in true statements of obligation, permission and prohibition of the shape "Agent α/group Γ obligates (permits, forbids) agent β/group Δ to see to it that A".

Perloff and Xu 2001), (Xu 1998)) a sentence A is agentive in agent α (group Γ) if and only if A is equivalent to "α (group Γ) sees to it that A". There are various formal concepts of seeing to it that. One is the deliberative stit operator suggested by von Kutschera (1986) and, independently, Horty (1989). I shall not repeat here the formal semantics of $[\alpha\ \textit{dstit}\colon A]$ ("α deliberatively sees to it that A") and $[\Gamma\ \textit{dstit}\colon A]$. For the present purpose it suffices to note that the semantics reflects the nondeterminism of agency. Models are based on trees of moments of time branching towards the future. Formulas are evaluated not at moments of time but at pairs (m, h), where m is a moment and h is a history, a linearly ordered set of moments that is not contained in any larger linearly ordered set of moments. If for every history h such that $m \in h$ a formula A is true at (m, h), then A is said to be settled-true at m. If a formula A is settled-true, then it is not agentive. Agentive sentences are history-dependent in the sense of not being settled-true at any moment m. Normative concepts *are* iterated in normative discourse, and nesting is possible only if obligation statements are agentive and are therefore not settled-true. If α is obligated to obligate β to see to it that A, then α is the authority who obligates β to see to it that A. Thus, iteration is a phenomenon that is there to be modeled, and making explicit the authorities who obligate, forbid or permit is a way of arriving at a formal representation of iterated deontic modalities. In (Wansing 1998) it is suggested introducing for every agent α an Andersonian sanction constant S_α. S_α is a propositional constant that, intuitively, is true at a moment/history pair (m, h) if there is wrongdoing of α at (m, h). Obligation statements are then to be represented according to the following schema:

$[\alpha\ \textit{dstit}\colon \neg[\beta\ \textit{dstit}\colon A] \supset S_\beta]$
α obligates β to see to it that A.

$[\alpha\ \textit{dstit}\colon \neg[\beta\ \textit{dstit}\colon \neg[\gamma\ \textit{dstit}\colon A] \supset S_\gamma] \supset S_\beta]$
α obligates β to obligate γ to see to it that A.

The obligation report "α ought to obligate β to refrain from smoking" can then be formalized as:

$$\exists x[x\ \textit{dstit}\colon \neg[\alpha\ \textit{dstit}\colon \neg[\beta\ \textit{dstit}\colon \neg[\beta\ \textit{dstit}\colon \beta \text{ smokes}]] \supset S_\beta] \supset S_\alpha]$$

This formula is a non-agentive existential statement, since the authority who obligates α to obligate β is left implicit. However, a further nesting of deontic operators as in "γ ought to obligate α to obligate β to refrain from smoking" is possible:

$$\exists x[x\ \textit{dstit}\colon \neg[\gamma\ \textit{dstit}\colon \neg[\alpha\ \textit{dstit}\colon \neg[\beta\ \textit{dstit}\colon \neg[\beta\ \textit{dstit}\colon \beta \text{ smokes}]] \supset S_\beta] \supset S_\alpha] \supset S_\gamma]$$

Moral 2: Take the iteration of normative concepts seriously; hence consider obligation normal forms as fundamental.

10.4 History Dependence

Whether or not it is true that an authority α obligates an agent β to see to it that Q may depend on the history under consideration passing through a given moment. In Wansing (1998) an example of the history dependence of obligation reports is presented. Central to this particular example is an attributive use of a definite description. Obviously, the denotation of a description like "the next president" at a certain moment of time may depend on the future course of events, i.e. on the histories passing through that moment. But there are also considerations that demonstrate history dependence and do not rely on using definite descriptions attributively.

Suppose that authority α obligates agent β to see to it that if at the next moment[6] A is true, β now sees to it that Q and if at the next moment A is not true, β now sees to it that not Q. Suppose that at the present moment, time branches into the histories h_1 and h_2 and, moreover, that at the next moment with respect to h_1, A is true, but at the next moment with respect to h_2, A is not true. Then, with respect to h_1, β is now obligated to see to it that Q, and with respect to h_2, β is now obligated to see to it that not Q.

There just seems to be no way around acknowledging that the truth of obligation reports may depend on histories. Therefore formal accounts of normative discourse ought to represent this history dependence. If obligation reports are taken to be agentive sentences and are formalized as suggested in the previous section, iteration of deontic modalities can be expressed, and history dependence is secured.

Brown (2001, Section 3) emphasizes the "distinct possibility that a personal obligation can be treated as an impersonal obligation that a personal agentive proposition be true". Also Horty and Belnap (1995) suggest interpreting statements of the form "α ought to see to it that A" as "It ought to be the case that α sees to it that A". Horty and Belnap consider a type of objection to representing personal obligations in terms of impersonal obligations that is ascribed to Peter Geach. They present the following argument:

[6] Recall that formulas are evaluated at moment/history pairs. With respect to a given history, "the next moment" is a referential expression. Also in a pre-theoretical context, the expression "the next moment, whichever it will be" seems strange.

Suppose, for example, that Fred ought to dance with Ginger, that Fred is obligated to do so. According to the suggested analysis, this should be taken to mean that it ought to be that Fred dances with Ginger. Now as it happens, the relation of dancing is symmetric. In any possible world in which Fred dances with Ginger, Ginger dances also with Fred, and vice versa; and so it seems that the two statements "Fred dances with Ginger" and "Ginger dances with Fred" are necessarily equivalent. It follows from standard deontic logic that if the statements A and B are necessarily equivalent, then the statement $\mathsf{O}A$ is likewise equivalent to $\mathsf{O}B$. We can thus conclude, since it ought to be that Fred dances with Ginger, that it ought to be also that Ginger dances with Fred; and then according to the suggested analysis, again, this would lead us to conclude that Ginger ought to dance with Fred. But of course, this conclusion is incorrect: it could easily happen that, because of the customs governing some social occasion, Fred is obligated to dance with Ginger even though Ginger is not obligated to dance with Fred.

Horty and Belnap (1995, p. 625) point out that this objection can be met "simply by noting that the argument fails to consider whose agency is involved in the complement of the ought". Suppose A expresses the statement that Ginger and Fred dance together.[7] $\mathsf{O}[\alpha\ \mathit{dstit}\colon A]$ and $\mathsf{O}[\beta\ \mathit{dstit}\colon A]$ fail to be logically equivalent, because $[\alpha\ \mathit{dstit}\colon A]$ and $[\beta\ \mathit{dstit}\colon A]$ fail to be logically equivalent. The ease with which Horty and Belnap can meet the Geach objection might seem to support representing statements of personal obligation in terms of history-independent statements of impersonal obligation. However, if in the above example "α obligates agent β to see to it that" is replaced by "It is obligatory that β sees to it that", the modified example still demonstrates that the truth conditions of obligation reports depend on histories. Moreover, the agentive conception of normative statements also meets the Geach objection. If again A expresses that Ginger and Fred dance with each other, then, assuming an authority α, we obtain the following distinction:

(1) α obligates Fred to see to it that A.

(1′) $[\alpha\ \mathit{dstit}\colon \neg[\text{Fred}\ \mathit{dstit}\colon A] \supset S_{\text{Fred}}]$

(2) α obligates Ginger to see to it that A.

(2′) $[\alpha\ \mathit{dstit}\colon \neg[\text{Ginger}\ \mathit{dstit}\colon A] \supset S_{\text{Ginger}}]$

Obviously, (1′) and (2′) are not logically equivalent.

[7] The symmetry of "dancing with" may be interpreted to imply that "Ginger dances with Fred" and "Fred dances with Ginger" are agentive only in the group {Ginger, Fred}.

Moral 3: Accept no formal representation of normative discourse, if in this representation for every moment m, obligation reports are either settled-true or settled-untrue at m.

HEINRICH WANSING
Dresden University of Technology, Institute of Philosophy
01062 Dresden, Germany
E-mail: Heinrich.Wansing@mailbox.tu-dresden.de

Bibliography

[1] N.D. Belnap. Backwards and Forwards in the Modal Logic of Agency. *Philosophy and Phenomenological Research* 51 (1991), 8–37.

[2] N.D. Belnap and M. Perloff. Seeing to it that: a Canonical Form for Agentives. *Theoria* 54 (1988),175–199.

[3] N.D. Belnap, M. Perloff, and M. Xu. *Facing the Future. Agents and Choices in Our Indeterminist World*, Oxford University Press, New York, 2001.

[4] M.A. Brown. Doing as We Ought: Towards a Logic of Simply Dischargeable Obligations. In: M.A. Brown and J. Carmo (eds.), *Deontic Logic, Agency and Normative Systems*, Springer-Verlag, Berlin, 1996, 47–65.

[5] M.A. Brown. Conditional and Unconditional Obligation For Agents In Time. To appear in: M. Zakharyashev, K. Segerberg, M. de Rijke and H. Wansing (eds.), *Advances in Modal Logic. Vol. 2*, CSLI, Stanford, 2001.

[6] B.F. Chellas. *Modal Logic: An Introduction.* Cambridge University Press, Cambridge, 1980.

[7] J. Horty. An Alternative stit-operator. Manuscript, Philosophy Department, University of Maryland, 1989.

[8] J. Horty and N.D. Belnap. The Deliberative stit: a Study of Action, Omission, Ability, and Obligation. *Journal of Philosophical Logic* 24 (1995), 583–644.

[9] F. von Kutschera. Bewirken. *Erkenntnis* 24 (1986), 253–281.

[10] J.J.Ch. Meyer. A Different Approach to Deontic Logic: Deontic Logic Viewed as a Variant of Dynamic Logic. *Notre Dame Journal of Formal Logic* 29 (1988), 109–136.

[11] D. Nute (ed.), *Defeasible Deontic Logic*, Kluwer Academic Publishers, Dordrecht, 1997.

[12] H. Wansing. Nested Deontic Modalities: Another View of Parking on Highways. *Erkenntnis* 49 (1998), 185–199.

[13] H. Wansing. A Reduction of Doxastic Logic to Action Logic. *Erkenntnis* 53 (2000), 267–283.

[14] G.H. von Wright. Deontic Logic. *Mind* 60 (1951), 1–15.

[15] M. Xu. Axioms for Deliberative *Stit*. *Journal of Philosophical Logic* 27 (1998), 505–552.

Index